CCCC STUDIES IN WRITING & RHETORIC

Edited by Steve Parks, University of Virginia

The aim of the CCCC Studies in Writing & Rhetoric (SWR) Series is to influence how we think about language in action and especially how writing gets taught at the college level. The methods of studies vary from the critical to historical to linguistic to ethnographic, and their authors draw on work in various fields that inform composition—including rhetoric, communication, education, discourse analysis, psychology, cultural studies, and literature. Their focuses are similarly diverse—ranging from individual writers and teachers, to work on classrooms and communities and curricula, to analyses of the social, political, and material contexts of writing and its teaching.

SWR was one of the first scholarly book series to focus on the teaching of writing. It was established in 1980 by the Conference on College Composition and Communication (CCCC) in order to promote research in the emerging field of writing studies. As our field has grown, the research sponsored by SWR has continued to articulate the commitment of CCCC to supporting the work of writing teachers as reflective practitioners and intellectuals.

We are eager to identify influential work in writing and rhetoric as it emerges. We thus ask authors to send us project proposals that clearly situate their work in the field and show how they aim to redirect our ongoing conversations about writing and its teaching. Proposals should include an overview of the project, a brief annotated table of contents, and a sample chapter. They should not exceed 10,000 words.

The Hands of God at Work

Islamic Gender Justice through Translingual Praxis

Amber Engelson
Massachusetts College of Liberal Arts

Conference on College
Composition and
Communication

NCTE
National Council of
Teachers of English

National Council of Teachers of English
340 N. Neil St., Suite #104, Champaign, Illinois 61820
www.ncte.org

Staff Editor: Cynthia Gomez
Manuscript Editor: Leigh Scarcliff
Series Editor: Steve Parks
Interior Design: Mary Rohrer
Cover Design: Pat Mayer
Cover Art: Alwai Artsagav

ISBN 978-0-8141-0176-6 (paperback); ISBN 978-0-8141-0177-3 (ebook);
ISBN 978-0-8141-0178-0 (PDF)

Library of Congress Control Number: 2023951160

BOOK COVER PHILOSOPHY

Mubadalah activist Nurul Bahrul Ulum describes in this way the symbolism in the cover art that artist Ilwas Alwi Artsagav crafted for this book:

The symbol of a tree is often employed to represent life. Its circular form signifies balance, underscoring the idea that both roots and branches are of equal significance for the tree's unceasing growth.

A key principle of gender equality in Islam is encapsulated in the Arabic verse from Al Hujurat 13: "inna akromakum indallah atqokum," (Arabic in the illustration) which translates as "Indeed, the most noble of you in the sight of Allah is the most righteous among you." This verse emphasizes that all individuals stand as equals before Allah, with the only distinction being the level of their righteousness.

In the illustration also there's the symbol of the hand, which signifies the omnipotence of Allah and concurrently reflects the symbiotic roles of men and women. It can be likened to the right and left hands working in unison.

The complete illustration bears resemblance to a falling water droplet, which metaphorically symbolizes Allah's boundless mercy.

The philosophy of this illustration also encapsulates the idea of translingualism, which entails understanding and appreciating the principle of gender equality in Islam across different languages and cultures. By simplifying and succinctly expressing these concepts in various languages, we can help expand the global understanding of the tenets of gender equality as practiced within the framework of Islam.

CONTENTS

ACKNOWLEDGMENTS

I WANT TO BEGIN BY THANKING THE many Indonesian friends whose voices and stories interanimate this book and my memories. From the laughter that echoed down the halls of ICRS, to the time these scholars and friends carved out of their busy lives to take tea with me and just talk, to the beautiful homes and lives I was invited into, to the many Indonesian cultural adventures organized for my benefit, my time at ICRS taught me what a culture of care and graciousness looks like in an academic setting. Faqih, Nina, and Ninik, your stories have forever transformed how I think about faith and activism: thank you for inviting me into your lives for the past thirteen years; and Tim, thank you as well for playing a major part in previous iterations of this project. I'd also like to thank all of the students in our 2009–2010 academic writing class for teaching me so much about how writing, religious faith, and dialogic engagement work in Indonesia. My gratitude extends well past the classroom; navigating and creating a home in a new culture is a complex endeavor, and I could not have done it without the friendship and support of Ingrid, Ipung, Elis, Ramang, Roma, Moko, and Marwan. Atun, Fatimah, Bernie, and Zainal, thank you for welcoming me to your institutional space and for taking the time to answer my questions about ICRS and its local-global identity. I'd also like thank those Indonesians who invited me into their activist spaces, with special thanks to the Fahmina Institute and Mubadalah, and to Nurul Bahrul Ulum, who was not only an excellent guide in Cirebon but who also put me in touch with Alwi Artsagav, who designed this book's cover art; special thanks also go to Ibu Nyai Hj. Masriyah and to the lovely children and faculty at Kebon Jambu al-Islami Pesantren.

To cite Nina, back in the United States it has been the "women, hand in hand" who have made this project possible. I want especially to thank Lauren Rosenberg for her support throughout the many years this book was coming into being. Every scholar needs a friend who is willing to print and comment in pencil on her book proposal and then mail it via post while on a road trip to a place without internet, and who is willing to talk at length about what it means to be a feminist in a leadership position, while at the same time attempting to write a book and take care of family. Your graciousness and love, Lauren, even when grieving, kept me on track. Thanks as well, Lauren, for introducing me to Katie Silvester, whose book journey has paralleled my own in so many ways; as a scholar exploring transnational feminisms; as a mother navigating COVID; and as someone who was also embarking on the rather labyrinthine process of writing her first book. Katie: our monthly meetups kept me going, and I know they will continue. The BIMR and Christine Tardy's "Moms Writing in 2020" Facebook groups, as well as a feminist writing retreat organized by Rebecca Dingo, also helped me carve out space and time for this book. And thanks as well to the women who supported me early in my project: my University of Denver writing group—Kara Taczak, Angie Sowa, and Julie Parrish—and my dissertation advisors Haivan Hoang and Anne Herrington. And thank you, Deirdre Vinyard, for being my mentor regarding all things related to multilingual writing.

I also want to extend special thanks to two scholars at Penn State, Xiaoye You and Suresh Canagarajah, who invited me into a scholarly community that I at first felt too timid to join. Xiaoye, thank you for asking me "Where's your book project?" every year since we met at the 2010 Watson Conference; for introducing me to publishers; and for sharing your book proposals for inspiration. Without your encouragement, I don't think this project would have happened. And thank you, Suresh, for moderating my 2010 Watson talk with such grace, a talk that I recall had three people in attendance, two of whom were the graduate students presenting; thank you as well for remembering me many years later and for inviting me into your home to enjoy a sumptuous feast, and for extending an invitation to join you at your place of worship (I'll take you up on that next time!).

My colleagues at MCLA, and especially Jenna Sciuto and Tom Whalen, also contributed to this project in innumerable ways. Jenna, your prolific publishing while working at our 4-4 teaching institution inspired me to write this book, and our long hikes and snowshoe excursions during sabbatical kept me on track. Tom, even though you're a business professor, you were the first person to read my book in its entirety and to comment on it, which very much helped me imagine where I might better cater to a non–writing studies audience. Thank you as well to Gerol Petruzella and Jessica Yurkofsky at Academic Technology for helping me with the digital portions of this book. Thank you, Zack Finch, Hannah (Noel) Haynes, and Jenna, for reading chapters, and thank you Carolyn Dehner and Ruby Vega, for being the supports that you are. Finally, thank you, Corin Carpenter, for helping me with my final citation checks.

I gratefully acknowledge the support of the United States Department of State for the English Language Fellowship that first brought me to Indonesia.[1] I'd also like to thank the University of Denver and MCLA for funding my 2014 and 2022 research trips; and Steve Parks, thank you for noticing my project and seeing its potential.

And finally, my family. Thank you, Nate, for tending our actual gardens as I cultivated my academic garden; and Aspen, thank you for lending me your crayons and construction paper while we were isolating for COVID, tools which helped me conceptualize the colonialist dualities I talk about here. I promise I'll add more pictures in the next one.

PREFACE: A TELLING OF THE TELLING OF THIS STORY

The decision to use English as the primary language of ICRS-Yogya was painful to decide since we are aware of the "imperialism" of English. Most people from any nation, including Indonesia, communicate most effectively in their mother tongue. However, English is now the single most effective language of universal communication. Indonesians must master English in order to participate in international discourse, including discourse with other Asian, African and Latin American scholars. ("Language Policy" 13)

This excerpt was drawn from the first official language policy of the Indonesian Consortium for Religious Studies (ICRS), the self-described "Indonesian, international, inter-religious PhD program," in Yogyakarta, Indonesia, where this ethnographic story begins. Like most ethnographies, the research presented in the following chapters embraces complexity—in this case, as the epigraph foreshadows, the complexity of English's complicated identity as symbol of Western[2] power, but also as the language best suited, at least for now, to writing toward global interrelation. English has long been used to forward Western ideology, and despite its position as global lingua franca the language continues to marginalize as many as it connects because of existing inequality. However, English can also be appropriated and resignified in order to serve non-Western purposes; as the language policy implies, English can no longer be tied solely to Western interests and, just as important, to Western *audiences* (see You, *Cosmopolitan;* Canagarajah, "Toward").

Since I first received this language policy in the predeparture welcome package sent to my Massachusetts mailbox, I've probably reread this text hundreds of times. And each time I reread it, the words themselves become more three-dimensional. It is more than *just a text* now; I hear the voices of my Indonesian research participants, their laughter and their creative, metaphoric language play, coupled with their astute observations regarding Western power; I can visualize how they write their voices into academic conversations about religious studies and feminism, integrating their Indonesian experiences and their Islamic faith with those of previously published scholars. And I can visualize the Indonesian spaces where our worlds—and words—met and intermingled: from the beautifully appointed classroom where I taught at ICRS; to the grounds of the Fahmina Institute and the Mubadalah activist site in Cirebon where Faqih works toward Islamic gender justice with local and global activists; to the homes I was invited into for Buka Puasa[3] during Ramadan; to the tiny apartment Nina and Ninik invited me to when they did their semester abroad at Boston University; to Nina's lovely orchid-filled patio in Yogyakarta. I can also now envision my research participants' faces framed by a Zoom screen because of COVID-19, continents apart in body but connected by memories and the affordances of digital technology. Eventually, the pandemic receded enough for me to visit Indonesia again in July 2022, emphasizing how simultaneously vulnerable and crucial the body—and in-person connection—are to my own research process. A *text* like the language policy can *inform* distanced audiences, but it's the human voices and the embodied experiences linked to the text that make it *live*, interanimating it with three-dimensional complexity.

The Hands of God at Work is my attempt to capture this three-dimensional complexity in book form. Drawing from ethnographic data collected in various sites across Indonesia (and via Zoom and WhatsApp) from 2009 to 2022, this book explores how an English-medium Indonesian PhD program with a religiously motivated social-justice mission, along with three Muslim scholar-activists I met there, activate knowledge where languages intersect, despite and in relation to shifting power dynamics, a process mediated by material circumstances within Indonesia and voices past, present, and future that both are audience to and transcend the traditional geographic and discursive borders associated with them. As the Indonesians with whom I worked negotiate translingually to make meaning at the borderlands where multiple and seemingly competing discourses intersect, they in turn throw into relief false divides between the rational and the religious; between the mind and the body and thus between thought and action; between signifier and signified; between female agency and Islam; and between English and non-Western audiences. By amplifying the scholarly-activist engagements of ICRS, and then tracing over the course of thirteen years how three Indonesian writers whom I met there perform what I term "translingual praxis" to catalyze Islamic gender justice, the ethnographic story I craft here illuminates new ways to better listen for meaning-making at the borderland of what is and what could be.

ON THE POSSIBILITIES AND PERILS OF "THINKING WITH"

This book is only a small snapshot of my experiences researching in Indonesia; I have multiple notebooks full of thick description and notes on my teaching practice, hours of recorded interviews, hundreds of pages of transcripts from student and faculty interviews, hundreds of pages of student texts written in multiple genres from my course, pages and pages of advanced academic scholarship from my case-study participants, photographs, brochures, and many vibrant memories not captured in text. To complicate matters, I've written a dissertation with the data collected from 2009–2010, conducted follow-up research at two points over the thirteen years since I started, and I've subsequently published snapshots of these data in journal articles and edited collections over the course of many years, a process that emphasizes how academic conversations are continually transforming themselves and being transformed by new and compelling research, which results in new and compelling theoretical questions. All the while, my research participants' lives and projects were transforming as well. How does one sort through this three-dimensional constellation of data? And how, from there, does one start telling an ethical ethnographic story for an external audience? In keeping with Mari Lee Mifsud's argument that a scholarship of feminist praxis requires "the telling of the telling of the story" (312), the story I craft here is both in response to and strives to be in active conversation with the language practices of my Indonesian research participants, while also taking into consideration how my own audience—which I hope comprises people from a diversity of backgrounds—might engage with *their* stories.

I want to begin, then, by telling you that this book is simultaneously a story of *my* unlearning *and* a story that strives to amplify the important work my Indonesian colleagues are doing to rewrite the world toward justice. More specifically, this book dwells at the borderlands of my own research about translingual agency and the scholarly-activist Islamic gender-justice work of Indonesian colleagues. To emphasize that our projects are different but also interrelated because of our many years of work together, with the structure of this book, I seek to perform what decolonial feminist theorist Catherine Walsh terms "thinking with." She argues, drawing from Arturo Escobar, that when it comes to scholarly research "there needs to be a rethinking of how and with whom we think (and understand) theory" (28). Scholars with my positionalities must move "from a posture of 'studying about' to 'thinking with'" (29) the humans we work with to create knowledge. "Thinking with" means acknowledging existing power relationships and making explicit the lenses I bring to interpretation, while also emphasizing that my work exists in dialogic relationship with that of my research participants—without appropriating their meaning-making as my own. The structure of this book seeks to reflect and perform this complex dance: I begin with my own lenses and end with the stories of my research participants.

Structuring my book in this way is not without its dangers: though Section I performs my belief that it's important to make my own positionalities explicit as a means of better "thinking with" the work of my research participants, I do fear that because I begin with my own lenses my readers will automatically center me—and the research paradigms *I* draw from—as the unquestioned locus for this book project. I hope that as you, my own audience, engage with this final version, you also try to "think with" and learn from the work of my Indonesian colleagues on *its own terms*, rather than always already in relation to the theories I've brought to their stories. It is in that excess where new meaning can be made and the conversation continued.

To help you access this excess, I took inspiration from Laura Gonzales's work in *Sites of Translation* to directly link this two-dimensional book to the living voices and scholarly-activist work of my research participants. To do so, I've embedded QR codes throughout that will lead you to audioclips from our 2022 interviews, as well as to digital materials research participants helped me cocurate in order to amplify their continuing work. As you will hear, the audioclips from our interviews are far from "polished," and that is intentional: the roosters that you hear, the wind rustling the leaves near the recorder, and the coughs and awkward jumps and starts as Faqih, Nina, and Ninik engage in dialogue with me about complex ideas emphasize the messy and dialogic "in-between" nature of reciprocal knowledge-making. On the most basic level, I include these 2022 clips as-is in the hope that my audience might also learn to listen to my research participants' English and the rhythms of their speech, rather than solely encountering their words divorced from the interview moment and written in my "unaccented" prose. These voice clips also, I hope, work performatively to emphasize the very theory I'm discussing in the book itself—that in fact, folks who study translingual negotiation need to move past the study of language itself to focus instead on studying language in relation to embodied human action and material circumstances. As Laura Gonzales argues, multilingual people "[carry] difference in their words and in their bodies" (*Sites of Translation* 2), which requires understanding that translation is a "culturally situated, embodied, lived performance" (3). And finally, though I *am* an active player in the meaning-making here, it is my hope that by linking to the projects and the embodied voices that exist in excess of this one static ethnographic story, I can in a small way challenge the often-extractive relationship between Western researchers like me and those with whom we strive to think with.

THE TELLING OF THE TELLING OF MY UNLEARNING

In Section I, "From Praxis to Theory and Back Again," I make explicit what Krista Ratcliffe would call my discursive energy field (*Rhetorical Listening*) as the first step toward Walsh's "thinking with." More specifically, in keeping with Mikhail Bakhtin's theory of dialogic audience negotiation, which suggests that as I write from this current moment I'm subject to the past voices working through me as well as to my perceptions of my future audience's apperceptive backgrounds, I try to make clear in this section both what I do and do not—or *cannot*—bring to my telling of this ethnographic story. No theory, regardless of its origin, can ever fully capture the complexity of experience. As my research participants emphasize as they grapple with terms like "feminism," the very process of naming—of ascribing words to what is *lived*—implies that there is meaning that exists in excess of the language chosen to fix this experience in space and time. With every word chosen, there are words—and thus worlds—left *unchosen*. This *inevitable* excess is further complicated by deliberately constructed and longstanding exclusions linked to coloniality, which position me— as a white, Christian-raised woman from the United States writing in what most might consider fluent Standard American English— as the unquestioned locus of meaning-making. The words in my repertoire often rely upon the *deliberate* exclusion of other ways of being, knowing, and doing for their meaning. Questioning the unquestioned is therefore a crucial means of moving from *theorizing about* to *theorizing with* one's research participants, to the extent possible.

My research journey reflects how easy it can be to center yourself and your own research paradigm when writing from a position of power, despite the best of intentions. Though I was careful in early iterations of this project to reflect upon power dynamics and reciprocity when it came to my own intersecting identities and the identities of those with whom I worked, the theory I developed from my initial data still centered the West as the locus against which to understand translingual agency. My initial project, crafted in 2009, focused on English as a language of Western imperialism, and how writers negotiated Western power to create meaning. As my previous publications show, I eventually came to the conclusion, like Min-Zhan Lu and Bruce Horner, Brooke Ricker Schreiber and Missy Watson, Anis Bawarshi, and others, that assimilation to dominant norms can be a form of translingual agency, provided writers are aware of their options and engage in critical praxis to make their choices (see "Hands"; "Resources"; "To Whom"). I still ascribe to this belief, but the unquestioned intellectual tradition against which I defined this agency has shifted with time and reflection.

As I read and translated and commented upon my participants' scholarly work on religion and gender over the course of thirteen years, as I talked with them about their activist work and visited their activist sites, I started to see *intersections between* discourses in their repertoires I hadn't yet considered together—relationships that exceeded the linkage between English and the West—which required I complicate my initial assumption that translingual agency, in whatever form it took, be understood solely in relation to how writers negotiated against Western power.

My questions shifted: Rather than measuring translingual negotiation solely by its oppositional relationship to English and the cultural-textual norms linked to Western audiences, could I map translingual agency in relation to the *actual theoretical content* of the texts my research participants composed and their *embodied performances*? For example, could I explore my research participants' orientations toward translingual agency in relation to their orientations toward religious practice and the theories of religious interpretation they drew from to perform their scholarly and activist work? In relation to the theories of feminist agency they constructed at the borderlands between their own Indonesian experiences and the theories they encountered in English-medium texts? Could I, in turn, explore whether their orientations toward translingual agency correlated with how they took agency to effect gender justice in relation to situational power dynamics in the material world? I could, and did, and decolonial theory, along with feminist and translingual theories, helped me give language to and reflect upon why these interrelationships were not immediately apparent to me when this project began.

To that end, in the first chapter, "Thinking with the Audiences That Precede Me," I make explicit the "hows" and "whens" and "whos" that informed my rereading of research participants' work over the course of thirteen years, while also emphasizing and performing my belief that knowledge makers should employ feminist rhetorical listening both in their literature reviews *and* when addressing empirical data in locales "elsewhere and otherwise" (García and Baca). By juxtaposing an epistemological blind spot made evident to me at the beginning of this project with a theory I encountered at the end of my ethnographic process, decoloniality, I emphasize the ways decoloniality helped me simultaneously understand the limits of my own epistemological lenses and to name what I had already seen happening in the scholarly-activist work of my research participants. After reflecting on how this book is positioned in relation to current debates about whose work can or cannot claim the terms "decolonizing" and "decoloniality," I focus in on which specific aspects of decolonial theory, when put in conversation with the feminist theories I brought with me, were relevant to my unlearning: in particular, the notion of transmodern border thinking and what new ways of being, doing, and knowing might emerge if theorists like me moved from interpreting from within a "theo/ego-logical" (see Mignolo) framework to instead adopt a geo- and body-logical understanding of the world. Unlike the theo/ego-logical framework, which relies on same-other divisions to tie "modernity" solely to Western thought, the latter frameworks acknowledge power while also forwarding an *interrelational* understanding of the world. I end by highlighting the ways feminist scholars working from the borders—some of whom claim the term "decolonial," and some of whom don't—take to task colonial dualities as they work toward gender justice.

The second chapter, "Thinking with and Working toward Translingual Praxis," draws from and seeks to illuminate how Freirean conscientização and translingual theory worked dialogically with the data I collected to help me map how my research participants circulated meaning between languages and audiences on both the discursive and material planes to effect social justice. I make explicit these theories because they, along with the theories in Chapter 1, contribute to how I define *translingual praxis*, a term that, to me, captures the type of intentional choices my research participants engaged in as they performed with, between, and beyond the many languages at their disposal to reach different audiences. To conclude, I suggest that drawing from—and expanding upon—

Bakhtin's theory of dialogic audience negotiation, and asking, "From whom?" "For whom?" and "With whom?" of writers' work can help illuminate the "how" of translingual praxis and its three-dimensional complexity.

The third chapter, "Ethnographic Matters," makes explicit my critical ethnographic approach to data collection. In this chapter, I discuss how evolving research epistemologies influenced my methods and the dialogic audience coding heuristic I used to explore moments of translingual praxis, which was developed from a complex thirteen-year journey between data and theory and back again. I also do some necessary critical self-reflection on my own identity as a scholar, and I end with a discussion about informed consent and risk when it comes to maintaining anonymity in a human-focused and multimodal project like this one.

The fourth chapter, "Negotiating Colonial(ist) Realities," outlines Indonesia's complex sociolinguistic history as a deeply religious, Muslim-majority country that, despite boasting from four hundred to seven hundred distinct language groups, is united by Bahasa Indonesia, a version of Malay first imposed by Dutch colonizers but then embraced in a postcolonial language policy lauded as one of most peaceful to date (Lowenberg). I then explore from a programmatic level how the English-medium Indonesian Consortium for Religious Studies, the site where this project began, situates itself in relation to this history, to English's imperialist past, and to its work toward interreligious harmony. I end by discussing the uneven globalization that the program negotiates through strategic and tactical networking so that they can access and contribute to global academic conversations in English, which in turn informs the work they do locally to foster social justice. English can no longer be tied solely to Western interests, as Xiaoye You suggests.

The fifth chapter, "Rewriting a Critical Pedagogy," discusses the critical pedagogy I crafted for ICRS in 2009 and 2010, in which I tried to take into consideration the complicated local yet global identity at ICRS, and the possibility that the first-year PhD students with whom I worked might rewrite the Western genre forms I introduced to reach the Indonesian English-using audiences many an academic and currently a two-term Congresswoman in Indonesia's House of Representatives—strategically cultivates audience to work toward a border and power-aware cosmopolitanism. The way Ninik performs translingual praxis shifts depending on situational power dynamics and whose voices she wants to amplify and how; at times, Ninik chooses to transcend linguistic borders—translanguaging through translation to acquire resources for her Indonesian activist work or to educate audiences from different cultural backgrounds with texts that appear to assimilate; and at times, she demands audiences shift their positions to be more receptive to her language work. At other times, however, she deliberately creates linguistic borders through her use of English, translanguaging through translation to protect her feminist message and her own experiences with gender-based violence from conservative local audiences. In so doing, she challenges traditional rhetorical models that link one language with one nation-state and thus one audience, while also making space in the ways we conceptualize cosmopolitan language use for the times when writers might want to *maintain* linguistic borders—which, if we look at translingual praxis from a spatiotemporal perspective (see Lu and Horner; Pennycook, *Global Englishes*), doesn't preclude the same writers from transcending those borders at another point as time and power shift around them. By exploring from a dialogical perspective Ninik's language choices in relation to the many audiences, both local and nonlocal, she imagines for her scholarly-activist work, this chapter adds nuance to recent conversations concerning cosmopolitan language use and the tension between those who trend toward linguistic borderlessness and those who caution against these models because of existing neoliberal or cultural power dynamics.

Finally, in the conclusion, I look back to the work showcased in the ethnographic story I construct here as a means of looking forward to what we *all* can do to better listen for stories long present, yet absenced, by epistemologies that paint the human experience in dualistic, rather than interrelational, ways.

SECTION I
FROM PRAXIS TO THEORY AND BACK AGAIN

Ethnographic Moment 1: The Watchmaker Analogy

Teaching Journal: February 4, 2010

Today I drew from Andrea Lunsford and her colleagues' Everything's an Argument *to create a handout listing the primary logical fallacies for each rhetorical appeal. For many of these fallacies, I revised her examples to be more appropriate to an Indonesian audience. However, when it came to the "faulty analogy," I used her example without thinking of my Indonesian audience. She describes the "faulty analogy" as an "inaccurate or inconsequential comparison between objects or concepts" that is "pushed too far or taken too seriously" and uses the following example to explain:*

> The universe is like an intricate watch.
> A watch must have been designed by a watchmaker.
> Therefore, the universe must have been designed by some kind of creator. (512)

After I had explained this "faulty analogy," immediately two students' hands shot up and they said this was an argument they had read somewhere about creationism and an interesting debate about the analogy sprang up where they didn't address the fallaciousness (or not) of the analogy, but rather, what it implied about religion and whose idea it was. I backpedaled a bit and explained that the analogy may hold true for some audiences because they assume a creator, but for others the logic might seem faulty. I mumbled something about the clock being a human creation and the analogy as well, and therefore relying on the clock to point to the presence of the divine wasn't logical since the clock and the divine aren't on the same planes of existence . . . but this discussion opened a whole can of worms I wasn't ready to discuss as someone used to leaving religion out of the classroom.

Despite my discomfort, this miscommunication as to what is "logical" and what is "fallacious" to different audiences led another student to ask if there was a "right way of doing logic," or something that was the "opposite of these logical fallacies" out there. Before I could answer, another student suggested that the "rhetorical appeals" might be a right way of arguing, but whether

they were logical depended on context. Another student then inter-
vened to suggest that some people's fallacies might be some people's
truths, and he suggested that the "Javanese way" of arguing might
be different from Aristotle's way.

Chapter 1

Thinking with the Audiences That Precede Me

THE MOMENT ABOVE, WHICH I RECOUNTED in my teaching journal in 2010 during the second semester of teaching a PhD-level academic writing class at the Indonesian Consortium for Religious Studies, illuminates a central claim of this book: that when studying global language practices in a world that is always already translingual, we must move past what we see in texts and even past language itself to understand knowledge-making from a *rhetorical* perspective—one that, as comparative rhetoricians argue (see Lloyd; Mao, "Doing;" Bo Wang), both includes *and* exceeds the culturally constructed "logics" long held unquestioned by Western epistemologies. In this particular classroom moment, the PhD students with whom I worked challenged, as audience members, the rational/religious divide written into this activity, taking the conversation in a direction that exceeded my epistemological grounding. Religion and intellectual inquiry, when viewed as interrelated rather than in opposition, can suggest new and more ethical ways of being, doing, and knowing in the world, this book shows.

This classroom moment also foreshadows another central theme of this book: namely, that scholars, like me, who hail from locales where Western epistemologies dominate, can no longer assume we are the intended audience for English communication. Though I introduced the clockmaker "fallacy" that sparked the discussion, the PhD students with whom I worked took the conversation in directions I hadn't intended. Essentially, this moment required of me what Krista Ratcliffe terms "rhetorical eavesdropping," or "standing outside, in an uncomfortable spot, on the border of knowing and not knowing, granting others the inside position, listening to learn"

("Eavesdropping" 91). It is at this border of knowing and not
knowing where this book dwells, with the hopes that the scholarly-
activist work of my Indonesian research participants opens up
new ways of understanding global knowledge-making for my own
audience.

By exploring moments of translingual praxis—a term I will
define incrementally over the next two chapters—and tracing how
humans move knowledge from the discursive plane to the material
plane and back again to effect social justice across multiple and
intersecting languages, audiences, and contexts, this book opens
up new ways of understanding translingual negotiation at the
intersections of feminist scholarly activism and Islamic belief. As
I intimate in the preface, this chapter will begin to make explicit
the English-medium theories that helped me to eventually name—
after thirteen years of back and forth between data and published
scholarship—the work that my research participants were *already*
doing. By engaging in the critical praxis required by "thinking
with," I hope that those people in my own audience who share
similar positionalities to mine might better "see" and question their
own interpretive lenses as they learn to listen to language use at the
border of knowing and not knowing.

ON LISTENING FOR MUTUAL COMMITMENTS

For me, this type of epistemic listening transcends the divide often
painted between published scholarship, what I term a writer's
citational repertoire, and empirical data. In a nod to the Bakhtinian
theory that interanimates this book, which posits that the many
past voices a writer has encountered prior to composing a text exist
in dialogic and mutually transformative tension, I try to perform a
listening stance both in relation to the scholarly conversations that
precede me *and* in relation to the ethnographic data presented in
Section II. By employing in our literature reviews what Sonja Foss
and Cindy Griffin term an "invitational rhetoric," which requires
that a "rhetor . . . not judge or denigrate others' perspectives but is
open to and tries to appreciate and validate those perspectives, even
if they differ dramatically from one's own" (5), scholars like me will

be better prepared to listen to empirical data they collect in locales long positioned as elsewhere and otherwise.

To that end, in the next two chapters, I hope to write into being a scholarly conversation that addresses how power constructs and maintains difference but that also performs my belief in crafting space for dialogic engagement despite difference when citing the scholarship of others. In an academic climate where exclusion when confronted with difference is perhaps the easier way out, learning to listen for mutual commitments despite difference is imperative if we truly want to rewrite the world toward justice. As an example, though the recent energy surrounding decolonial theory might encourage my own audience to center that conversation as I begin the "telling of the telling of [this] story," I want to emphasize that how I interpret the decolonial theory outlined below cannot be divorced from my previous longstanding engagements with feminist rhetorics and translingual theory. Despite differences in language, in terminology, in loci of enunciation, in each of these conversations there is a commitment to creating a more socially just world. As the work of my Indonesian colleagues will also show, it is possible to respect epistemological differences *and* to believe that mutual transformation can happen at the borderlands of *seemingly* discrete, yet interrelated, conversations.

Though Ratcliffe's theory of "feminist rhetorical listening" originated in and is in response to systemic racism and white feminism in North America, I do think it has merit—to foreshadow a term Islamic feminist Leila Ahmed employs—in helping those interpreting from my positionality to move toward the type of intersectional listening required to *hear* the work of scholars interpreting both closer to home and from elsewhere and otherwise. In *Rhetorical Listening*, Ratcliffe urges feminists to reimagine the past voices—or discourses—that move through us as *discursive energy fields*, which allows us to "[shift] the place of identification" between writer and audience from the Burkean "common ground" metaphor, which flattens power relationships, to "shared atmosphere" (71). Importantly, Ratcliffe argues that the concept of "shared atmosphere" allows communicants to simultaneously identify *and* disidentify with the discourses that move through the rhetorical situation, which are by nature polyglot and populated by contradictory voices. Acknowledging such interpretive contradiction as the norm rather than the exception is necessary to unearth and amplify voices long silenced by normative interpretations. Essentially, Ratcliffe argues that by reimagining the space between writer and audience (and the multiple discourses that work through them) as "shared atmosphere" knowledge makers can better acknowledge both unequal power relationships and productive dissonance.

Engaging with productive dissonance, in turn, is vital to understanding the body's role in meaning-making—and thus a means of moving toward what Walter Mignolo terms a body-politics of knowing. Once these "discursive energy fields become embodied in people," Ratcliffe writes, "the discourses are channeled and changed—sometimes greatly, sometimes minutely—by the bodies they occupy" (70). Bodies are moved and move differently in the world, and thus bodies inscribed by differing cultural logics and different material realities move knowledge differently. As an example, my Indonesian research participant Nina and I may read Sherry Ortner's feminist theory in the same historical moment—we share an "atmosphere," after all—but, because of our very different lived realities as a white woman from the United States and a brown woman[4] from Indonesia, and the many voices—religious, scholarly, familial, linguistic (and so forth)—we each bring to the text, our interpretations inevitably differ, affecting how we *move* Ortner's voice into the world. This difference in movement or form need not obviate our shared commitments to gender justice, though the why of that difference needs to be acknowledged.

Acknowledging the "why" is a first step to challenging problematic discourse, if necessary. Although Ratcliffe is careful to acknowledge power differentials that shape any particular historical moment, she also argues that humans can "reinforce, revise, and/ or resist the discursive energy fields in which they find themselves" (70). Reframing the dialogic contact zone between writer and audience and the discourses that shape them in terms of "shared atmosphere," even if there is dissonance, is central to Ratcliffe's argument for renewed focus on rhetorical listening (34). In her words, rhetorical listening is

> [A] trope for interpretive invention, that is . . . a stance of openness that a person may choose to assume in reaction to any person, text, or culture; its purpose is to cultivate conscious identifications in ways that promote productive communication, especially but not solely cross-culturally. (25)

Consciously and deliberately taking on a "stance of openness," Ratcliffe argues, need not lead to *consensus* between writer and audience, or between scholars from differing schools, or between researcher and research participant. To avoid appropriation, it is crucial for meaning-makers to avoid collapsing difference into the same in the desire to challenge systemic oppression. Instead, rhetorical listening involves communicants' "listening to discourses not *for* intent, but *with* intent," a process of "standing under" discourses that requires "consciously acknowledging *all* our particular—and fluid—standpoints" as they "wash over, through, and around us" (my emphasis 28). Critically reflecting upon points of identification *and* disidentification allows meaning-makers to acknowledge power differentials while simultaneously working toward meaning-making that is interrelational rather than reifying—collaborative rather than appropriative.

ON REVISITING ORIGINS

To establish context for the "standing under" I'm about to do and its connection to the watchmaker moment above, let me tell you what I *did* know at the point this classroom discussion happened in 2010. Because my initial project was informed by Suresh Canagarajah's and Catherine Prendergast's critical ethnographic monographs (*Resisting Linguistic Imperialism in English Teaching* and *Buying into English*, respectively)—and because of my awareness of ways Orientalist discourse permeates the Western research tradition (Said; Spivak; Bhabha)—prior to leaving for

Indonesia, I delved deeply into the English-medium secondary research on Indonesia's geopolitical positioning. As Chapter 4 details, I knew, for example, that the Indonesian nation-state hosts the world's largest Muslim population; that Islam likely arrived in this diverse archipelago of seventeen thousand islands through contact with Arab, Indian, and Chinese traders in the twelfth century, at which point it intermingled with indigenous religions and existing Hindu-Buddhist practice to form the complex religion it is today; and that the country had long been working toward the religious, ethnic, and democratic pluralism postcolonial leaders had written into the nation's founding document, Pancasila, in 1945 (see Ricklefs). I brought this historical content, along with the work of contemporary anthropologists Anna Tsing and Tania Murray Li, whom I cite in future chapters, to Indonesia with me in 2009.

Prior to departure, I also knew that the Indonesian Consortium of Religious Studies (ICRS) was, and is, cosponsored by three universities, Gadjah Mada University (UGM), which houses ICRS; State Islamic University Sunan Kalijaga (UIN); and Duta Wacana Christian University (UKDW), making it the only PhD program in the world supported by an interreligious partnership among a national-secular, a Muslim, and a Christian university. This self-described international, interreligious PhD program in Yogyarkarta, Indonesia, was explicit from its inception in 2006 about its desire to promote interfaith dialog within Indonesia and beyond through scholarly research and local-global collaborations. Again, I brought this knowledge with me to Indonesia, thanks to the comprehensive welcome package I was sent prior to my departure from Massachusetts. As I began my work at ICRS in August of 2009, my knowledge about religion and its role in Indonesia deepened further, as I attended ICRS's weekly Wednesday Forum lectures on local and global religious practices and as I talked with faculty colleagues and staff about their scholarship and religious studies courses.

Fast-forward to February 4, 2010, and the ethnographic moment excerpted above, which happened in my academic writing class at ICRS: at that point, I had been teaching and revising the critical pedagogy I describe in Chapter 5 for about six months. I had also by that point already closely engaged with the religious studies scholarship of the graduate students in my class across multiple projects—some composed for my class and some for other classes that they shared during individual writing consultations. And I had started to see emergent themes in the content of Faqih's, Nina's, and Ninik's work (the writers whose scholarly activism I showcase in Section II), who were then in their first year of their PhD programs. In particular, I had noticed they were all exploring female agency and Islamic belief, which furthered my knowledge about the role religion plays in Indonesia and of the published scholarship written by and about female Muslims and religious gender justice in non-Western contexts.

Now let me highlight some of what I knew about *language* prior to my departure to Indonesia (in brief, as language theory is interwoven throughout). As Chapter 4 will explore in more depth, I was aware that Indonesia is an incredibly diverse language ecology, with Bahasa Indonesia (a version of Malay first institutionalized by Dutch colonialists, but then appropriated by the postcolonial leaders as the lingua franca of the new nation-state), the official language, making the majority of Indonesians at least bilingual. I was also well-versed in the conversations at that time about the imperialism of English (Phillipson; Pennycook, *Cultural Politics*; Skutnabb-Kangas; Canagarajah, *Resisting Linguistic Imperialism*) and its potential for global possibilities (Crystal). As the language policy quotation with which I began this book attests, I was aware from predeparture documents that ICRS as a program was also quite critical in its published statements of English's imperialist legacy, criticism that I viewed as an invitation to craft the critical pedagogy outlined in Chapter 5. This pedagogy, which I brought with me and revised throughout the 2009–2010 academic year, drew in part from Connor's work on intercultural rhetoric; Kubota and Lehner's call for a critical contrastive rhetoric; and Min-Zhan Lu's and Canagarajah's work at the time, which foreshadowed future conversations on translingualism. (As I mention in the next chapter, the term "translingual" had not yet entered the lexicon of rhetoric and writing studies.) In sum, when I went to live in Indonesia in 2009, and throughout early iterations of this project, I was quite aware—and critical—of the English language's ties to Western imperialism. Simultaneously, I was also aware of the ways writers could appropriate and resignify the language for their own purposes—a possibility I deliberately wrote into the critical pedagogy I developed.

The question remains, then: if I was already attuned to the importance of religion in Indonesia *and* to how established ways of thinking and doing with English are linked to Western imperialism, why—to return to the ethnographic moment above—was I blindsided by the ways the Indonesian graduate students in my classroom took the watchmaker "fallacy" in unexpected directions?

To put it bluntly, I knew at that time that religion was central to the Indonesian social fabric, but what I couldn't or didn't see was that religion, in fact, was more than academic *content* for the people with whom I worked. Religion was a *resource*, among many others, that my research participants drew from in every context they moved through; Islam intersected with and interanimated the multitude of discourses—local, global, in English and otherwise—that they drew from to interpret and rewrite the world toward gender justice on both the discursive and material planes.

Essentially, without reimagining religion as more than an object of study or as more than a discrete performance in a place of worship, I was incapable of understanding how religious faith might interanimate and inform my research participants' orientations toward language itself—negotiations that required tracing how writers moved meaning, both with and in excess of language, between text and body and back again. Without, in turn, understanding that *values* linked to specific discourses overlap and move—just as their attendant language systems can and do—I was likewise incapable of anticipating how my research participants might take a Western-derived fallacy, written in Standard English, in new directions—a translingual resignification in *value*, if not in linguistic form, that initially went unmapped in my project.

From my vantage point thirteen years later, I can see that when this project began, the logics of religion and the logics of language existed in discrete spaces for me, likely because academia (and thus my academic research questions related to language) had long been positioned as discrete from spiritual belief and embodied performance. Likewise, in my initial project, I failed to see the slippery relationship between signifier and signified—between lexical markers and the values or experiences they sought to fix in time. In hindsight, I realize that this initial blind spot was likely related to my reliance on linguistic models that position lexical markers, the values linked to these markers, and their place of origin—in this case, English and the West—as immutably tied and thus incapable of overlap and resignification by contact with values that have different geopolitical origins. To return to Ratcliffe, truly "listening to learn" required I question and complicate not just the *content* I brought with me to Indonesia and how it interacted with the knowledge of my research participants, but also the epistemological lenses that initially obstructed the possibility of truly "thinking with" and learning from my Indonesian colleagues.

ON NAMING WHAT I DO AND DON'T KNOW

How, then, did this process of unlearning and reseeing unfold? As I attempt to perform here Mari Lee Mifsud's call for a "praxis of being self-reflexive that is at once feminist and rhetorical" (308), the fraught question of *time*—and the complexity of telling an ethnographic story that avoids recreating a Western progress narrative when it comes to *my own* unlearning and reseeing—arises. Since stories themselves do unfold in real time, as we read and write from one word to the next, stepping outside of time seems impossible. What *is* possible for me to do as a storyteller is to emphasize that the process of composing this ethnographic story was complex, recursive, and necessarily incomplete. By throwing into relief here the "whens" and "hows" and "whos" that went into constructing this book, I hope it is clear that this story is *constructed* and that other stories and ways of telling *do* exist. If, then, in the previous section of this chapter, I looked backwards from the current moment to what I brought with me to Indonesia, in this section, I'll fast-forward from where I began back in 2009 to what could be viewed as the *end* of my ethnographic process in

2022—and to one of the final theories I drew from to construct the ethnographic story you're reading: decolonial theory.

As I worked to finalize this ethnographic story, decolonial theory helped me understand my initial blind spots and to better name what I had *already* observed my research participants doing with their words and actions. In the first draft of this book, which I completed in 2019, my recursive coding process had already helped me see, for example, correlations between how my research participants defined Islamic feminist agency in their published texts and their orientations toward linguistic agency, both in-text and in-process, as they negotiated audiences past, present, and future to effect social justice. What I hadn't yet seen—or reflected upon—were the epistemological lenses that initially blinded me to these connections, which led to my unconscious centering of the West as I sought to understand translingual agency. Decolonial theory, when layered upon my existing citational repertoire, helped me understand and name these blind spots. By naming here, in 2024, the specific aspects[5] of decolonial theory that informed the final telling of this story, I hope to help those in my own audience who interpret from similar positionalities also to engage in critical praxis as they seek to understand global meaning-making in interrelational, rather than dualistic, ways.

But first, given that colonialism spans the discursive and material planes, how we name the work being done to transform its effects on multiple fronts is important. As Eve Tuck and K. Wayne Yang assert, the term "decolonization" refers to the work of activists in lands still victim to settler colonialism, where, "in order for the settlers to make a place for their home, they must destroy and disappear the Indigenous peoples that live there" (6). Decolonization, they argue, has been turned into a metaphor to inaccurately describe work being done in locales with different colonial histories—like Indonesia, which, as Chapter 4 explores, was victim to an exploitative Dutch colonialism but not to settler colonialism. To avoid "colonial equivocation" (17), I want to emphasize the distinction between "decolonization" and "decoloniality." Decolonization refers to the important work of reclaiming Indigenous land and sovereignty in settler-colonial contexts. Decoloniality, on the other hand, explores the underlying structures of knowledge—or the *epistemic circumstances*—that continue to justify the colonial matrix of power in the many contexts, including Indonesia, that experienced European colonization (see Quijano; Mignolo, "Delinking").

In fact, though the question of origin when it comes to knowledge-making is fraught, Mignolo argues that the concept of decoloniality actually originated in Bandung, Indonesia. He writes:

> Decoloniality has its historical grounding in the Bandung Conference of 1955, in which 29 countries from Asia and Africa gathered. The main goal of the conference was to find a common ground and vision for the future that was neither capitalism nor communism. ("Geopolitics" 130)

This theory of decoloniality has since been reinterpreted in locales across the globe by scholars, like Tuck and Yang, who are invested in employing what Romeo García and Damián Baca term the "rhetorics of elsewhere and otherwise" to challenge oppressive colonial legacies. Thus, in settler-colonial contexts, the two terms—decolonization and decoloniality—can and should work in tandem, as they do in the scholarship of Baca; Baca and Victor Villanueva; Iris Ruiz and Raúl Sánchez; Kevin Adonis Browne; Ruiz and Sonia Arellano; Steven Alvarez, and others. Because Indonesia does not have a settler-colonial past, the term "decolonize" is inaccurate, as Tuck and Yang assert; the nation-state does have a colonial history, however, and thus, as with the work of Fatima Zahrae Chrifi Alaoui, Shyam Sharma, and others who explore rhetorics in non-settler-colonial contexts, knowledge-making there can inform and be informed by theories of *decoloniality*.

There is still the question of whether *my* knowledge-making about Indonesia can be called decolonial in either sense of the word. Like Kate Vieira in "Writing about Others Writing" and Anna Plemons in *Beyond Progress in the Prison Classroom*, I don't believe I can claim these terms for this project, no matter how careful I try to be with methodology. Given my positionality as a white female scholar from the United States who is publishing her work in a prominent book series, I cannot claim to be writing from anywhere but the "center." What I can do is acknowledge that theories of decoloniality, among others, interanimate my own admittedly Western theoretical lenses to inform the way I tell this ethnographic story and then draw from my privilege to *amplify* the scholarly-activist work of my Indonesian research participants. To do so, I've integrated QR codes throughout this book that lead directly to the voices of my research participants and their activist organizations. Their scholarly-activist work might, I contend, contribute to *theories* of decoloniality by throwing into relief what Mignolo terms the geo- and body-politics of knowledge-making ("Delinking").

I emphasize the word *theories* above because I am cautious of naming—again from my admittedly Western perspective—my research participants' scholarly-activist work *itself* as "decolonial," especially given this book's focus on critical intentionality when it comes to meaning-making. Can work contribute to decoloniality if, in fact, the writers who produced it—like my own research participants, who don't see decoloniality as the central theory or purpose of their scholarly-activist work; like Gloria Anzaldúa or Paolo Freire—*don't name* their work as such? Or conversely, if a writer claims their work *does* add to theories of decoloniality, does that necessarily make it so? The difficulty in answering these questions can be seen in the recent friction between scholars who wish to define decoloniality in opposition to cultural rhetorics because the latter "employ a method of storytelling that routes the locus of enunciation of knowledge to the author of the piece" (Cushman, Baca, and García, "Delinking") and those who see space for such person-centered storytelling in a world that so often demands that minoritized "voices should stop being voiced" (Hidalgo).

If we move past the question of naming specific scholarly constellations as belonging or not, which seems exclusionary, and move instead to consider from where an audience member is interpreting, a different question emerges. One of the major claims of this book is that in a translingual world we must question from a dialogical perspective how audience works when it comes to global rhetorical practices. What if we move past the question of whether a *writer* can or cannot, should or should not, claim decoloniality, to consider the audience's role in the interpretive process? Couldn't, or shouldn't, the determination about whether scholarship contributes to decoloniality also be understood in relation to the position from where *an audience member* is interpreting? For example, knowledge-making that seems decolonial to me, a scholar interpreting from (and admittedly trying to get outside of) a Western paradigm that has long defined "rationality" and religion as mutually exclusive, may not appear to be "decolonial" to writers and audience members like those Indonesians with whom I worked, who, because of the ways religion is deeply embedded in their lives, *already* view religion and scholarly work as mutually transformative.

Though questions concerning intentionality and audience permeate this book, I myself cannot—indeed, I believe I should not—definitively name other people's work as decolonial or not. Rather, what I *can* do, in the words of Mignolo, is ask, "Who is doing it? Where? And why?" in relation to the Indonesian literacy context I study—questions, he argues, that move us past abstract universals when it comes to "local histories, memories, [and] body politics" ("What Does It Mean to Decolonize?" 108). Then, I can let you, as my audience members— people undoubtedly interpreting from a diversity of global perspectives—decide whether the translingual rhetorical practices of the Indonesians showcased here contribute to, or challenge, *your own* epistemological lenses when it comes to understanding how people make meaning in locales that were once colonized.

ON THE PROMISE OF CRITICAL BORDER THINKING

The dialogic practice of border thinking, to my mind (and rather performatively), serves as the central connective tissue among the feminist, decolonial, and translingual theories in my citational repertoire. Though Mignolo's theory of border thinking is an important part of the telling of this story, it was Anzaldúa's work in the poetics of border thinking and Mestiza consciousness that first performed, for me, what a border-thinking praxis that acknowledges power and existing borders, but also hopes for epistemic and material transformation, might accomplish. In *Borderlands/La Frontera*, Anzaldúa writes,

> The answer to the problem between the white race and the colored, between males and females, lies in healing the split that originates in the very foundation of our lives, our culture, our languages, our thoughts. A massive uprooting of dualistic thinking in the individual and collective consciousness is the beginning of a long struggle, but one that could, in our best hopes, bring us to the end of rape, of violence, of war. (102)

Though they don't necessarily claim the term "decolonial" for their work, Anzaldúa and other Third World feminists, the Islamic feminists showcased below, and the translingual theorists in the next chapter all believe that we can—and should—acknowledge the stories that exceed the limits of dominant discourse *and* critique the very systems that create that exteriority in the first place. This is also, as García and Baca have recently asserted in *Rhetorics of Elsewhere and Otherwise*, "the hope and vision of decoloniality: where the possibility of new stories exists" (3).

Reinterpreting border thinking through the lens of trans-modernity—a concept central to decolonial theory—and reflecting on how transmodern border thinking might help challenge the dualities Anzaldúa refers to has helped me better understand the scholarly-activist work of the Indonesians showcased in this book. In the words of Madina Tlostanova and Mignolo, "Trans-modernity is the space of the borderlands, the space where exteriority becomes visible" (19). Illuminating new stories about what it means to be human, they argue in "On Pluritopic Hermeneutics, Trans-modern Thinking, and Decolonial Philosophy," requires interrogating long-held, rigid understandings of the "other" that continue to maintain notions of exteriority. "'Otherness' as we sense and think about it today," Tlostanova and Mignolo assert, "is a Western construction from the Renaissance on and is constitutive of the Western concept of 'modernity'" (12). In other words, Western meaning-makers created the notion of "other" in order to paint their culture as more "modern" than those whom they sought to dominate.

The concept of "otherness" still allows for the successful reproduction of Western notions of modernity. For this reason, Tlostanova and Mignolo critique poststructuralist and postmodern theorists who reify the difference between the "same" (the humanitas, or those with power to define) and the "other" (anthropoi, or those who have long been defined by the "same"). They first take to task theorists who position the "other" as *unknowable*—a stance that harks back to "the Lévinasian thesis that any contact with otherness ends in violence" and that, they argue, allows those in the position of "same" to continue to interpret the "other" by translating the "other" into the "same" (14). They also take to task theorists who, "although [they] reject absolute otherness," still draw from "modernist progressivist thinking" that positions the other as being somehow at an "earlier stage of development" than the more "enlightened" humanitas (14). Transmodern border thinking requires that knowledge makers recognize, rather than ignore, the experiences of humans long "othered" by the "same" *and* that knowledge makers also interpret the meaning-making practices of those othered as existing on the same spectrum of knowing as their own: as existing in the same "now," but perhaps with different questions and answers, rather than as always already in contrast with the somehow more "modern" humanitas. To do so, knowledge makers must delink from the same/other dualities that continue to define dominant thought.

Although it is important to acknowledge that "other truths . . . exist and have a right to exist" (18) it is also important to avoid falling into the modernist myth that there is some sort of pure, alternative truth that exists external to dominant discourse. Both the prefix "trans" and the concept of "border thinking" assume that there is overlap and connection and that discursive borders are permeable—despite the rigid same/other binary that is continually reinforced as a means of positioning Western interests as inevitably more "modern." To apply this notion to the watchmaker moment above, both I and the Indonesian graduate students in my class were interpreting the *same* Western-derived text, in the same "now," but because of our differing epistemological lenses, new ways of seeing this text—and our differing cultural logics—emerged.

Interpreting the meaning-making practices of humans defined as "other" means, for this particular project, first acknowledging power differentials and then acknowledging that knowledge traditions long imagined as "exterior" to Western modernity—for example, Islam—exist on the *same continuum* as, not in opposition to, knowledge traditions linked to Western philosophy. Rasha Diab's *Shades of Sulh*; Maha Baddar's "From Athens (via Alexandria) to Baghdad"; Lahcen Ezzaher's "Alfarabi's *Book of Rhetoric*;" and Shane Borrowman's "The Islamization of Rhetoric" have opened up space for an interrelational understanding of Islamic and Western knowledge-making in primarily Arab contexts, and it is my hope that the research here does similar work from a Southeast Asian locality. The Indonesian scholar-activists showcased here emphasize that those long "written about" can employ border thinking to circulate concepts across *seemingly* discrete languages, audiences, and knowledge traditions in order to resignify Western definitions of "modernity" and "progress" in ways that challenge inequality.

ON ISLAM AND THE GEOPOLITICS OF KNOWLEDGE-MAKING

Understanding how colonial dualities work is important for scholars interpreting from positionalities similar to my own to both *see* this type of transmodern border thinking and to reflect on their own blind spots. Though this book illuminates how research participants draw from multiple discourses in their repertoires to rewrite what it means to "know," religion—and in this case, Islam—plays a central role in their meaning-making practices. As I intimated previously, specific aspects of decolonial theory were central to helping me name and reflect upon my initial blind spots when it came to the complex translingual work my research participants were *already* doing to enact Islamic gender justice. Mignolo's theorization of the long-upheld and socially constructed divide between religion and "rationality" and how this duality continues to reconstruct the colonial matrix of power was particularly illuminating.

In "Delinking," Mignolo takes a historical look at how the coloniality of power and the coloniality of knowledge are intertwined, constructed, and maintained through Western-derived notions of what's "rational" and what is not. To decolonize knowledge, Mignolo argues, scholars must both acknowledge and delink from the "theo-logical" (Christian) framing of the modern/colonial world that reigned from the sixteenth to the eighteenth century *and* from the "ego-logical" Cartesian understanding of the rational human subject that began to arise in Europe at the beginning of the seventeenth century, to eventually spread to Asia and Africa in the nineteenth century (460). During this epistemological transition, European colonialists repositioned the "rational" and the "religious" as oppositional (while veiling the intersection between those who were now deemed rational and their existing Christian identities), which helped them relegate Islamic knowledge-making to being always already in opposition to modernity.[6] In Mignolo's words, "[a]s they became hegemonic, Theology and Secular Philosophy grounded by Christianity formed the Master Voice through which the people, regions of the world and other religions would be classified, described and ranked" (471). As Figure 1 shows, although the rhetoric used to describe "civilized" and "modern" meaning-making may have shifted, the locus of modernity was merely transferred from the theo to the ego (with the latter veiling, but not replacing, the former); the rhetoric may have shifted, but the *bodies* signified by that language, and their locations, remained in the same positions in the same/other binary, a phenomenon only noticeable if one looks past language itself to the humans being described—or at those who are doing the describing—and their lived geopolitical realities.

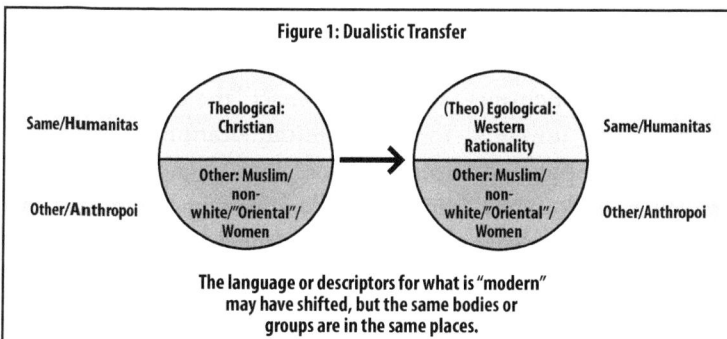

Figure 1: Dualistic Transfer

Figure 1: Dualistic Transfer		
Same/Humanitas	Theological: Christian	(Theo) Egological: Western Rationality	Same/Humanitas
Other/Anthropoi	Other: Muslim/ non-white/"Oriental"/ Women	Other: Muslim/ non-white/"Oriental"/ Women	Other/Anthropoi

The language or descriptors for what is "modern" may have shifted, but the same bodies or groups are in the same places.

Figure 1: Dualistic Transfer

Chapter 2

Thinking with and Working toward Translingual Praxis

THIS EXCERPT FROM FAQIH'S OPINION PIECE, which he wrote in 2010 in (mostly) English for a local Indonesian audience in an op-ed assignment for our academic writing class, helps to illuminate the central theoretical lenses of this book. To apply a purely text-based, *secular* analysis of the opinion piece excerpt above, we can see that when addressing a local Indonesian audience in English, Faqih code-meshes—interspersing Arabic words, like "khalwah," and even perhaps "Hira" (though it is a geographical term)—into his predominantly English syntax. In so doing, his text could be considered "translingual." This analysis, however, if not taken further, flattens the rhetorical complexity of this excerpt.

If we look to the *content* of this opinion piece we can see that understanding global language practices also requires moving past a purely *language-based* understanding of translinguality. To comprehend moments like this one, we must focus on the ways writers interanimate English with *knowledge* drawn from traditions often positioned by the colonial matrix of power as "at odds" with Western culture and the languages associated with it. The cave of Hira, for example, is the location near Mecca where Muhammad, who was in seclusion (*khalwah*), first received divine revelation from Allah, according to the Muslim faith. And the intimate moment Faqih describes between Muhammad and 'Aisha is drawn from the Hadith, the Islamic prophetic tradition Faqih studies in his scholarly work. Faqih draws from a religious text as a legitimate means of substantiating his argument, similar to how one practicing from within an ego-logical tradition might draw from a peer-reviewed locate points of transformation in language—and importantly, my research shows, in the values and knowledge traditions represented by those languages.

As I now move to define "translingual praxis" through an extended process of what Catherine Walsh calls "thinking with," I'll take Bloom-Pojar's theory to heart: I'll emphasize the "contextual embeddedness" of any language act by first defining my understanding of "praxis"—which is deeply contextual and ever-shifting—and then I'll move to exploring how I see theories of translinguality interanimating the definition of "translingual praxis" I'm building toward—thanks, of course, to the scholarly-activist work of my research participants and to the meeting of our respective "discursive energy fields" (Ratcliffe, *Rhetorical Listening*).

DEFINING PRAXIS

The definition of translingual praxis I'm working toward is deeply informed by Paolo Freire's body of work, which, in text and performance, challenges long-held divides between the mind and the body, religion and rationality, what is known and what is felt. Though his theory has been critiqued by some decolonial scholars for its Western, Marxist influence (see Sandy Grande, "Red Pedagogy") and by others for the way his liberation theology seems to position humans as above the nonhuman natural world (see Tuck and Yang 20), to me, the ways religion interanimates Freire's theories rewrites the problematic rational/religious divide promoted by coloniality, and the material embeddedness of his theories the false divide between the ego and the body, mirroring, in some ways, my research participants' work. For these reasons, his definition of "praxis" informs how I read the data collected here, and thus the definition of the term "translingual praxis" I'm working toward.

Religion, though formative when it comes to the rhetorical practices of many, including Freire and the Indonesian scholars showcased here, is often ignored or reviled in Western academic circles (see DePalma and Ringer; Vander Lei and Kyburz). When it comes to Freire's theory-building, Priscilla Perkins argues that rather than viewing his critical Catholicism as a discourse central to his theory-making—among the many discourses he drew from—leftist academics in the United States have instead tended to view his religious beliefs as a "birthmark that disfigured and obscured his theories" (590). To counter this view that progressive theory-building and religious discourse are incommensurate, scholars like Shari Stenberg, Beth Daniell, and Amy Goodburn draw from Freire's work to argue that, in Stenberg's words, "[R]eligious literacies . . . are not only deserving of study and reflection but may in fact serve as a resource for critical projects" (282). Ignoring how Freire draws from his religious identity as a resource in his scholarly-activist theory-making reinforces the rational/religious duality forwarded by coloniality. A word of caution, however; though Freire's work seems salient to my project, when it comes to aligning his theory with the knowledge-making of Muslim Indonesians, it is crucial to take a comparative approach rather than a deficit approach; as Muhammad Agus Nuryatno, Kholidi Ibhar, Ahmad Warid, and others argue (see Nuryatno, "Education" 83), the concept of a critical consciousness catalyzed by religion *already* exists within Islam. Though Brazilian Catholicism and Indonesian Islam developed (and continue to develop) in vastly different contexts, some of the *values* linked to these religions do transcend both the originating discourses *and* the languages associated with them, suggesting interrelation rather than division between these seemingly disparate faiths.

Freire and the writers whose work is showcased in this book, then, are interrelated in the ways they integrate beliefs forwarded by their respective religions with academic discourse to effect social justice. The material world affects human action, but humans, with their beliefs and actions, can and do affect the world in a recursive, never-ending process. In a distinction crucial to the definition of translingual praxis I'm building here, for Freire, *action* is inevitable as bodies move through the world, "but action is *human*," he asserts, "only when it is not merely an occupation but also a preoccupation, that is, when it is not dichotomized from reflection" (*Pedagogy of the Oppressed* 53, my emphasis). Freire terms this type of intentional human agency *conscientização*, or praxis, which he defines as "an act of knowing that involves a dialogical movement that goes from action to reflection and reflection upon action to new action" (58). With this careful distinction between action that occurs inevitably and the type of critical action that occurs with reflection and human intent, Freire anticipates the distinction I will make between translingual agency and translingual praxis.

Opportunities for this type of intentional—and human— reflection occur when an actor is confronted with what Freire calls a limit-situation, or a limitation linked to existing power relationships.[11]Freire argues that a human has two options at this point: submersion in the situation and thus tacit acceptance, or confrontation through critical reflection. This reflection on existing discourses, for Freire, is crucial to understanding that history, and thus humans themselves, craft "the very condition of existence" (109), which concomitantly implies that humans can also work to change that existence. In Freire's words:

> Only as this situation ceases to present itself as a dense, enveloping reality or a tormenting blind alley, and they can come to perceive it as an objective-problematic situation— only then can commitment exist. Humankind emerge from their submersion and acquire the ability to intervene in reality as it is unveiled. (109)

Once people discover themselves to be merely "in a situation," which involves pausing to name and reflect on its human construction, Freire asserts they can imagine and bring to fruition other, more ethical possibilities in the future. As the portraits in this book will show, this type of praxis can lead to different sorts of action depending on situational power dynamics and the many dialogic audiences, past, present, and future, who mediate each limit-situation.

Importantly, the action that precedes and proceeds from moments of praxis, as the work of my research participants shows, both encompasses *and* transcends discursive negotiation to reflect and affect the *material* world. Freire's emphasis on material intervention, however, is sometimes ignored. As Antonia Darder, in "Freire and a Revolutionary Praxis of the Body," and Tricia Kress and Robert Lake, in "Walking with Freire," have pointed out, many theorists who draw from Freire's work seem to sidestep the crucial role embodied action plays in Freire's theory of praxis. Citing the scholarly tendency to focus solely on cognitive reflection when it comes to praxis, Kress and Lake argue that "one of the great misconceptions about critical pedagogy is that transformative learning is an activity that takes place in the *mind*" (49, my emphasis). Placing primacy on thought and internal reflection—at the expense of material action—they argue, is a symptom of and works to entrench the European Enlightenment's (what Walter Mignolo would call the "ego-logical") project of separating the mind from the body—a problematic duality that upholds the colonial matrix of power. "The effect," they assert, "is an undermining of the end goal of humanization, which is fundamental to Freire's philosophy: mind is divorced from body, content is divorced from context, and students and teachers cannot be fully human as beings *in* and *with* the world" (49, original emphasis). The relationship between word and the material world permeates Freire's pantheon, as Darder emphasizes. In *Pedagogy of Hope,* for example, Freire argues that "a critical understanding of the situation of oppression does not yet liberate the oppressed . . . Now the person who has this new understanding can engage in a political struggle for transformation of the concrete conditions in which the oppression prevails" (24). In *Pedagogy of Freedom,* he argues that "words not given body (made flesh) have little or no value" (39) and in *Pedagogy of the City,* that "[i]t is [through] this process of change, of transforming the material world from which we emerged, that creation of the cultural and historical world takes place" (108). Praxis, as Freire defines it, requires that humans acknowledge and challenge in word and action the mind/body separation that has long propped up notions of Western rationality, a formulation that has in turn allowed for the subjugation of bodies marked as other, as decolonial feminists argue.

My research participants' scholar-activist work very much emphasizes the transformative potential of this dialogic interplay among reflection, discursive knowledge-making, and material practice. In Walsh's words, "It is in this concrete making and doing, in embodied practice, that theory is crafted and that theorizations are continually made" (35). To return to Freire, "To exist, humanly, is to name the world, to change it. Once named, the world in its turn reappears to the namers as a problem and requires of them a new naming. Human beings are not built in silence, but in word, in work, in action-reflection" (*Pedagogy of the Oppressed* 88). This human naming of the world does not create a static, long-lasting truth but rather requires a continual, processual movement among naming, reflection, and action.

Given the theory/action focus of my Indonesian research participants' scholarly-activist work, it is important to conceptualize their translingual action in relation to the material, embodied circumstances in which—and because of which—they engage in praxis, while also tracing how they use language to move the many knowledge traditions in their citational repertoires from one context to the next, across multiple languages, through time. To return to Bloom-Pojar, taking a rhetorical approach to translingual negotiation is necessary to understand this type of critical praxis; we need to acknowledge situational power dynamics but also the human capability to rewrite them as new situations arise. Freire's theory of praxis, when put in conversation with the other theories I outline here, helped me understand this complexity and to more fully "see" the work of my research participants.

DEFINING TRANSLINGUAL PRAXIS

I begin this chapter by defining the term "praxis" in the concept of translingual praxis to emphasize my rhetorical approach to translingual negotiation and also to situate how this theory speaks to the distinction I will make between translingual praxis and translingual agency. But first, though part of me wishes to say, like Walsh, that "it is not the use of words that matters here; what matters are the perspectives, processes, prospectives, actions, and thought" (49) underlying any chosen signifier—a sentiment that my research participants echo in their chapters—given the many voices currently discussing how best to link the affordances signified by the prefix "trans" to some form of the base word "language," it seems important to make explicit whose voices inform my definition of "translingual" in "translingual praxis."[12]

Although the "turn toward trans-" emerged in Western conversations *after* I began collecting data in 2009, the "perspectives, processes [and] actions" (Walsh 49) signified by "translingualism" were *already* evident at ICRS. As Bruce Horner and Sara Alvarez argue, citing José Ortega y Gasset (8), the lived reality preceded the terminology. I am also careful to emphasize "Western conversations" here, because, as Setiono Sugiharto argues in "The Multilingual Turn in Applied Linguistics?" the idea of a scholarly "turn" in academia is dependent on locality and positionality. When it comes to Indonesia, he argues:

> [T]he local applied linguistic practices have long been and will always be multilingual, and in fact multilingualism is at the heart of the Indonesian multiethnic communities. Thus, the term "turn" as in the "multilingual turn" seems rather vacuous and misleading, as far as my perspective from the periphery is concerned. (417)

From an Indonesian perspective, there was never a need to "turn toward" translinguality; as Suresh Canagarajah has also long emphasized, translingualism is the norm, rather than the exception, despite the monolingualist ideology forwarded by Western hegemony (see *Translingual Practice*). For scholars interpreting from positionalities similar to my own, however, the "turn toward trans" was and is a necessary one, if indeed we want to notice and then help transform the oppressive systems we've long upheld, whether knowingly or not.

At its heart, for me, translinguality involves the questioning of socially constructed yet still powerful borders, whether linguistic, ideological, or geographical, with the aim of promoting more equitable global (language) relations. This sentiment surfaced repeatedly in programmatic documents at ICRS, like the "Language Policy" excerpt with which this book began, and in the practices of my research participants. To return to Ahmed, regardless of when the term surfaced or from where it originated, to me the term "translingual" seems to have merit when it comes to describing the rhetorical practices of my research participants—at least in the way I'll now define the term and its corollaries here, by trying to "stand under" the work of various theorists who've contributed to my discursive energy field.

Both my research participants' rhetorical practices and multiple theorists—some of whom *seem* at odds with one another—interanimate how I understand translingualism. Perhaps the most widely read definition of "translingualism" is that which emerged in Bruce Horner, Min-Zhan Lu, Jacqueline Jones Royster, and John Trimbur's "Language Difference in Writing": "Tak[ing] the variety, fluidity, intermingling, and changeability of languages as statistically demonstrable norms around the globe" (305), they argue for an "approach [that] sees difference in language not as a barrier to overcome or as a problem to manage, but as a resource for producing meaning in writing, speaking, reading, and listening" (304). As Canagarajah, Xiaoye You, Nancy Bou Ayash, Sugiharto, and others show with their empirical research, reconceptualizing the many languages in our repertoires as resources that coexist on the same linguistic spectrum, and as overlapping and mutually transformative, both reflects the way language actually works and challenges notions of deficit often mapped onto those long "othered" by dominant monolingualist discourse.

Not surprisingly, since the publication of "Language Difference in Writing," scholars have continued to build upon, to apply, and to seek clarification when it comes to the concepts theorized in the "turn toward trans-". Disagreements when it comes to the existence of "borders," as well as who (or what) can claim translingual agency abound (see Matsuda; Gevers; Schreiber and Watson). In "Defining Translinguality," for example, Horner and Alvarez accuse Vershawn Young and Li Wei, among others, of suffering from "confusion" (14) because, in their respective theorizations of code-meshing and translanguaging, they mention the existence of "codes" and "boundaries" between languages. In so doing, Horner and Alvarez argue, they "appear to be dependent on, and react[ing] to, the boundaries" they seek to "'challenge,' and thereby, perversely if inadvertently, risk reinforcing those boundaries" (14). Because of Young's and Li's seeming reliance on "borders," Horner and Alvarez choose to craft an epistemological border between their own definition of "translinguality" and Young's and Li's theories of code-meshing and translanguaging.

Because of my theoretical leanings—both border-thinking and feminist rhetorical listening require acknowledging existing epistemological and material differences while *also* locating interrelations that exceed those differences—and because of the Indonesian context where I research, where borders both material and discursive *do* have impact, I take a more inclusive approach when it comes to terminology. In this book, I assume that the term "translingual" encompasses the productive aspects of all three theories. Li's argument when it comes to "translanguaging"— that "human beings think beyond language" (18)—is central to understanding the work of my research participants and the ways that interrelated *values* in their repertoires intermingle in excess of societally named "languages." Translanguaging, to me, is the process of putting translinguality—the natural state of language (more on that below)—into action. Likewise, the way Young theorizes code-meshing is central to understanding how the writers with whom I worked deliberately chose to mesh codes—or at least what society deems as codes—into their texts or not, depending on power relationships. Code-meshing cannot and should not be conflated with translingualism itself, as Brooke Ricker Schreiber and Missy Watson assert, but it *can* be one indicator of a writer intentionally negotiating between the actuality of their interior language processes and their audience's (possibly erroneous) perceptions regarding language and the language user producing it. To put it all together, for me code-meshing is a means, and not the only one, of translanguaging in moments that are always already translingual.

The question of translingual agency—of who or what can perform it, under what circumstances, and how and where to locate it—is also under debate. The authors of "Language Difference in

Writing" emphasize that *all* language users, not just those marked as "other" when it comes to dominant discourse, engage in translingual agency—a claim Horner and Alverez repeat to forward a labor-focused, rather than identity category–focused understanding of translingual agency. The latter formulation, they argue, and rightfully so, singles out people with nondominant discourses, creating an unquestioned "normative" English user, and thus a border. Indeed, if we subscribe to Gee's assertion that discourses inevitably overlap within a language user's repertoire, and if we look to how languages have historically shifted as discourses and their attendant languages come into contact (Canagarajah, *Translingual Practice*), it makes sense that *everyone* engages in translingual agency. It's unavoidable. If, then, *all* communication is translingual—and I believe it is—and all communicators engage in translingual labor when they make meaning—and I believe they do—the question remains: how can we account for power differences when it comes to who does the labor, how, and under what circumstances? It still seems problematically pluralistic, for example, to place my own language practices as a white woman fluent in what society views as Standard American English on the same level with the deliberate negotiations among English, Indonesian, and Arabic that the scholars highlighted here perform as power shifts around them and they, in turn, shift power. As Keith Gilyard asserts in "The Rhetoric of Translingualism," "We don't all differ from the standard in the same way" (286).

In addition, if we understand discourse in the way Gee does—as representing the dialogic relationship among language, values, and the material environment—the question of whether translingual agency resides solely with humans arises. In an effort to challenge the ego-logical ontology forwarded by the Enlightenment, scholars like Pennycook in his *Posthumanist Applied Linguistics*, Jay Jordan in "Material Translingual Ecologies," and Jody Shipka in "Transmodality in/and Processes of Making" want us to move beyond "human-centered or human-centric" notions of agency (Shipka 253)—an argument that Canagarajah has also recently taken up in "Translingual Practice as Spatial Repertoires," in which he argues that to avoid "methodological individualism," we need to acknowledge the "agency of material and spatial features" (50). If, however, we view translanguaging as a dynamic, mutually constitutive dance that unites writer, text, and audience at particular points in time as mediated by the agency of material and spatial features, how then can we account for the type of critical *human* agency required to reflect upon and challenge human-created systemic inequality?

We can turn to an extended example drawn from the research of one of my case-study participants, Nina, to understand what I mean. In Chapter 7, Nina discusses how the Fahmina Institute, the feminist activist organization cofounded by Faqih, Chapter 6's case-study participant, helped minority Muslim Ahmadi women in her community understand their legal rights in relation to Indonesian laws concerning religious practice; this activist work I consider a discursive intervention since these legal rights are codified in written law. This discursive intervention, in turn, encouraged these Ahmadi women to act on their material world; with an increased understanding of their rights as written in legal texts, they took embodied agency to remove physical barricades put up by conservative Sunni Muslims that kept them from worshiping at their Ahmadi mosque. The discursive and material planes work recursively here, as Canagarajah and others suggest, with the initial material oppression in the form of physical barricades inspiring discursive intervention by a feminist NGO, and this discursive intervention spurring these particular Ahmadi women to eventually take material, embodied agency, which, to follow the chain further, led to Nina's discussing this moment with me (in English) as she paraphrased her scholarship on feminist agency and subsequently, to this very chapter you're reading.

Although in this case material and spatial features exist in recursive tension with the humans interpreting and acting on the limit-situation, I hesitate to ascribe the *same type* of agency to them, despite their *impact*. To my mind, imbuing the mosque blockades with agency—as opposed to the conservative Muslim groups who put them up—sidesteps culpability. Shifting agency from the oppressors to the material objects used for oppression diffuses blame, while equating the agency of Ahmadi women with the material objects they interact with and successfully oppose seems to be an objectifying move in the most literal sense. In this particular situation, objects have *impact*, I contend, while the humans, as Freire argues, exhibit agency through their *intentionality*, which is, of course, still mediated by situational power dynamics.

By asking questions of theories that establish translinguality for all and imbue objects with agency, I do not intend to discount these theories' validity wholesale; after all, theories should be drawn from specific contexts, and the Indonesian context showcased here and the contexts from which the theorists above draw to craft their theories differ dramatically. Rather, I wish to add a bit of terminological nuance to the conversation.

One way to better account for the type of translingual action I see my research participants taking is to make a distinction between *translingual agency* (which is open to all) and *translingual praxis,* which I define as follows:

> Translingual praxis is the dialogic process by which a writer critically reflects upon situational power dynamics in relation to audience, purpose, and the diverse voices at their disposal to make intentional rhetorical choices at particular moments in time.

Reserving the term *translingual praxis* for moments, or limit-situations, when writers use language intentionally in relation to the many voices in their repertoires to rewrite existing power relationships is a way to highlight the extra labor scholars like the ones in this book do to negotiate with power to produce meaning. Importantly, these rhetorical choices occur on both the discursive *and* material planes as writers move knowledge across languages and audiences as time and context shift around them.

Indeed, by emphasizing particular moments, this definition aligns with what Lu and Horner term a "temporal-spatial" understanding of language and, later, Horner and Alvarez a "spatiotemporal" understanding (which I'll use). Locating moments of translingual praxis in both space *and* time, and "acknowledging we can never step into the same river twice" (Lu and Horner 589), allows us to acknowledge that each utterance is "by definition phenomenologically different from others in spatiotemporal location and, therefore, in sociopolitical significance" (Horner and Alvarez 12). In Anis Bawarshi's words, we need to acknowledge "asymmetrical relations of power" ("Beyond" 246) and "shift the locus of agency from the genres themselves . . . to their users, who are constantly having to negotiate genre uptakes across boundaries" (248). Translingual praxis happens both textually *and* extratextually, in text *and* in process, as writers negotiate language, identity, and power in relation to their particular historical moments and, as I'll argue next, in relation to the many voices that precede and proceed from these moments—what Mikhail Bakhtin theorizes as a process of dialogic audience negotiation.

LOCATING TRANSLINGUAL PRAXIS

Translingual praxis as I define it above is a critical form of translingual agency that centers human intention at the contact point between material reality and discursive possibility. Translingual praxis can happen both in text and in process, and how writers perform it shifts as discourses collide and time and the material world shift around them. Given these variables, *locating* translingual praxis is a complicated endeavor. Though Bakhtin was shaped by Western discourse, his theory of dialogic audience negotiation helped illuminate, for me, the "how" of my research participants' translingual praxis.

Despite his being a literary theorist, Bakhtin's theoretical lenses have since transcended disciplinary borders (in a way he'd likely support) to inform the work we do in Western rhetoric and writing studies circles. As Kay Halasek suggests, "by turning to language, the single most constitutive element of the rhetorical situation, Bakhtin redefines the other elements—author, audience, and subject—in terms of sociological dialogism, for each is constructed by and through language" (20). We can see Bakhtin's sociological understanding of language and how his theory might connect to border thinking and translinguality quite explicitly in his *Dialogic Imagination*. He argues that

> [a]t any given moment of its historical existence, language is heteroglot from top to bottom: it represents the co-existence of socio-ideological contradictions between the present and the past, between different socio-ideological groups in the present, between tendencies, schools, circles, and so forth, all given a bodily form. (291)

Language represents multiple voices and thus differing "socio-ideological traditions" from the past that language users must navigate as they work from the historical present to make future meaning. These past and present voices "coexist" because discourses and the values linked to them overlap, as Gee suggests. Because language always "exists in other people's mouths, in other people's contexts, serving other people's intentions, " for a writer to wrest language from past audiences in order to negotiate present and future audiences involves negotiating power and ideology (Bakhtin 293–94).

How writers negotiate competing discourses and their mutually constitutive language/value relationships—the focus of this book— can be understood as a process of dialogic audience negotiation. Bakhtin argues that because of the heteroglossic and thus "intertextual" nature of language, past voices as well as present and future voices are simultaneously present in—and thus are *audience to*—any textual production: "any concrete utterance is a link in the chain of speech communication of a particular sphere" and, as such, "each utterance is filled with echoes and reverberations of other utterances to which it is related by the communality of the sphere of speech communication" (91). Not only are past voices— the audiences that populate a writer's citational repertoire—part of and thus audience to every utterance a writer creates (there's no such thing as "original" language) but as writers produce text, they also predict their future addressee's—their intended audience's— "apperceptive background" or their "prejudices" and "specialized knowledge" (96). A writer must pull from what has been said or written to make meaning in their present, a process that also mediates the choices they make in relation to their intended audience as they imagine that audience's response; this process is both diachronic and dialogic in that a writer must inevitably draw from past utterances to anticipate their intended audience's apperceptive background, which in turn mediates how a writer invokes both that audience and their own identity in the text itself. Bakhtin argues that audience both precedes and proceeds from a writer as they write from their historical present, a process mediated by shifting power relationships.

Understanding translingual praxis in relation to *audience*—a term that invokes, for me, the *humans* past, present, and future who work with and on language—helps to emphasize that critical human agency is necessary to challenge the colonial matrix of power, without devolving into the what Mignolo would term the "ego-logical" notion of the rational human shaping the world. Importantly, Bakhtin, like Freire, also emphasizes the importance of exploring human *intentionality* when it comes to textual choice—a concept central to my definition of translingual praxis *and* to dismantling systemic oppression. He writes, for example, that lexical markers are merely

> the sclerotic deposits of an intentional process, signs left behind on the path of the real living project of an intention, of the particular way it imparts meaning to general linguistic forms. These external markers, linguistically observable and fixable, cannot in themselves be understood or studied without understanding the specific conceptualization they have been given by intention. (292)

The linguistic markers themselves, Bakhtin argues, though inherently heteroglossic, are themselves merely the rigid "sclerotic deposits" of an author's agentive choices in relation to their context or "living project." A writer doesn't stand above context, of course, just as an audience member doesn't; they intentionally situate themselves within a diachronic chain of signification to make language *live*. Bakhtin continues: "As a living, socio-ideological concrete thing, as heteroglot opinion, language, for the individual consciousness, lies on the borderline between oneself and the other" (293). By emphasizing the relationship between self and audience from a dialogical and diachronic perspective—with language as the concrete or material connection between writer and those voices past, present, and future who are audience to and thus mediate textual production—Bakhtin avoids falling into power-flattening humanism, while still reserving space for authorial intention when it comes to textual choices. Intention, in turn, is a necessary component of translingual praxis, which requires we understand how writers move between reflection and *action* on both discursive and material planes as time and contexts shift.

One way to illuminate the process of translingual praxis, this book shows, is to draw from Bakhtin's theory of dialogical audience negotiation to ask of ethnographic data "from whom," "for whom," and "with whom" do writers negotiate, and how? These questions, which I drew from the friction between my Indonesian data and my own theoretical lenses, informed the coding processes I employed and thus the fabric of the ethnographic story I tell here, illuminating the "how" of my research participants' translanguaging as they moved between the discursive and material planes to promote social justice. Indeed, as a testament to the affordances of border thinking—and, in a rather performative way, to the salience of Bakhtin's theory of intertextuality itself—in this book the voices and theories of my Indonesian research participants, as well as the theorists I cite above and elsewhere, work to interanimate and transform Bakhtin's primarily discursive theorizing to also encompass the materiality promised by translingual praxis. Though springing from vastly different contexts, the Indonesian voices and the voices of the theorists I cite above were audience to the theory of translingual praxis I build here, which in turn affects, in a dialogical way, the very telling of the telling of this ethnographic story I'm doing for you, my own audience. The next chapter will discuss how I gathered the ethnographic data that informed this telling.

Ethnographic Moment 3: A Very American Process
Teaching Journal: September 11, 2009

Students seem to be aware that I am a researcher even though it's the first week. After I introduced the plan for the day and asked whether there were any questions, a male student wearing a brightly colored batik shirt asked tentatively, "What will you research?" I explained that I would be doing ethnographic teacher research with our class to explore the relationship between culture and language practices and that I'd be talking more about my project at the end of class . . . . To end class, I introduced my research project at more length. After explaining the IRB process in the United States, I handed out the informed consent forms and read them out loud.

There was an interesting moment when I read the informed consent section about this teaching journal:

> Although I will take research notes throughout the semester, to ensure that your choice to participate in this research is entirely voluntary, and will not affect your grade in any way, this consent form will be collected by [the ICRS office manager] and kept locked in her office until after December 17, 2009, when grades have been submitted. At this time, I will look at the consent forms and include you in my analysis only if you have consented to participate.

One student interrupted and exclaimed, "This paperwork is very American." I could only admit that it was, while emphasizing ethics as important. After class, I discussed this moment with a professor from the United States who has been at ICRS for quite some time, and he explained that many Indonesians are still scarred by the authoritarian regime they just overthrew, where signing one's name to an official university document could be dangerous.

I hadn't thought about requesting an exemption for informed consent when I submitted my materials back at UMass. Luckily, though, the students seemed excited about my research: in fact, they asked me to send them my proposal so they could understand my research project as a whole and so they could use it as a model. It's nice to be at the same level as my students so that I can know what they're going through . . . I hope some sign the form . . .

Chapter 3

Ethnographic Matters

I INCLUDE THE PREVIOUS ETHNOGRAPHIC excerpt not to denigrate the "very American" IRB process, but instead to highlight, like Anna Plemons and my US-born colleague at ICRS, that what constitutes "ethical research" is very much tied to context. The moment above highlights what can happen when a researcher from one context brings her ethical assumptions to another. Luckily, this moment spurred a rather reflective discussion rather than a cultural disconnect, and all ten students in my PhD-level academic writing class eventually chose to participate. Interpreted a bit more broadly, this anecdote also suggests, to me, that we view all interactions between researcher and research participants—and the data that arise from these interactions—from a border-thinking framework, where we must, from an ethical standpoint, acknowledge power and ensure the safety of our research participants when crafting our projects, but also the fact that research is inevitably a dialogic, mutually transformative process as discourses meet and intertwine.

Thinking with, as Catherine Walsh asserts, involves dwelling at the borders of self and other—not to reify difference or to ignore power but instead to explore connection despite difference *in relation to* power. Rather than ignoring the lenses with which I see the work of my research participants, I must acknowledge and reflect on my own discursive influences and what happens when my admittedly Western scholarly engagements, language practices, and life experiences encounter those of my research participants. To return to the Bakhtinian lens I use to understand translingual praxis, disavowing the many past voices who are audience to this research not only reinforces the ego-logical notion that researchers, as "rational" beings, can remain neutral but also denies the transformative possibilities opened up when seemingly distinct discourses, in this case my own and those of my Indonesian research participants, are reimagined as relational and mutually transformative. To that end, this chapter makes explicit what methodological lenses I brought to the ethnographic story I tell here, and thus how I eventually came to understand the complexity of my research participants' rhetorical practices through the lens of "translingual praxis."

To review, translingual praxis, as I define it in the previous chapter, is a critical form of translingual agency that centers human intention at the contact point between material reality and discursive possibility. In keeping with the spatiotemporal understanding of agency forwarded by translingual scholars (Lu and Horner; Pennycook; Horner and Alvarez), translingual praxis can happen both in text and in process, and how writers perform it shifts as discourses collide and time and the material world shifts around them. As Anna Tsing argues, an "ethnographic account" is particularly suited to exploring points of friction when it comes to global intersections and the new formulations of power and possibility that proceed from these points of friction (*Friction* 6).

SAME QUESTIONS: EVOLVING LENSES

The ethnographic data in this book were collected over the course of thirteen years: during the 2009–2010 academic year, when I first began teaching and developing curriculum at ICRS as a US Department of State English Language Fellow,[13] in July 2014, when I returned to ICRS for follow-up research, and again in July 2022 for a final follow-up study, which, because of COVID-19, began via Zoom but ended on-site in Indonesia. Given ICRS's complex local-global identity, which I'll discuss at length in the next chapter, my project sought to answer these research questions:

- How has the English language been positioned as both local and global in a specific Indonesian literacy context?
- How, in turn, do writers, as they use English, negotiate the point of contact between local and global?

As the data showcased in this book illuminate, answering these questions involved exploring how writers negotiated power in relation to the multiple languages and audiences (in dialogical terms) at their disposal. Though, as mentioned previously, the "translingual turn" in Western conversations occurred after my initial study began in 2009, my project essentially sought to illuminate what translingual negotiation looked like in this particular Indonesian context. My follow-up projects focused more specifically on the relationship between religion and my research participants' scholarly-activist work as it pertained to the many languages and audiences they negotiated as they finished their dissertations and moved into their post-PhD lives.

Though my overarching research questions didn't change from one research moment to the next, as I discuss in the preface, my epistemological lenses did. Even though they represent only a snapshot of my larger data-collection process (more on that below), a look at the general script for my case-study interviews across the three studies (excerpted in full in the Appendix), illuminates how a project initially constructed within the confines (whether explicitly named or not) of English's Western imperialism—and which premised textual negotiation—shifted incrementally to a model in which religion and scholarship, scholarship and activism, and, with that, English-medium, Indonesian-medium, and Arabic knowledge were viewed *relationally*.

In my first set of interview questions, which moved from language histories and motivations to audience negotiation, and then to discourse-based questions in relation to texts they'd written, there *was* actually space for participants to discuss their writing lives in relation to discourses and audiences *not* linked to Western power. For example, because of a colleague's asking, "But to whom do we have students write?" at an academic board meeting (a moment discussed in Chapter 5), I asked, "What audience do you imagine most often when you write in English? Why?" This question left open the possibility that English could be delinked from the Western nation-state to reach localized audiences. The question of audience, in fact, was a central thread in all points of the study. However, at this point in the study my questions about audience also forwarded a contrastive rather than comparative approach, as evidenced in the question where I ask about publishing: "How much of this was in English vs. Indonesian? Can you compare the different writing styles to different audiences?" With the "vs." comes the assumption of immutable difference and no overlap.

Also notable in this first round of interviews is the fact that although I didn't ask about imperialism, my research participants still brought it up in their answers (likely because of conversations spurred by the critical pedagogy I developed for the academic writing class described in Chapter 5). Acknowledging Western power and English's links to imperialism *is* important, though from a border-thinking perspective, acknowledging what might come of meshing seemingly discrete discourses—and audiences—is also necessary. Overall, though the 2010 questions left space at some points for participants to talk about the interrelational aspects of their writing practices, at other points my dualistic orientation is clear. It is not surprising, then, that as I interpreted the data, I also brought epistemological lenses linked to coloniality to it, which resulted in a dissertation that focused mostly on research participants' local-global textual negotiations with the English language in relation to Western power, with very little focus on religion or activism or the possibility of interrelation (see "Writing the Local-Global").

It wasn't until after recoding data for what would turn into my 2014 *College English* article, "The 'Hands of God' at Work," that I began to see and thus ask about the complex intersections among research participants' Islamic faith, the Western academic knowledge they had garnered from their English-medium dissertation projects, and their local gender justice endeavors. This evolution can be seen in the 2014 questions, where I move from discussing participants' beliefs about English's imperialism (explicitly this time), to their dissertation projects, to how they circulate knowledge to different audiences, and finally to the relationship between religion and English writing. The final iteration of this project, in 2022, continued this interrelational exploration, with an additional focus on naming—of specific terms like "feminism" and "decolonial"—

and how, whether, and when participants translated or claimed these terms and for what audiences. As I discuss in the previous chapter, decolonial theory, which I had encountered just prior to this July 2022 trip, helped me reflect upon my original blind spots *and* better see how participants circulated knowledge in excess of linguistic origins among contexts long defined in opposition to one another.

METHODS MATTER

Though in the moment of praxis above I discuss shifts in interview questions to illustrate my shifting epistemologies, interviews were only a small part of my larger project. The following methods, which involved a careful "back-and-forth among historical, comparative, and current fieldwork sources" (Heath and Street 33) helped me locate, trace, and interrogate multiple points of friction at the institutional level and in three writers' lives over the course of thirteen years. Overall, my project involved the following methods of data collection:

- *Secondary research* on Indonesia's history and its sociolinguistic context, past and present, which I'll outline in the next chapter.
- *Observational research* of sociolinguistic practices at ICRS and at various activist sites of my research participants (2009–2010, 2014, and 2022).
- *Program-related document collection* of faculty handbooks, promotional brochures, and other hard-copy materials only available on site, and of digital program-related documents (2009–2010, 2014, and 2022).
- *Semi-structured interviews with administration and faculty* about institutional history and global literacy sponsorships (2009–2010, 2014, and 2022).
- *Teacher research* on classroom conversations that happened as PhD students took part in a yearlong academic writing course I developed and taught, recorded in a triple-entry notebook (2009–2010). (See Engelson, "To Whom," for a robust discussion of this process.)

- *Semistructured interviews* about writers' individual literacy histories and writing practices, in English, Arabic, and Indonesian, at three checkpoints across thirteen years, with the first two iterations on site and the final follow-up via Zoom because of COVID-19, followed by in-person, on-site member checks in July 2022 (2009–2010, 2014, and 2022).
- *Multimodal cocuration of digital texts*: of the audioclips and web texts linked to this book, which are meant to connect my own audience directly to my research participants' scholarly-activist work (in 2022).
- And *rhetorical analysis of my participants' written work*, of both formal and informal texts written in the course I developed and taught during the 2009–2010 academic year (literacy narratives, cover letters and their respective assignments, generative writing) and of texts written for wider audiences as they advanced in their academic and civic careers (dissertations, academic publications, and publications for civic audiences).

These methods and my overall ethnographic approach helped me to explore how writers negotiated across, between, and within languages both textually *and* extratextually, as they negotiated their linguistic choices in the drafting process and through conversation, and, just as importantly, as they moved knowledge in text and body from one rhetorical situation to the next across languages and audiences over an extended period of time.

CODING MATTERS

To sort through all of these data, I took an inductive approach to analysis (see Kamberelis and Dimitriadis) with "multiple phases of coding and categorizing" (48). The process began right when data collection began in 2009, when I began taking notes in my teaching journal, which in turn helped me reflect upon and revise my course, as Chapter 5 will explore (see Nunan). As I collected more qualitative data over the course of thirteen years, and as published knowledge of global writing practices evolved, so too did my analysis.

With Kay Halasek's *Pedagogy of Possibility* as an inspiration, I ended up creating a coding process that drew from but also exceeded Bakhtin's dialogic audience heuristic to encompass material interventions as well as discursive ones. Importantly, rather than being *applied to* my Indonesian data, this admittedly Western heuristic was *drawn from* my coding process and the questions of audience my research participants continually returned to. From a border-thinking perspective, Bakhtin's voice was *already* audience to *my* understanding of audience negotiation, but I made sure also to allow the Indonesian data I collected to transform Bakhtin's dialogic audience heuristic in new ways. The results of this coding heuristic will emerge organically, as this book progresses, but in the meantime, here are the questions I asked of the data showcased here:

- *"From whom?"* Asking *from whom* writers drew their knowledge was central to locating the past voices that preceded, and were audience to, the texts research participants created and thus to understanding pretextual translanguaging, or what Li terms "thinking beyond language," to illuminating how the writers with whom I worked drew from subjugated knowledge to inform their texts, to finding "interrelations" despite perceived difference when it came to overlapping discourses, and to emphasizing global inequality related to the material access to literate resources.

- *"For whom?"* As Chapter 5 will discuss, inspired by an Indonesian colleague's question at an academic board meeting about the location of English-using audiences, asking *for whom* writers intended their knowledge helped me map textual choices in relation to these writers' intended audiences and to challenge longstanding links among language, audience, and nation-state.

- *"With whom?"* Inspired by my Indonesian research participants' activist intentions, this question helped me locate the embodied, real-world audiences research participants wished to serve with knowledge drawn from their written work, regardless of originating language, and, concomitantly, to reflect on how this book itself might, in some small way, amplify my research participants' work, challenging what has been traditionally an extractive relationship between the West and the "rest."

As I coded using these questions to guide me, I began to see broad patterns of engagement—or ways of negotiating with audience—when it came to each of my case-study participants' portfolios, which, as I'll argue in their respective case-study portraits, are likely linked to situational power dynamics and their differing identities. When it came to what emerged from moments of translingual praxis, Faqih seemed to *serve* his audiences; Nina, to *access* audiences; and Ninik, to *cultivate* audiences. These orientations toward audience suggest new ways of understanding the "how" of translingual praxis, provided, of course, that knowledge makers learn to listen for and past colonialist dualities.

IDENTITY MATTERS

In addition to its value in mapping global interrelations, taking an ethnographic approach, with its multiple points of data collection, was crucial because of my own positionality as a white "native-speaking" English user from the United States with beginner-level Bahasa Indonesia (Indonesia's official lingua franca). Bruce Horner, Samantha NeCamp, and Christiane Donahue, as well as others, have suggested—and rightfully—that to truly understand translingual negotiation, more multilingual research is necessary. In "Toward a Writing Pedagogy of Shuttling between Languages," for example, Suresh Canagarajah argues that multilingual scholars are best suited to comparative textual analyses given their ability to, in Canagarajah's words, "study the author writing in relatively the same genre though for different audiences and languages" (591). A multilingual researcher *would* be ideal for such research, particularly when comparing textual differences across different language traditions. Though online translation tools *did* help me translate some of my research participants' texts from Bahasa Indonesia to English, my translation work relied on my preexisting knowledge of their English-medium work; thus, I still had to rely on the writers with whom I worked to make up for my linguistic deficit—an approach their fluency in English, Arabic, and various Indonesian languages allowed.

The mixed methods forwarded by ethnography also helped me paint a more three-dimensional picture of the writing lives of Muslim writers than is often seen in dominant Western discourse. As Catherine Pavia emphasizes in "Taking Up Faith," when researching religious identities it is especially important to engage in reflection about how one's own terministic screens, to employ Kenneth Burke's term, affect our methodologies and interpretive processes. Engaging in this type of reflection, and then coupling it with multiple types of data collection, is crucial when someone like me, who grew up in a Christian-centered community, seeks to study the rhetorical practices of Muslims—a group often reviled or, at best, essentialized by dominant Western discourse. Though my research questions did not originally focus on religion, religious discourse permeates almost every level of Indonesian society, as the next chapter will show. The fact that my research participants were earning PhDs in religious studies meant that local religious data were embedded in almost all of the English texts they produced, an affordance for me, as it allowed me to center their Indonesian interpretations of Islam in my own analysis, which I then put in conversation with secondary research on Islam's role in the national imagination. This published scholarship, we will see, was expanded upon—and at times challenged—by the academic and activist work of my research participants. The collaborative, emic approach ethnography encourages—and the qualitative methods required to center research participants' knowledge—allowed me to take a writer-centered, as opposed to a researcher-centered, approach to understanding Indonesian rhetorical practices. Importantly, I do not claim to be a scholar of Islamic rhetoric or Islamic gender justice myself; however, those whom I showcase here *are*, and at the borderland between their expertise and my own, new knowledge can be produced.

Indeed, in a nod to the productive friction that can happen when discourses collide during the research process, my own research project appeared to help at least one of my research participants reflect in new ways about themselves as language users. At the end of my initial 2010 interview with Faqih, he exclaimed,

> This interview is a good idea because I can know myself when you ask me and interview me . . . . Can you write about the idea that I just think about intimate people even when I make a decision for my life? This is about writing, of course, but I will try to make it a theme for my life . . . . It's like I can know myself, from this research, from the questions, without going to a psychologist!

Indeed, intimate audiences are central to Faqih's chapter. At the borderland where different discourses meet—in this case, where his religious studies scholarship meets my writing studies scholarship—new knowledge is created. The Indonesian writers showcased in this book are, like me, "persons in process . . . recomposing themselves toward their futures" (Herrington and Curtis 354). Making this mutual transformation evident involved, for me, "thinking with" the work of my research participants, a process I'll continue as I seek to reflect upon the voices, past and present—from Western contexts and Indonesia and beyond—that contribute to this ethnographic story.

RISK MATTERS

By highlighting this mutually dialogic transformation, I don't mean to diminish the risks research participants took when they chose to take part in this project. As the ethnographic moment above describes, my initial project did pose a risk because of its teacher ethnography focus and the power differences between students and teachers as well as the unique nature of ICRS—a program that, because it's the only one of its kind in the world, would be easy to locate even with a pseudonym. The data collected in my 2014 and 2022 follow-up studies further complicated matters, especially for the three ethnographic case-study participants I chose to focus on. My focus on their published scholarship and the feminist-activist organizations they are a part of—data that are easily searchable on the web—could pose a risk because even with pseudonyms, they are easily locatable with the titles and content of their texts. Though they have already published their work widely, the content of their work itself might also pose a risk: Faqih, Nina, and Ninik are vocal public intellectuals writing at the intersections between Islam and gender justice in a country that, as the next chapter will explore, is still working against conservatism and toward its promise of religious plurality. These risks to anonymity were made explicit in the informed consent processes across the thirteen years we've worked together, and all participants have chosen to participate in each portion of the project using their names.

The multimodal nature of the current project, with direct links to their voices and their scholarly-activist organizations, makes anonymity impossible. However, as Laura Gonzales emphasizes in *Sites of Translation*, it is "a way to give additional credit to the people who inform this work" so that they're not "merely . . . representations of my authorship" (66–67). Amplifying their scholarly-activist work—and reframing them as participants in, rather than subject to, my research project—was a central goal of this book. To accomplish this goal ethically, for the 2022 portion of this project I broke the informed-consent process into multiple parts, across two different forms. The first form had two parts, with the first section asking them to agree to being videorecorded and to participate using the names they publish under or, alternately, to suggest pseudonyms. The second section focused on the multimodal aspect of this project, and I emphasized that it was entirely optional because anonymity would be impossible at this point. And, finally, once I received consent for the optional multimodal portion on the initial form and after cocurating the digital texts linked here, I disseminated a second form; taking a cue from Gonzales's process, I employed a recursive consent process ("Designing") whereby I asked permission to publish each digital text prior to publication of this book.[14]

Though risk is inherent when taking part in qualitative research and power dynamics inevitable when a person like me, who springs from an extractive Western research tradition, seeks to conduct research "elsewhere and otherwise," I do hope that making explicit this risk to my research participants and then amplifying their scholarly-activist work with my own helps to bend this project toward "inter-relationality" rather than extraction.

PROCESS MATTERS

The writing of an ethnography is inevitably recursive and complex. As I mentioned in the preface, the fact that I've structured this book by forefronting the theories that contributed to my understandings of "translingual praxis" and the dialogic audience coding heuristic I used—both of which I *drew from* the qualitative data I collected—challenges linear notions of time. To return to Mari Lee Mifsud's argument about the importance of "telling the telling of this story" and to foreshadow the ethnographic excerpt that follows, this research and the process of constructing this ethnographic story has been one best described as a dialogic and diachronic "jalan-jalan."

Ethnographic Moment 4: Jalan-Jalan
Teaching Journal: September 7, 2009

Today I had my first "official" day at ICRS, though I don't teach until tomorrow. As I walked there, I found myself negotiating numerous temporary street stalls lining the sidewalk, which required me to step off the sidewalk into the hectic street traffic of one of Yogyakarta's main thoroughfares, Jalan Kaliurang. The streets were busy even at 7:30 a.m.; many of the Indonesians I encountered likely had gotten up before 5:00 a.m. for the first morning prayer. As I jumped back and forth between officially sanctioned foot paths and the speeding traffic, merchants and other folks going about their morning shopping asked me, "Mau ke mana?" Translated literally, this phrase means "Where are you going?" I knew enough from my first Bahasa Indonesia lessons to know that this phrase isn't meant to be taken literally and is instead just a general greeting, similar to "What's up?" in US English. Luckily, I had practiced the appropriate answer, "jalan-jalan," which translates roughly to "I'm wandering" or "taking a stroll." Eventually, twenty-four-hour "fotocopy" shop signs indicated I was getting close to the University of Gadjah Mada (UGM), which houses ICRS, where I am going to spend the next year researching and teaching PhD-level English academic writing. The fotocopy shop signs pointed to numerous services and were mostly in English: "Free Wi-fi," "Copy," "Print," "Scan," "Laminate," "E-book." And

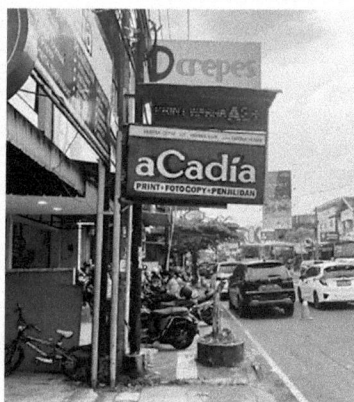

as I peeked into these well-lit, spacious, tile-floored shops—which was easy to do from the street, since storefronts are open-air—I saw lines of Indonesian students waiting patiently for the giant machines to create their hardcopy and e-book academic books, for a price that is likely much cheaper than "official" versions sold through publishing houses and bookstores.

I had been told UGM was the "Harvard of Indonesia" because of its position as the top-ranked and oldest university in Indonesia, and the entrance to the Pascasarjana, the UGM graduate school building where I was to work, signaled this reputation. Stepping from the vibrant, dusty, noisy street into the grounds of UGM was like passing from one world to the next. The official entrance which I reached by crossing a bridge flanked by beautiful white arches, then continuing along a path shaded by palm trees and redolent with the smells of tropical flowers, took me to a light-filled atrium and a grand split spiral staircase, and eventually, three floors later, to ICRS. Once I got there, the office manager gave me a tour and showed me where I was to teach. The classroom is better-appointed than my classrooms at UMass. It has a gray slate tile floor, comfortable, padded desks, an air conditioner, and, unlike at UMass, a laptop projector built into the classroom (which you need to turn off with a giant pole, because, they explained, the remote keeps on disappearing). And my favorite: a whiteboard (which sure beats the chalkboards I'm used to in Bartlett Hall!).

Video Clip of Midday Prayer from ICRS Entrance

Chapter 4

Negotiating Colonial(ist) Realities*

I BEGIN WITH THIS ETHNOGRAPHIC MOMENT (and the video clip) both to give my audience a glimpse into the embodied, material reality that shaped my initial research project and because the scenes presented here work on both the metaphorical and literal levels to illuminate central tensions and possibilities highlighted in this chapter and beyond. Overall, this first "jalan, jalan" to ICRS emphasizes how economic inequality exists in dynamic tension with educational possibility. Just as material circumstances forced me as a pedestrian to move back and forth between where I was *supposed* to be and where I *had* to be in order to move forward on my walk, so too do material circumstances force Indonesians, like the temporary street stall vendors and those students in the photocopy shops, to engage in tactics that exist outside of those sanctioned by the powers that be. To employ Michel de Certeau's terms from *The Practice of Everyday Life,* although powerful institutions may sanction certain "strategies" for accessing resources—often to these institutions' economic benefit—individuals in developing countries also take agency to negotiate "tactically" with and against these top-down strategies to achieve their scholarly and civic purposes. As de Certeau emphasizes, such tactical maneuvers are opportunistic in nature and act as a form of creative resistance to hegemonic power, in the street stalls' case to the more expensive rent of the brick-and-mortar shops and in the students' case to the role global publishing houses play in dictating who can afford new knowledge.

*Portions of this chapter were drawn from "'Resources Are Power': Writing across the Global Information Divide." *Thinking Globally, Composing Locally: Rethinking Online Writing in the Age of the Global Internet.* Eds. Rich Rice and Kirk St. Amant. U of Colorado P, 2018.

As this chapter looks back into Indonesia's sociolinguistic past, we will see that when it comes to language, Indonesians also have a long history of disrupting hegemonic strategies through the tactical appropriation of the resources at hand.

This ethnographic anecdote also emphasizes the unevenness of globalization. My walk from the chaotic street-life of Jalan Kaliurang into the pastoral spaces of the Pascasarjana works metaphorically to emphasize the uneven flow of global resources, both economic and linguistic, in this one literacy ecology. As John Trimbur argues, globalization is a "contradictory and uneven process operating through transcultural localizations" ("English" 113). Not everyone in a society has equal social or economic footing, as Jan Blommaert, James Ferguson, and others have shown. In Ferguson's words, "the 'global' does not flow, thereby connecting and watering contiguous spaces; it hops instead, efficiently connecting the enclaved points in the network, while excluding (with equal efficiency), the spaces that lie between the points" (47). ICRS, as my anecdote shows, was better-appointed technologically than the spaces where I taught at the University of Massachusetts Amherst, and it certainly was a much more beautiful space architecturally. However, as the photocopy shops just outside the graduate school walls indicate, global inequality and thus unequal access still affects the scholarly work done at ICRS, no matter how beautiful the space. It is to the ebb and flow of resources—and to the often-tactical ways Indonesians have sought to fill with their words and actions the spaces that "lie between the points," or what might be termed the "excess" of coloniality—that this chapter will now turn. By acknowledging the conditions that brought about and continually reinforce global inequality under the guise of "neutrality" and "improvement" and "rationality," and then acknowledging that which inevitably exceeds this formulation, we can help foster new understandings of what it means to create knowledge globally.

LINGUISTIC TACTICS IN THE
FACE OF COLONIAL POWER

To understand the complicated role that English plays in the writing lives of the Indonesians at ICRS, it is important to understand

Indonesia as a sociolinguistic context, which necessitates delving into the nation's complex language history. As Subhan Zein explores in depth in *Language Policy in Superdiverse Indonesia*, the Indonesian archipelago has a long history of negotiating externally imposed languages, a history which, Peter Lowenberg shows, is in turn complicated by an equally long history of appropriating and resignifying these languages to serve Indonesian purposes and the values Indonesians hold dear. This give-and-take between colonial strategy and on-the-ground tactics, I argue, likely informs the ways contemporary language users at ICRS negotiate with the imperialism of English to achieve their religiously motivated academic and civic purposes.

ICRS's desire to use English as a means of writing Indonesian scholarship on religion into global academic conversations is likely tied to the continued reverberations of Dutch colonization, which intersects more recently with globalizing discourses that paint developing countries like Indonesia in terms of deficit. What constitutes "progress" and thus deficit is, of course, constituted by a colonial matrix of power that has long defined the concept of "modernity" and "progress" using Western knowledge as the measuring stick, as Aníbal Quijano asserts—whether in relation to the "ego-logical" separation between religion and rationality or in relation to language standardization. When it comes to Indonesia, Tania Murray Li in *The Will to Improve* shows how various actors, whether colonial officials in the past or current global developers, use Western-constructed notions of "expertise" as a justification for intervention in Indonesia's cultural and political fabric. These interventions, Li argues, are justified by what she terms "the will to improve" (5). Li points to two key practices that work in conjunction to justify intervention: *problemetization*, or identifying "deficiencies" often based on preconceived notions about "proper" ways of being and doing, and *rendering technical*, or "defining boundaries" for action by assembling data about the "problem." This "technicalization" works, in turn, to justify any intervention as neutral, commonsensical, and thus apolitical, leaving power relations between trustees and those receiving "aid" unquestioned (7). Of course, the very fact that "technicalization" and the strategic creation of boundaries is required suggests a reality that exceeds what is "rendered technical" and thus the possibility of delinking from it to form new ways of knowing.

Regardless of this inevitable excess, in her ethnography Li establishes numerous ways this "will to improve" justified oppressive colonial policies. Beginning in 1800,[15] the Dutch rendered technical Indonesia's "never quite there-ness" to justify colonial intervention, whether that intervention involved "helping" Indonesians become more "white" and thus more "civilized" or helping them return to an "authentic" native state by "being true to their own indigenous traditions" (15). To showcase the latter, for instance, Li highlights how colonial officials used "research" to almost entirely *invent*— and thus "discover"—traditions of "communal life" and an Indonesian collectivist mentality that justified forced migration and restructuring of *already* structured communities.

Language, in turn, was a particularly important means of controlling the seventeen thousand islands and over four hundred distinct language groups[16] the Dutch encountered in their colonial enterprise (Lowenberg). The Dutch language policy, I would argue, was implicated in Li's notion of the "will to improve" because of the standardizing and codifying processes implemented to control who was allowed to make meaning. Though there has been little theorization of the role this technicalization of language played in the Indonesian colonial project, Alastair Pennycook points quite powerfully to the ways this "will to improve"and the "rendering technical" of knowledge through the process of standardization played into British colonial language policies (*Cultural Politics*). He takes to task the mistaken notion that English was promoted in British colonies as a blanket policy. In fact, English was meted out to only a select few elite colonial subjects because of possible incendiary effects if it became too widespread: after all, those with the tools of the colonizers could challenge the colonizers' justifications for oppressing them. Such withholding, in turn, created the desire in non-English using colonial subjects to learn English and thus "improve" their social positionings. This desire—a deliberate colonial strategy—has long fueled notions of deficit when it comes to those without access to the language of power. And for those who did have access to English, Pennycook shows how what Li would call the "rendering technical" of English worked to maintain notions of never-quite-thereness: during the same time period, the burgeoning of English studies and linguistics worked to "standardize" English through codification, a process that "held the language and its desired meanings firmly in the hands of central colonial institutions" (*Cultural Politics* 104), and left little room for culturally specific uses of English.

Though it's important to avoid "colonial equivocation" (see Tuck and Yang 19), the Dutch enacted similar practices in terms of language policy. Like their British counterparts, the Dutch also withheld Dutch from the vast majority of Indonesians, despite the fact that they proclaimed Dutch as the national government's official language. In fact, fearing the same incendiary effects as did the British, they established only two hundred and fifty Dutch-medium primary and secondary schools for the Indonesian elite and a few "academically promising non-elite" (Lowenberg 61). To implement their "improvement" agendas efficiently in what was then a loosely aligned archipelago, in 1865 they made Malay the official language for commerce and local administration because it had already acted as a lingua franca for traders in Southeast Asia for thousands of years. The language was so useful, in fact, that the Dutch made Malay the official language of commerce and local administration in 1865 (61).[17] As had the British, they then "rendered" the language "technical," operating under what could be considered the "will to improve": Lowenberg shows that once Malay was made official "the Dutch found themselves continually having to modernize and standardize the variety of Malay," a process that involved imposing a standard Latinized alphabet in 1901 and eventually forming Malay-medium publishing houses in 1908 (62). The Dutch, it seems, had the same impulse as the British to "standardize" their colonized subjects' language use, perhaps, like the British, so they could maintain control of colonial meaning-making. This standardization, however, also helped work against the Dutch colonial project, uniting once-disconnected islands in a

of national unity brought two successive dictators, Sukarno and Suharto,[18] both of whom killed, terrorized, and relocated hundreds of thousands of Indonesians. Amid the political, economic, and religious strife of the past sixty years (factors that, as I'll discuss next, encouraged the founding of ICRS), Bahasa Indonesia remains a success story[19] and one of the most powerful tools in unifying an extremely diverse archipelago as it has grappled with what it means to be a newly democratic nation since Suharto's overthrow in 1998.

Through this brief overview of a complicated history, then, we can see the ways that language has been used as a colonial tool—enabling colonizers to more easily navigate and control the colonized under the guise of "improvement"—and, more important, the ways that Indonesians took agency and resignified this colonial tool as a revolutionary one, capable of articulating their own interests. Though this linkage between language and nation-state will be problematized throughout this book, as Anna Tsing argues in *Friction*, this sociolinguistic snapshot emphasizes that with every local-global encounter there is the possibility that power can be reconfigured.

NEGOTIATING RELIGIOUS BORDERLANDS

Not surprisingly, ICRS as an academic institution must negotiate in similar ways with English—a language long linked to Western imperialism, but also a language the program sees as necessary to achieve the inter-religious harmony promised by Pancasila. As evidenced by the placement of "Belief in one God" as the first tenet of Indonesia's democracy, religion permeates the warp and weft of almost every institution in Indonesia. The reference to "God" rather than to a specific religion in this founding document is especially significant because Indonesia boasts the world's largest Muslim population, the majority of whom identify as Sunni, with other minority Islamic traditions, like the Ahmadi community of which Nina is a part, also making up a small percent of the overall Muslim population. Rather than privileging Islam because of its majority status, postcolonial leaders were careful to craft space for other religions to coexist, in a pluralistic democratic state, with Islam.

Although Pancasila clearly values monotheistic religions since it doesn't name one specific religion as primary, it leaves space for the country's six major religions to practice their beliefs in tandem: ideally, then, those practicing Islam (87 percent of the population), Protestantism (7 percent), Catholicism (3 percent), Hinduism (1.5 percent), Buddhism (1 percent), and Confucianism (less than 1 percent) would peacefully coexist in the pluralist and democratic country Pancasila envisions (US Department of State).

In recent years, however, religiously motivated violence has escalated, as evidenced by the bombings of Western hot spots in Bali and Jakarta by Islamic extremists (in 2002, 2005, and 2009, respectively) and by the multiple interreligious riots that continue to happen in places throughout Indonesia. Indeed, despite Pancasila's promises, in 2012 alone seventeen Christian churches were forced to close in Aceh, the only island to embrace Shariah, or Islamic law; and liberal Muslim activist Irshad Manji, a Canadian, was assaulted during her visit to the country, purportedly by the militant Islamic Defenders Front (Kuhn). As Nina's portrait will attest, there is also violence perpetrated by extremist Muslim groups against minority Muslim communities, like the Ahmadiyya. Extremist violence, which belies the pluralist views of Pancasila and the beliefs of the majority of Indonesia's population, spurred the founding of ICRS in 2006 and continues to motivate the scholarship happening there.

Despite this local exigency, in their mission statement ICRS self-identifies as an "Indonesian, International, Inter-Religious Studies PhD program," a local-global institutional identity that has long been reflected in their program goals, though recently the balance has shifted toward locality. Their founding goals, which I first encountered in 2009, were as follows:

- To provide a setting for PhD research on religions that is rooted in Indonesian culture and religious beliefs but in dialogue with the international community.
- To produce a PhD program in religious studies that maintains international standards of academic excellence but is controlled and directed by Indonesian scholars.

- To promote North-South and South-South exchanges with good universities in different parts of the world. (*Introducing ICRS-Yogya* 7)

ICRS shows in these original goals a clear desire to be rooted in Indonesia and run by Indonesians but also to be connected to international academic conversations, an orientation that is complicated to maintain when confronted with economic inequality and the reality that because of English's global hegemony, the language—long linked to Western interests—is a must. In fact, as I show in the preface, the program's first language policy explicitly emphasizes "the imperialism of English" and how "painful" the decision was.

Despite the ways the program imagines itself as both international *and* Indonesian in its published goals, because of its international connections (and, tangentially, its use of English), ICRS has been accused in more conservative Indonesian circles of being an "agent of the West." Such complaints are often linked to the Western funding required to establish an "international program" in Indonesia. Though initially founded in 2006 with the funding support of three Indonesian universities—one Islamic (Universitas Islam Negeri Sunan Kalijaga), one Christian/Protestant (Universitas Kristen Duta Wacana), and one secular (Universitas Gadjah Mada)—to defray costs linked to internationalization, the founders of ICRS applied for and were granted a five-year, one-million-dollar endowment from the US-based Ford Foundation to help foster international connections through South-South networking; staff development; student scholarships; and South-South exchange programs. Although this Western sponsorship was undoubtedly implicated in the "will to improve"—indeed, it could be and has been viewed as one way to further US interests in the developing world— without this support, the continuance of ICRS, at least internationally, would have been much more difficult.

Dr. Fatimah Husein, the assistant director of ICRS, described in a 2010 interview how ICRS's local-global positioning makes some Indonesians wary of ICRS's goals with an anecdote about her initial trip to Jakarta to accept the Ford Foundation funding.

She explained in her interview that as she outlined the "golden goals" for their Indonesian international program, the official in charge of distributing their money "did not seem interested at all." Remembering from past experience with the already developed MA program (CRCS)[20] that "many people will probably think we are leading to weakening of Muslim—and not only Muslim, but all religions' faith—trying to say that all religions are the same" and that the MA program had been viewed in the past as "a challenge to Muslim faith by the West," she rushed to reassure him. "Look," she explained, "as a Muslim, I wouldn't exchange my faith for this kind of thing. If this program actually led students to become less Muslim or less Christian, I wouldn't join this." In response, the official pulled out a giant pile of documents from his desk, "which prior to this he had prepared about news related to ICRS and CRCS." She explained that she was not surprised by some publications put out by a well-known conservative Muslim group against the programs; however, she was quite surprised to find that "it's not only people you anticipate to hear from, but people from the State Department who wonder why the Ford Foundation is going to give us this money and what kind of activities we'll do." Such resistance points to many Indonesians' valid fear that as a postcolonial, developing country, Indonesia has been and still is vulnerable to non-Indonesian ideologies circulating with global capital such as that donated by the Ford Foundation.

The Indonesians at ICRS have long successfully navigated this frictive tension between coloniality-cum-imperialism and the locality of their interreligious goals, a reality the program made quite explicit in 2022 when they rewrote their program goals as follows:

- To create an interdisciplinary and interreligious dialogue between scholars from different academic, religious, and cultural backgrounds in the study of religion.
- To educate Indonesian and international teachers, leaders, and scholars of religion who are skilled in interdisciplinary and interreligious communication.

- To produce outstanding research and publications that promote constructive understanding of the roles of religions in the world.
- To promote international cooperation between universities and maintain international standards of academic excellence and financial responsibility.
- To develop Indonesian resources and practices of community engagement that support reconciliation, justice and peace (*ICRS Doctoral Handbook* 6).

The first four goals are in some regards an echo of the previous goals but with a greater emphasis on the *action* implied—though not explicitly stated—in the original goals; namely, the active *doing* of interreligious dialogue across contexts both geographical and disciplinary. This shift from what the program *is* to what it *does* is likely a testament to the fact that the program of study (the "what") is fully established; in fact, ICRS has just earned UGM, where it is housed, a global ranking in the QS index when it comes to religious studies—forty-seventh in the world, and first in Indonesia, which shows their success in achieving "international standards of academic excellence" (ICRS.or.id).

This more explicit focus on *doing* in the revised program goals is also, I contend, reflective of the way ICRS has always challenged the academic/activist duality long maintained by the colonial matrix of power, which positions the rational/embodied and the academic/spiritual in *opposition* as opposed to in dynamic interrelation (see Mignolo, "Delinking"). The final goal, above, now makes explicit how actors at ICRS have long worked to promote interreligious harmony within Indonesia itself. A brief glimpse at the program's "Research and Projects" page showcases the type of local engagements ICRS takes part in, from projects exploring the effects of COVID-19 on religious faith in Indonesia; to a collaborative urban development program meant "to engage schools, universities, civic organizations, NGOs, and faith-based communities . . . to develop [and] co-design strategies and recommendations to foster sustainable, just and smart urban living"; to a religious literacy training program for religious extension officers/religious councilors

ICRS Research and Projects Page

ICRS Religion & COVID 19 Project

ICRS Co-Designing Sustainable, Just and Smart Urban Living Project

ICRS Religious Literacy for Social Justice Program

(penyulu agama) at the Indonesian Ministry of Religious Affairs focused on the principles of interreligious dialogue and social justice, a program which reached 1,177 individuals in eleven cities, and included both the targeted civil servants at the Ministry of Religious Affairs and "religious teachers, representations of religious institution, youth organizations, academics, and non-governmental and civil society organizations." At ICRS, scholarship, religion, and social justice exist in dialogic, as opposed to dualistic, relations.

REROUTING LINGUISTIC "STANDARDS"

Despite ICRS's desire to promote social justice locally, and the success of Bahasa Indonesia as a national lingua franca, ICRS's doctoral handbook and website are written in English because the English language, of course, is tied up with—and often reconstitutes— the colonial matrix of power (see Canagarajah, "Challenges"; Sugiharto, "Enacting"). Long used to reinforce Western interests, English has a history of being linked to Christian proselytizing (see Bhabha; Varghese and Johnston), and to development initiatives that Robert Phillipson has shown were deliberately put in place to shift from the overt exploitation of colonization to ruling "the empires of the mind" (131). This linguistic imperialism also solidified English as the global lingua franca when it comes to the circulation of academic knowledge across borders.[21] As ICRS's former director, Dr. Syamsiyatun, explained in 2014, "Most Religious Studies scholarship that takes an anthropological view of religion is published in English," a testament to the language's links to the economic power of the United States and Great Britain. To "maintain international standards of academic excellence," English ability is a must, particularly for those wishing to access and contribute Indonesian knowledge to internationally indexed conversations in religious studies.

As Theresa Lillis and Mary Jane Curry, in *Academic Writing in a Global Context,* have shown, because of English's predominance, scholars in non-Anglophone countries are often expected to publish in English to be considered "credible" (see also Pedersen's "Negotiating Cultural Identities through Language"). Indonesian scholars are no exception. In 2012, the Indonesian government became interested in "maintaining international standards" when it comes to academic publishing. The Indonesian Director General of Higher Education issued a mandate, Dikti 152, requiring all undergraduates, graduates, and faculty to publish their research before receiving their degrees or promotions (Sugiharto). Though undergraduate and MA students can submit their work to Indonesian-medium journals, both PhD students and current faculty are required to publish in scopus-indexed journals, most of which are English-medium, either to receive their diplomas or to advance from lecturer to full professor (McAdams). This mandate has caused a stir in academic communities across Indonesia because it assumes that all Indonesian faculty have the linguistic fluency to publish in internationally indexed journals—again, most of which are in English—and that Indonesians have the same access to academic resources that those working from more privileged countries do (McAdams). No wonder the authors of ICRS's first language policy called the decision to use English a "painful" one.

That English is linked to Western power and thus Western understandings of the world, and that it can reify existing inequalities, is undeniable; however, painting an overly deterministic picture of the English language denies the agency of global language users to negotiate power and, at times, appropriate language—and knowledge itself—for their own purposes. To return to Indonesian history, actors within this diverse archipelago have a long history of subverting the strategies of the more powerful to redirect resources. The way that ICRS has shifted its language policy from 2009 to 2022 is indicative of this type of situated agency. Despite the founders' explicit mention of English's imperialism in the language policy, when I arrived in Indonesia in 2009, all students were required to write their dissertations in English, which was simultaneously a pragmatic move given English's academic power *and* an idealistic one given the program's global aims and the fact that some students do hail from non-Indonesian countries. The 2022 ICRS doctoral handbook indicates that the program has adopted a more flexible, yet still pragmatic, approach. The new language policy first begins by asserting that:

The language of instruction at ICRS is English. This means that lecturers in all ICRS courses use English; all papers, other assignments as well as dissertation proposal and literature reviews as part of the comprehensive examination must be also written in English. Required reading assignments should mainly consist of materials published in English. In cases where Indonesian materials are assigned, alternative English materials should be indicated. (13)

These requirements, which echo the earlier iteration of the language policy, position English as the primary language, although there is mention of the possibility that Indonesian materials could be assigned, albeit alongside English materials. The new policy when it comes to dissertations, however, is more flexible. It states that

> students may use Bahasa Indonesia in writing their dissertations. The decision about this will be decided by the program together with the promoters and the student. For students who write their dissertations in Bahasa Indonesia, at least one of the required publications must be written in English. All dissertations, regardless in what language they are written, must have both English and Indonesian abstracts. (13)

This current policy builds in flexibility, provided that students first have direct conversations with faculty and staff at ICRS about the affordances and risks of choosing Bahasa Indonesia over English. To satisfy DIKTI 152—and the expectations for English fluency hiring institutions might have when considering prospective job candidates—students are still required to write a portion of their dissertations in English.

REROUTING PUBLISHED RESOURCES: NEGOTIATING MATERIAL ACCESS

Even if scholars are fluent in English, accessing global academic conversations from Indonesia is complicated by economic inequality. As Canagarajah's (*Resisting*), Lillis and Curry's, and my own research has shown (see "Resources Are Power"), unequal access to published academic resources belies claims that English and the digital turn have truly leveled the playing field when it comes to the circulation of knowledge. Accessing and then contributing to global academic conversations involves more than linguistic fluency; getting published often requires access to recently published scholarship, which too often is unavailable to scholars working in developing country contexts like Indonesia's. Despite this information divide, scholars at ICRS showed an adeptness for rerouting resources to the benefit of their Indonesian community.

Gaining access to English-medium global conversations at ICRS involved multiple types of networking, on the personal level—what de Certeau would call tactical networking—and at the institutional level—what de Certeau would term strategic networking. Perhaps the most obvious way ICRS students engaged in tactical networking was by sharing university library logins garnered either from Indonesian friends who had studied abroad or from international students or lecturers visiting from the Global North. In fact, as Chapter 8 shows, Ninik even writes this tactic into her literacy narrative. Time and again students came to my office hours, not to discuss the actual texts they were writing but to get help accessing the *content* they would use in their texts. Together we would navigate my US university's library website, locating and downloading peer-reviewed articles and ebooks that might contribute to their scholarly work, not just for current assignments but for the dissertations they anticipated writing three or four years in the future.

This type of networking was often only possible with the institutional support of ICRS and its Ford Foundation funding. In addition to personal networking, writers also relied on more formal institutionalized networking strategies to access resources— what Deborah Brandt terms literacy sponsors, or "agents, local or distant, concrete or abstract, who enable, support, teach, model, as well as recruit, regulate, suppress, or withhold literacy—and gain advantage by it in some way" (166). Literacy sponsorships are often in the economic best interests of the sponsor, but Brandt is careful to acknowledge the agency of those sponsored to "reroute" the sponsor's resources to forward "self-development and social change" (166). Today's multiple and intersecting literacy sites and the complicated sponsoring networks that come with them, whether "secular, religious, bureaucratic, commercial [or] technological," open up avenues for the appropriation of resources for purposes sponsors might not originally intend (166). Those with the economic means may have the power to implement their interests, but because of the overlapping nature of discourse, those sponsored can also appropriate the resources offered in one context to benefit another.

As mentioned above, ICRS was initially funded by a grant from the US-based Ford Foundation, a powerful literacy sponsor. Former Director Dr. Syamsiyatun explained in 2014 that the founders used the money not only to provide student tuition scholarships for "Indonesian, and other students from Asia and Africa," but also to connect the program "to international student exchange programs." This initial funding has since been supplemented by the US-based Henry Luce Foundation, which helps foster student exchanges with such universities as Temple University, Georgetown University, and Boston University by providing tuition waivers, housing stipends, and travel money. These exchanges—made possible through the English language and, ironically, the *physical* movement of bodies in an age when digital "flow" is often assumed—are one way that the scholars working at ICRS can access the university passwords and current academic texts necessary to contribute to global written conversations.

ICRS does more than foster embodied knowledge-sharing, however; with the help of global literacy sponsors, the program has also built global partnerships that make written resources digitally—and legally—available to Indonesians. In 2009, ICRS became part of an open access project, Globethics.net, which began as a legal, open-access, multilingual online library focused on sharing global research in ethics across the information divide.[22] ICRS curates the organization's multilingual Islamic ethics library, and in so doing is able to work toward the cosmopolitan ideals set out in its mission statement and its language policy. Although

Globethics.
net Library
Page

this networking involves engaging with powerful Western literacy sponsors, this opportunity also opened up avenues for ICRS to "participate in international discourse, including discourse with other Asian, African and Latin American scholars" ("Language Policy").

As the Globethics website explains, "The founding conviction of Globethics.net is that having equal access to knowledge resources in the field of applied ethics enables individuals and institutions from developing and transition economies to become more visible and audible in the global discourse" ("Globethics.net"). As a testament to the program's reach, currently there are 47,319 registered users worldwide, with Indonesia coming second after India for the most users, at 25,248 (*Ethics* 19). As of 2021, Globethics has made legally available, free of charge, 3.6 million documents pertaining to ethics, "including articles, books, reference works, dissertations, conference papers, case studies, and educational resources . . . via a multilingual portal accessible free of charge" (*Ethics* 12).

With over two hundred global partnerships, which include IFLA, Sage, Gale/Cengage Learning, UNESCO, the World Council of Churches, and the Swiss-based Linsi Foundation, Globethics.net has helped create a network of resources among academic institutions in Switzerland, China, India, East and Francophone Africa, Russia, Argentina, Turkey, and Indonesia. These partners, in turn, reach out to universities and libraries in their respective countries to gather resources to share across borders. A promotional brochure from the organization (not surprisingly, in English) puts it this way to prospective scholarly donors: "GIVE your articles and books for *their* studies, research, teaching, decision-making, action; TAKE *their* articles and books for *your* studies, research, teaching, decision-making, action" ("Your Offer; Your Benefit" ad, original emphasis,). Though clearly the brochure targets English-using academics, the audience the "you" refers to and their geopolitical location is deliberately unclear—a move that seeks to erase the distance between the haves and the have-nots. This rhetorical move reframes the conversation in terms of interconnectivity and mutual knowledge-sharing, reaching toward the cosmopolitan connection

English has long promised but failed to deliver.

The fact that those long constructed as "other" can be audience to other "others" with this type of digital networking also indicates that English can no longer be tied to Western interests. Scholars who study global literacies, such as Pennycook, Canagarajah, and Xiaoye You have echoed Brandt's claim that resources can be appropriated and resignified for purposes not intended by the originating literacy sponsor. As You argues in his *Writing in the Devil's Tongue,*

> Each nationality exposed to English finds a way to repurpose it to their own needs, to exercise control and a degree of sovereignty over the language. English becomes a technocultural means owned by its users, regardless of their national, racial, linguistic, class, or gender background. Rhetorical and sociolinguistic factors associated with people's use of English, rather than the old monolithic notion of language, are central to understanding the ownership of English. (167)

Making a claim he returns to at length in his more recent *Cosmopolitan English*, You takes to task the "old monolithic notion of language" that suggests that English can only represent Western interests (and to which Phillipson seems to ascribe with his notion of linguistic imperialism). As Indonesia's language history indicates, and as the case-study portraits in this book show, when English comes into contact with the myriad identities that You suggests global language users perform (to which I would echo Brandt by adding religious background as well), the language is repurposed, challenging, in turn, the West's "sovereignty" over the language.

REROUTING KNOWLEDGE: TOWARD THAT WHICH EXCEEDS LANGUAGE

Importantly, though, to challenge the long-held link between English and the West, we must also understand how *knowledge* that originates in English interacts with knowledge traditions long positioned by the colonial matrix of power as being in opposition to Western "modernity." This focus on that which exceeds language itself—on the values, the beliefs, and the lived, embodied experiences of humans in the world—is central to rewriting global power relationships that have long been defined by the same/other dualities promoted by coloniality: the dualities that position rationality and religiosity (and especially Islam) as dichotomous; that divorce the mind from the body and thus academia from the material world; that assume passivity in non-Western women as a means of justifying intervention; all for the purpose of defining what's "modern" and what needs to be "improved." This is the promise of ICRS: that at the borderland between colonial dualities and that which exceeds them, social justice is possible on both the discursive *and* the material planes. As the next chapter will explore, the critical pedagogy I crafted for this complex literacy ecology built in moments for praxis and *textual* innovation but failed to account for the ways seemingly discrete content and value systems intertwined to suggest new ways of thinking and moving "in and with the world" (Freire, "Cultural" 452). Reflecting on this epistemic blind spot in my pedagogy in relation to the multiple forms of data I collected across thirteen years eventually helped me to develop the concept of "translingual praxis" that interanimates this book.

Ethnographic Moment 5: But to Whom Do We Have Students Write?
Teaching Journal: November 18, 2009

I was invited to present at ICRS's Academic Board meeting today; when they invited me to attend last week I was told that they wanted me to discuss the English writing pedagogy I was developing for students in my academic writing class, and that was about it. Given how vague this request was, I decided to just disseminate my syllabus and introduce faculty to the CARS model as a way into discussing cultural differences—or alignments—when it comes to genre moves in different rhetorical traditions. I was quite nervous, actually, especially given that there were around fifteen faculty members from each of ICRS's sponsoring institutions! Given my other interactions with my Indonesian colleagues, I needn't have worried, though. There was much laughter and good discussion. After I discussed the CARS model with them, there was quite a lively discussion (which I recorded, luckily!). One faculty member raised his hand and explained, "When I assign a paper, they are invisible. They quote many authors, but their voice is barely there," and another gave an extended example: "Let's say someone wants to write about a religious event using semiotics. And the student tries to write about that. And you know that he or she would probably write about everything else about this topic, the whole history of semiotics, but actually you don't need all that information, so actually there is a lack of focus." They both suggested this was a cultural predilection—to respect the work of others and downplay the individual. To complicate matters a bit, I replied that it could also be about audience—and perhaps not knowing to whom they were addressing their knowledge, which is a great way to narrow down a lit review. In response, a faculty member raised her hand and asked:

> "This is about the move of 'establishing a territory,' isn't it? How wide or far should we talk about our field of study? Should we start with general international scholarship when we want to talk about politics of religion in a specific area? To whom do we have students write?"

This moment illuminated something that I hadn't thought about but that I should have when crafting the course. To whom were students to address their English words in this local-global literacy site? To Indonesian English users? To the West? To the Global North? To the Global South? To an international audience? What does that even mean—international? I'm going to have to do some reframing of my course . . .

Chapter 5

Rewriting a Critical Pedagogy*

THE ETHNOGRAPHIC EXCERPT ABOVE POINTS to the complexity of imagining audience in a program that is both Indonesian and international, with English as its lingua franca. Given English's still-troubling hegemony and the sociolinguistic context I outline above, the pedagogy I developed for ICRS sought to acknowledge that power exists—making an awareness of dominant English genres necessary—with the possibility that students might appropriate and resignify these genres for their own purposes. Taking into consideration the multiple audiences the program wished to reach and the faculty's critical view of English's imperialist legacy, the curriculum I developed for ICRS wed a rhetorical genre-based approach with critical contrastive rhetoric. Though, as the excerpt earlier suggests, I didn't initially question my assumptions regarding the link between English and Western audiences; as the semester progressed, I made space for explicit discussions of genre norms in relation to culture, power, and ideology, while also openly addressing the possibility that students might challenge dominant textual norms to reach the audiences of their choice. As we'll see, I assumed this critical pedagogy would encourage students to alleviate identity friction through the *genre moves* they made; however, the way students actually chose to take agency and negotiate among language, genre, and audience was more complicated than that. Agency manifested itself both textually *and* extratextually, as the writers with whom I worked rerouted the resources at hand to

---

*Portions of this chapter were previously published in "'To Whom Do We Have Students Write?': Exploring Rhetorical Agency and Translanguaging in an Indonesian Graduate Writing Classroom." *Literacy in Composition Studies* 6.1 (2018): 39–61.

circulate knowledge to academic and civic audiences, from one moment in time to the next, across multiple languages—a process I now term "translingual praxis."

ON NEGOTIATING GENRE

That explicit teaching of genre to help students access dominant discourses has long been established by scholars working in rhetorical genre studies (see Bazerman; Devitt; Bawarshi), and, when it comes to multilingual writing, in the field of English for Specific Purposes (see Cope and Kalantzis; Hyland; Swales).[23] In ESP circles, John Swales has been instrumental in forwarding a genre-based pedagogical approach to teaching multilingual writers (in fact, the pedagogy I outline below draws in part from Swales's work). He positions genres as tools at work within discourse communities or "sociorhetorical networks that form in order to work towards sets of common goals" (9). His theorization of discourse community and his notion that to obtain insider status community members must master the genres at work there (27) have been taken up by many who wish to help both multilingual *and* monolingual students gain access to disciplinary knowledge and thus become "insiders" within academia.

Although explicit genre instruction works to enculturate students into academic discourse communities, others have argued that when taught in a rote, static way, genre knowledge can also limit possibility and with that, students' rhetorical agency (see Coe; Devitt, Bawarshi, and Reiff). Prescriptively teaching dominant genres without discussing language, identity, and power can forward assimilation as the goal at the expense of nondominant identities and rhetorical practices. To return to Tania Murray Li's theory, by "rendering technical" and thus neutralizing these culturally inscribed forms, we risk forwarding what translingual theorists dub a monolingualist approach.

To negotiate the pragmatic need to introduce students to dominant genres *and* the need to acknowledge the identity friction involved, global-literacy scholars have called for a critical reframing of explicit genre instruction (see Pennycook, "Vulgar

Pragmatism"; Kubota and Lehner, "Critical"). Ryuko Kubota and Al Lehner, for example, argue that traditional contrastive rhetoric's focus on the teaching of explicit and clear-cut genre differences between multilingual students' "original" cultures and English often creates a falsely monolithic and essentialist perception of rhetorical situations and the actors that work within them. And with this explicitness comes the idea that students must understand these broad rhetorical differences not so they can question power, but so they can *assimilate* to Western audiences (14). They argue instead for a "critical contrastive rhetoric" that makes distinctions between rhetorical traditions explicit so students can critique their ideological underpinnings and then make the choice to assimilate or not as they compose. Such a pedagogy would give students the tools to "both resist assimilation and appropriate the rhetoric of power to enable oppositional voices" (20). A critical contrastive rhetoric "call[s] into question traditionally assumed rhetorical norms [to] explore rhetorical possibilities" (20). In keeping with the critical praxis Kubota and Lehner and others have long advocated for, the pedagogy I developed for ICRS deliberately built in discussions of language, identity, and power when it comes to genre—with invitations to engage in critical praxis through reflective writing and discussion. As I'll outline below, this pedagogy evolved as the year went on and I reflected on some central (and problematic) assumptions; furthermore, as is often the case with qualitative research, as I began coding the data what I expected to find was not reflected in what I *did* find—an epiphany that led to the theory of translingual praxis I develop in this book.

REFLECTING ON A MONOLINGUALIST FRAMING

Although most of the two-semester course I developed focused on genres commonly expected of PhD students in religious studies,[24] students began by writing a critical literacy narrative. I wanted, in Kubota and Lehner's words, to have them "write about how they perceive[d] the ways in which they [wrote] . . . in their first languages and critically bring their perceptions to bear on the work of composing texts" in my course (21). To help them draft their texts, and to avoid promoting essentialist understandings of language and culture, I developed activities that helped students critically reflect on the multiple and coexistent "cultures" and identities they might move among as they composed their English texts.

To begin, I asked students to read Fan Shen's "The Classroom and the Wider Culture," in which he contrasts the ideologies influencing Western genres with those of Chinese genres to reflect upon his difficulties acculturating to American composition practices. He explains that the personal experience and voice valued in Western writing—the "I" that "promotes individuality (and private property)"—was, in Communist China, "always subordinated to 'We'—be it the working class, the Party, the country, or some other collective body" (460). This Chinese ideology, he argues, was reflected in Chinese genres that encouraged him to suppress the "I," making his transition to US-based "individualist" writing practices difficult. Ultimately, he argues, writing in English meant "creating and defining a new identity and balancing it with the old identity" (466). As dated as Shen's 1989 text is, it opened up conversations about "culture" and "identity" in class discussion, where many of my students linked practices in their Indonesian genre repertoires to the "we-centered" Chinese practices Shen outlines.

However, because Shen compares only the *national* cultures of China and the United States, he creates a monolithic and essentialist model for students; as Roz Ivanič and others argue, students bring multiple identities and "cultures" to their writing practices. To challenge this one-culture-equals-one-identity binary, we then discussed Swales's definition of "discourse community," a concept students grasped easily as the majority of students were fluent in at least three languages, as well as in the languages of their professions and academic disciplines.

Once they were comfortable with the concept, I asked students to brainstorm multiple discourse communities in which they participated and, for each, to answer the following questions:

- How do the language practices in these discourse communities interact with each other?

- And how might they interact with your writing identities in English?

This reflective writing activity spurred a lively discussion on the ways students' already-existent discourses might affect their discoursal selves as they wrote in English.

As recorded in my teaching journal, when we reconvened one student explained that he had connected his Javanese discourse community[25] and his professional discourse community as a licensed therapist; he linked the hierarchical respect for authority in Javanese culture to what he described as a "culture of listening" in his therapist community to argue that both encouraged a more indirect notion of critique than might be expected in an "I"-centered culture (see my "I Have No Mother Tongue" for how he concretized this discussion in his literacy narrative). Another student, Chapter 6's case study, Faqih, put in conversation his identities as a feminist activist and Muslim imam to discuss how moving between these discourse communities might help him navigate a new, more "I-centered" identity in English. And another discussed how the hierarchical nature of Javanese might complicate the less hierarchical syntax of English. Yet another student, Chapter 8's case study, Ninik, contrasted her experiences studying abroad in Hawaii and her experiences with English at ICRS and the ways West-based assumptions about language mediated the texts she produced in these different countries (7 September 2009).[26] These discussions, the portraits in the following chapters will show, helped generate ideas for students' more formal literacy narratives.

Given these vibrant discussions, I initially deemed this assignment sequence a successful one in my teacher's journal; it highlighted for students the notion that language *is* culture while simultaneously making Western genre norms explicit, and it also encouraged students to think about discourses as coexistent—a step toward helping students build bridges between their existing discourse practices and the ones I planned to introduce in the class.

RETHINKING AUDIENCE

It wasn't until the academic board meeting focused on the program's writing curriculum that I began to question its success. As the ethnographic moment above indicates, after a vigorous discussion about voice negotiation in literature reviews, an Indonesian colleague asked me, "But to whom do we have students write?" Indeed. Upon reflection, I realized my opening assignment sequence might be construed as very West-oriented and monolingualist in nature because we didn't explicitly discuss which English-using audience students might reach with their knowledge, and with that the possibility that they might negotiate with textual form depending on the rhetorical situations they imagined. Shen's focus is very "East writing to West" and unidirectional, probably because he writes as a US immigrant; though he urges teachers to make the connections between composition practices and ideology explicit, his overall argument is that this might better help students create an English identity that can assimilate to Western practices. Similarly, because we didn't explicitly discuss audience in the discourse community activity, I realized it might have been interpreted as an activity meant to locate and "fix" students' non-Western textual moves when those moves bled into their English texts—to make it easier to adopt the Western identity Shen embraces.

This activity sequence, upon reflection, took a monolingualist approach to genre and audience. As evidenced by my colleague's question at the academic board meeting, such a unidirectional, East-converting-to-West approach to English writing is challenged by ICRS's positionality as an Indonesian yet international site. It is problematic to link one language to one discourse—in this case, English to the West—without considering audience and the fact that English is capable of appropriation and rearticulation by non-Western writers.

For the remainder of the course, I developed activities that allowed for the possibility that students' Indonesian audiences might dictate the way they negotiated Western genre conventions in English. Given expectations that I would teach students genres necessary to English-using religious studies scholars, many of these activities involved pairing short critical reflective writing activities with explicit genre instruction and discussions about textual negotiation. These activities both elicited vibrant class discussions *and* highlighted the limitations of locating rhetorical agency solely in the genre moves students chose to make.

An activity sequence I developed for a research article unit illustrates this claim. Given my initial West-centered framing, openly discussing the question of audience with the graduate students in my class seemed imperative. Therefore, to begin this unit, I asked students to do a reflective writing activity in response to these questions:

- Whom do you imagine as your English-using audience for this paper?
- And what country or countries does this audience come from?

Students' answers to these questions point to the important role Indonesian audiences played in their composing processes: four of the five students[27] taking part in the activity reported that they imagined Indonesian audiences, with only one imagining a Western audience because, he explained, "English is a Western language."

That the majority of students chose to imagine a local Indonesian audience—as opposed to imagining advanced academic literacy as an interaction with significant *texts* in the field—could be symptomatic of students' identities as novice academics seeking to enter a conversation where they felt less than authoritative (see Irene Clark). To use Ivanič's terms in *Writing and Identity*, because they were uncomfortable with the "discoursal selves" expected of them when writing in English—whether because of cross-cultural differences or being new to the field—it could have felt more comfortable imagining an intimate audience as they sought to construct "self as author," at least for the time being. However, that they were writing as Indonesians in an Indonesian context could also have influenced these conceptions of their target audiences. As this book will explore in detail, many of these students were engaging in advanced academic literacy not just to engage *textually* in larger academic conversations but to use their *knowledge*, regardless of genre or language, to foster concrete social change for real people in their Indonesian communities.

Given that the majority of students imagined Indonesians as their target audiences in this class activity further reinforced the importance of considering audience and textual negotiation when framing this research article assignment. Therefore, the next activity sequence I introduced paired explicit genre instruction with a discussion of critical negotiation.

RELOCATING AGENCY

I first introduced students to John Swales's CARS (Create a Research Space) Model, which outlines common moves in Western academic introductions (Swales and Feak). We then went over a list of common Western academic genre features compiled by Swales and Christine Feak in their *Academic Writing for Graduate Students*, which aligned—albeit with more specificity—with Shen's article in the prior unit.

In addition, to avoid the monolingualist approach the literacy narrative unit took, we also discussed the following excerpt from Suresh Canagarajah's *Critical Academic Writing and Multilingual Students*:

> It is possible in critical writing for multilingual students to tap the resources of English and use it judiciously to represent the interests of their communities. An uncritical use of the language, on the other hand, poses the threat of making the individual and community prone to linguistic domination (17).

This excerpt fostered a discussion that drew from the identity work students had done in their literacy narrative unit and highlighted their complicated beliefs about assimilating to Western norms as Indonesian writers.

An excerpt from my teaching journal reads as follows:

> One woman talked about power and the English language and how it eradicated other ways of thinking. They must learn

English and its ways of being, she explained, because they wanted to do well in school. I asked if assimilation was the only option and students had mixed reactions—one student argued they should just be aware of audience and that he could keep two identities, like Shen, and switch in between them. Other students said it was complicated because sometimes the languages mixed with each other—English bled into Indonesian writing practices and vice versa, showing they had mixed identities. Another student then brought up linguistic standardization and that Standard English rules were often enforced by instructors unaware of the "cultural aspect" of language. Yet another student thought that they should be able to write in an Indonesian way to Indonesian people. (16 November 2009)

This excerpt highlights that when given designated space within the classroom to do so, students were ready to discuss ways they might negotiate audience and textual identity when engaging with English genres. That students were so ready to engage in this discussion indicates their already existent translingual orientations toward knowledge and the importance of making space for such extratextual conversations in the classroom.

Given the vibrancy of this discussion, it seemed important to move toward ways students might take agency in the actual texts they wrote. Since students were getting their degrees in religious studies, I assigned for homework Ahmar Mahboob's "English as an Islamic Language: A Case Study of Pakistani English," in which he shows how English language textbooks written in Pakistan incorporate Islamic sayings—in their original Arabic—despite being written primarily in English, what translingual scholars would term "code-meshing."

To help frame discussion of the rhetorical moves Mahboob highlights, in class we discussed another excerpt from Canagarajah's *Critical Academic Writing and Multilingual Students,* in which he outlines ways multilingual writers might negotiate dominant English language forms:

- *Accommodation:* following the rules and assimilating to dominant language forms, even if at the expense of one's own beliefs or linguistic traditions.
- *Opposition:* ignoring the rules by refusing to adopt any dominant practices because they are against one's own beliefs or linguistic traditions.
- *Appropriation:* bending the rules and negotiating between one's own linguistic traditions and dominant language forms; in Canagarajah's words, "Although [writers using this technique] establish a discourse counter to that of the dominant conventions, they still establish a point of connection with the established genre conventions." (116)

Taken together, these texts spurred a lively discussion about the risks and rewards linked to accommodation, opposition, or, in the case of code-meshed texts like the ones Mahboob explores, appropriation of dominant Western norms.

Here is an excerpt from that day's teaching journal:

One student asked [in relation to Canagarajah's heuristic], "Which do you think is the easiest to do?" I threw the question back at the class and another student replied that accommodation is the easiest because you "don't have to think." Another student said that emotionally, though, accommodation was more difficult, even if writing in this way was easier, because of cultural differences. Another student countered and said that opposition might be easiest because you can do whatever you want without taking into consideration genre requirements. The student who asked which was the easiest ended the discussion with, "Sometimes it is very hard to do when you are new to writing." (18 November 2009)

From this extratextual interaction, it is clear that students were working through the relationship between genre and textual identity negotiation—and that they had different views concerning the feasibility of code-meshing and genre-bending.

Furthermore, as the final student suggests, critical appropriation—at least at the textual level—might take time for people "new to writing" in English, an argument for considering agency from a spatiotemporal framework. That seemed to be the case as we moved to our next activity, which was meant to bridge this discussion with choices they might make in their own texts to reach specific audiences.

To link back up to the first reflective assignment in the unit—and to catch up those students who had missed the opening activity—we once again brainstormed as a class multiple English-using audiences that might benefit from their research projects. Students came up with the following list: Amber as instructor; Indonesian instructors at ICRS; Indonesian English-users; a Western academic audience; and a Southeast Asian academic audience.[28]

Though their monolithic conceptions of audience might be considered problematic given the complexity of our global academic conversations, I did want students to take agency and define their own rhetorical situations for this assignment. Therefore, I asked students to choose one of these audiences and to reflect on the following questions in relation to that audience:

- Why might you share your research with this audience?
- What info can you assume they know? What info do they need to know?
- What kind of textual identity will you convey?
- How might you begin your text? What writing moves might you use?

As with their work in the first activity, most students (nine out of ten this time) chose to write about and address their texts to Indonesian audiences.

Notably—at least in hindsight—the discussion this activity spurred indicated that students were more interested in the first two *content-based questions* than the final two genre-based questions. Students were particularly interested in the way that they might transmit Indonesian religious studies content from local to global audiences and vice versa. One student, for example, shared how her research on Islamic boarding schools (pesantren) might be important to share with Western audiences, but it would be "old news" to Indonesian audiences (a question this student, Ninik, also addresses in her literacy narrative, as Chapter 8 will explore). Another student also drew from our previous discussion of the CARS model to postulate that putting Indonesian voices into conversation with Western ones might be a way to add new information to global conversations (22 November 2009). *Knowledge itself*, rather than form, took primacy in this discussion.

Though I viewed this discussion as productive, I still wanted to help students link their genre choices to the audiences they were imagining before they began crafting their texts. Therefore, I asked them to do one more reflective writing activity, for which I asked:

- Do you think it's OK to deviate from the CARS model? Why or why not?
- And for what reasons might you do so?

This reflective activity highlighted that although most students believed it was appropriate to deviate from the CARS model, they thought assimilation to Western norms was their best choice—for the time being.

One student, for example, wrote:

I think it is fine to deviate from the CARS model as long as we have supportive knowledge to do it. However, I will not deviate *at this time* since I think this model is easy to understand as a new English writer and also fluid if I want to later on. We can follow the model but we can still be creative in doing it. The reasons for wanting to deviate, I think, are the different nature of academic culture, audience and purposes. (My emphasis)

This student signals her belief that it is acceptable to deviate when considering different cultures and audiences, but because she is so new to academic writing in English, she won't deviate yet. Another student pointed to the model's newness as his reason for assimilating: "I think CARS model is really new for me and it can enrich me how to create a research space." These students see the CARS model as a "fluid" heuristic, and as a way to "enrich" their existent rhetorical repertoires. In keeping with a translingual orientation, rather than viewing this Western model in an either/or relationship with their existing linguistic traditions, these students view it as another part of their toolkit that they might draw from again—or challenge— in the future. For now, though, these students chose to assimilate, regardless of the audience they imagined.

Other students, however, pointed to power and to English's ties to the West as their reason for assimilating. One student wrote, "It is hard to deviate from CARS because it is such a 'universal guide' in Western research writing. I do not want to deviate. I just want to follow this model. Maybe in a perfectly new territory, it can be deviated." Though signaling the possibility for new rhetorical situations to expand textual possibilities, he has no desire to deviate because of the CARS model's "universalized" acceptance in English conversations long linked to the West. Another student echoed this belief that deviation from dominant norms can be difficult: "The risks for deviating from the CARS is our research is likely to be considered as nonacademic." Power matters, particularly to these novice academics.

Thus, although aware of English's ties to Western ideology and that they might negotiate with Western norms to reach their imagined Indonesian audiences, students were willing—for now—to assimilate in their research projects: a testament, it could be argued, to the West's power to define "good English," to their own identities as new graduate students wanting to try out a new genre prior to challenging it, and likely to a translingual orientation toward language use that positions new genres as additive rather than subtractive. That we began the course with a unit that assumed a de facto Western audience and that they were being evaluated by a "native speaker" might also have spurred their decisions, despite my efforts to revise the course in a way that encouraged critical negotiation with audience and genre conventions.

Were these critical genre activities, then, a waste of time? No. These conversations about textual form and audience weren't meant to forward a particular, "correct" way to negotiate English genres; rather, they were meant to encourage students to engage in critical praxis and then to make conscious rhetorical choices as they wrote their "discoursal selves" into English. And my students *chose* to assimilate in their research articles, regardless of their intended Indonesian audiences, at least for the time being. As Anis Bawarshi suggests, in a translingual world, agency is located not in the final product but in the writer's choices as they negotiate "memory, emotion, . . . sense of self, available discursive and linguistic resources, embodied dispositions, [and] histories of engagement" (247) in their particular historical moment. Assimilation *can* be a critical choice. As the case-study portraits in the next section will show, "assimilating for now" does not preclude writers from making different choices in the future as the translingual "river" (Pennycook, *Global Englishes* 35) shifts around them.

RECIRCULATING KNOWLEDGE

Indeed, though I didn't cue into it at the time, students' vibrant discussion about the role that Indonesian *knowledge* might play in expanding global conversations about religion points to the importance of moving past a focus on academic product and toward an understanding of the ways that *knowledge itself* circulates across languages, audiences, and genres. Prior to enrolling at ICRS, most of my students had been activists in their local communities, working with various Indonesian NGOs to forward such issues as religious tolerance, women's rights, and community literacy. As my pedagogy developed, I began to reflect in my teacher's journal on the way students' work on the ground fed into their academic scholarship, making me question my initial assumption that the only genres they would need to write would be academic in nature, scope, and audience. This assumption forwarded a one-way, extractive relationship, where students' community activism fed into their scholarly work but not vice versa. This realization, and midyear evaluations requesting more "public" texts, spurred me to incorporate nonacademic genres into my pedagogy. To better understand for whom students were writing and to bring their choices to the fore, I also began asking students to submit reflective cover letters with all formal assignments to help me "read" their choices—assimilative or not—from the perspective of the audience they were imagining. One of the most popular of these assignments (according to final evaluations) was the opinion piece, in which I asked students to revise the research article they produced in the unit described above to reach a public audience of their choice. Not surprisingly, the majority of students chose to write to an Indonesian English-using audience, though their rhetorical choices varied based on their positionalities in relation to that audience.

Attention to *form* is important; however, research and pedagogical lenses that highlight text at the expense of process—that focus on static product at the expense of movement and transformation—run the risk of "rendering technical" the subversive and responsive potential of translingual praxis. The desire of the writers with whom I worked to get past isolated textual moves and focus on what knowledge can *do* in the world can be attributed to the religious and activist identities they brought with them to the classroom and subsequently transferred back into their community activism. Though it *is* important to acknowledge the implications of students "integrating faith *into* their academic writing," as Jeffrey Ringer suggests in "The Consequences of Integrating Faith into Academic Writing" (292; emphasis added), we must also flip the script to explore the ways writers circulate knowledge garnered *from* academic literacy into their local communities and back again using the many languages at their disposal. It is to this movement between text and material context—and to the performance of translingual praxis by three case-study participants—Faqih, Nina, and Ninik, whom I first met in the course described here—that Section II will attend.

A DIALOGIC INTERLUDE: A "CONTINUOUS DYNAMIC OF TWO HORIZONS"

BUT FIRST, I WANT TO PAUSE HERE AT THE borderlands between Sections I and II. As I conclude the section of this book focused on which voices and what contexts—epistemological, methodological, geopolitical, and pedagogical—shaped my understanding of translingual praxis, and before I move into the next section, which explores the complex literacy lives of Faqih, Nina, and Ninik, I want to emphasize that the process of "thinking with" has been a dialogic and mutually transformative one. By dividing this book into two sections, I don't mean to imply that the voices of my research participants are *unmediated* by my scholarly lenses or that their projects were not influenced by my own. To return to the idea of "thinking with," my research participants' voices—and their engagements with the world—were inevitably transformed by my research lenses, just as my own engagements were transformed by their work.

Faqih highlighted this mutually transformative process in the WhatsApp conversation excerpted below. For some context, I received this text after our final in-person conversation on the last day of my three-day visit to Cirebon in July of 2022. Knowing that Faqih valued in-person dialogue when it came to member-checks, we had met that morning for an expansive Indonesian brunch and to discuss a draft of the chapter you're about to read, which I had sent him to look over prior to my trip. What ensued was a three-hour conversation about our projects—mine about translinguality and his about his theory of gender reciprocity, *mubadalah*—and the intersections between them.

This WhatsApp conversation, which Faqih sent after our brunch conversation, works in two ways to emphasize Faqih's interrelational understanding of knowledge-making: first, he signals his belief that in fact our projects, though asking different questions, still exist in dialogic relationship. As our "two horizons" met that morning, our respective projects were given new life, a testament to the power of "theorizing with" as opposed to writing about.

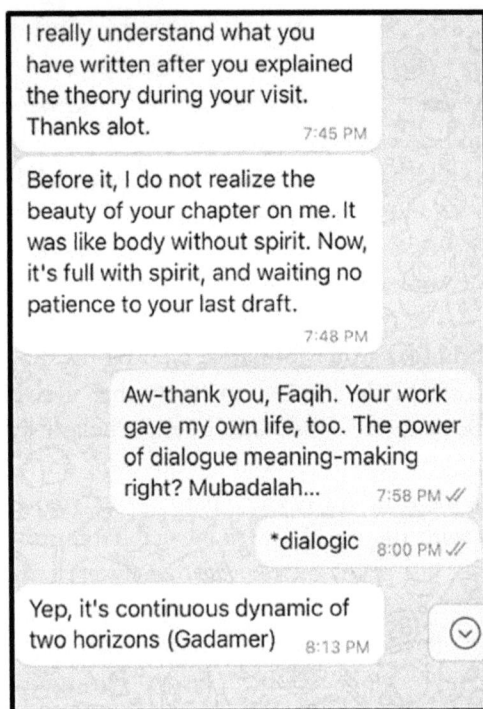

I really understand what you have written after you explained the theory during your visit. Thanks alot. 7:45 PM

Before it, I do not realize the beauty of your chapter on me. It was like body without spirit. Now, it's full with spirit, and waiting no patience to your last draft. 7:48 PM

Aw-thank you, Faqih. Your work gave my own life, too. The power of dialogue meaning-making right? Mubadalah... 7:58 PM ✓✓

*dialogic 8:00 PM ✓✓

Yep, it's continuous dynamic of two horizons (Gadamer) 8:13 PM

This WhatsApp text also works on the content level to foreshadow my research participants' interrelational understanding of discourses long positioned as discrete and oppositional by the colonial matrix of power—between "rationality" as defined by Western powers and Islamic thought, between the religious and the academic spheres, between the written and the embodied.

With Faqih's reference to my visit to Cirebon and how our in-person conversation—what he calls "the continuous dynamic of two horizons"—gave spirit to the body of the written chapter I'd sent him, he emphasizes the importance of moving past the textual, cognitive realm to perform embodied dialogue: a relinking of the mind and the written with the body and the performed that challenges colonial dualities *and* hints at his broader orientation toward language itself. With his reference to the spirit and the body, Faqih also places a religious metaphor alongside the work of German philosopher Hans-Georg Gadamer, who plays a central role—along with the Qur'an and the Hadith and feminists both Islamic and not— in his theorization of *mubadalah*. Religious faith and scholarly voices exist on the same spectrum of knowing for Faqih, as they do for Nina and Ninik as well.

Indeed, as the next chapters unfold, my own readers will see how the scholarly-activist lives of all three of the Indonesians showcased here are deeply intertwined, despite their differing positionalities in the Indonesian geopolitical landscape. Continuing the close relationship I first observed in our academic writing class in their first year of graduate school, in the thirteen years following, Faqih, Nina, and Ninik repeatedly referenced one another and one another's work, emphasizing that when their "horizons" met (and meet), their lives were (and are) mutually transformed. To cite a moment from Nina's 2022 interview, focusing on interrelations despite difference is crucial to rewriting the world toward gender justice: "Now is not the time for competition, but for collaboration. Because women, we need many hands to work as one." As the following chapters will show, Faqih, Nina, and Ninik use all of the linguistic resources they have on hand to do just that.

SECTION II
TRANSLINGUAL PRAXIS IN ACTION

Chapter 6

"Mubadalah Is In-Between": Translanguaging to Serve*

> *While in doing business is a proverb that "customers are kings," it is true also in doing communication. I do serve people when I communicate to them. In many cases, I shift deliberately from my way of writing to that owned by people to whom I write . . . Moreover, if I do serve a community with my writing, I should please them by changing my style of writing; words, sentences and structures; in order to serve them.*

*Portions of this chapter were published in "The 'Hands of God' at Work: Negotiating between Western and Religious Sponsorship in Indonesia." *College English* 76.4 (2014): 292–314.

THIS EXCERPT WAS DRAWN FROM A LITERACY narrative that this chapter's case study, Faqih, whose full name is Dr. Faqihuddin Abdul Kodir, wrote during his first year as a PhD student, in his very first essay for my PhD-level academic writing class at the Indonesian Consortium for Religious Studies (ICRS). In this passage, Faqih articulates a desire to assimilate to dominant norms to serve his audiences, and he uses a business metaphor to explain his communicative approach. When placed in conversation with English's ties to global economic power, the fact that Faqih uses this economic metaphor to explain his choice to assimilate could suggest that he is capitulating to power dynamics linked to English's imperialism. As scholars like Robert Phillipson, Theresa Lillis and Mary Jane Curry, and others have shown—and as Faqih himself admits—English does dominate global academic conversations, often increasing the distance between the haves and the have-nots when it comes to global academic knowledge production. Scholars like Faqih often *must* assimilate to dominant English norms and the Western audience implied thereby to be published in internationally indexed journals, a reality, as discussed previously, made more pressing because of Dikti 152, which requires that all Indonesian academics publish in internationally indexed journals, most of which are currently in English.

The assimilative force exerted by Western academic publishing expectations cannot be denied; however, as this chapter shows, attributing Faqih's desire to assimilate solely to Western power is problematic. Assuming a one-to-one correspondence between a global English-user's rhetorical choices and an assumed and monolithic Western audience flattens nuance and denies the frictive possibilities opened up by the multiple and competing discourses that interanimate a writer's "discursive energy field," to use Krista Ratcliffe's term. Faqih's desire to assimilate to his audience's needs transcends the isolated texts he produces—whether in English, Indonesian, or Arabic—pointing to an orientation toward knowledge production that is both agentive and translingual in process, if not in form. Faqih's desire to serve his audiences, this portrait will show, is very much linked to his Muslim faith and to his advocacy for gender justice, discourses that exist in dialogical relationship with the scholarly epistemological lenses he adopts in his religious studies scholarship, which in turn interanimate his relationship to English.

By assuming that discourses—and the languages linked to them—overlap and mutually interanimate each other as a matter of course, and, with this in mind, examining the way Faqih negotiates audience from a dialogical perspective, by asking *from whom* he draws his knowledge, *for whom* he composes his texts, and *with whom* he sees his knowledge circulating, and then focusing on intersections between seemingly disparate voices, this chapter illuminates a model of translingual praxis that places primacy on meaning-making that exceeds originating text and language. Faqih's focus on interpretive interaction, as opposed to concretized text—what he calls the "in-between" space—interanimates *mubadalah*,[29] the theory of Islamic gender he both theorizes and performs *and* the ways he engages with the English language and its ties to the West, suggesting that translinguality be linked to broader epistemological leanings that exceed language itself. Enacting Paulo Freire's belief that "words not given body (made flesh) have little or no value" (*Pedagogy of Freedom* 39), Faqih first dwells at the borderlands of seemingly discrete knowledge traditions and then uses the many languages in his repertoire to enact Islamic gender justice on both the discursive *and* the material planes. In so doing, he rewrites dualities long used to prop up the colonial matrix of power: between rationality and religion; between the mind and the body; and between feminism and Islam. All the while, he enacts a form of translingual praxis that deemphasizes form and authorial control in the service of his intended audiences and the actions they might take.

PERFORMING THE "IN-BETWEEN": IT'S NOT THE LANGUAGE, BUT THE *SUBSTANCE*

Indeed, throughout our time together, Faqih emphasized his desire to serve audiences with his words *and* actions, which often meant relinquishing authorial power to his audiences, either by assimilating to their expectations when it came to textual norms or allowing *their* interpretations to supersede his own. Faqih feels little friction relinquishing control because what matters to him is the movement—the dialogic interaction, the *feeling*—that occurs in the spaces "in-between" his language work and his audience's interpretations, which, he hopes, moves the world toward gender justice, regardless of the language used. A look at Faqih's orientation toward his own intersecting identities—which some might label religious, scholarly, or activist, but which he'd just call "Muslim"— illuminates the intersecting audiences that precede him and thus influence his language work, while also reflecting his broader orientation toward translingual praxis, which is deeply informed by his Islamic faith.

Given the many roles Faqih plays in his community—as religious leader, lecturer, and activist—I was curious about how he defines his vocation. Our ensuing conversation about the inadequacy of existing language to name what he *does* illuminates his orientation toward serving his audiences. When I asked him in 2022 if he would call himself a "kyai," or religious leader, he demurred, explaining, "No, no, no, no. Because a kyai is like a social attribute. A social position. . . . They call me kyai, but to me I'm not." Faqih admits that others call him that, foreshadowing his acceptance of others' labels, but also that he himself feels the term inadequate. He continued, explaining that his identity is "in between people. Between activist, kyai, scholar. To me, there is beauty in Islam, but people do not get it. So I want to preach and call people to that beauty. To that gift. To that virtuosity of Islam." Faqih views his identity as existing in excess of the discrete terms people use to define social identities—as *in-between* and linked to how he performs his faith.

Faqih: On Identity as "In-Between"

Faqih then pointed to a conversation we had just had about translating the Arabic term "Da'wah" into English in an article he had just asked me to look over before it was published. He had initially translated the term "Da'wah" as "calling," which, when paired with religion in the context he was using it, seemed to me, as a Western non-Muslim audience member, to indicate when a person received a specific "calling" from God. I explained this, and he replied: "Oh, like the Prophet." In this context, "calling" wasn't quite right. After a bit of back and forth about whether "Da'wah"

was a discrete moment with God or a continual action with others, he decided to use the word "preaching."[30] He settled on that word in his article, but in his interview he emphasized that "preaching" was still inadequate to describe his own work: "I don't know a proper word for that. That's why I say I don't know!" When I asked him if there was a word in Indonesian to describe Da'wah, he emphasized: "No, because in Indonesian, also Indonesian term also has its own meaning. And even here, maybe like in the West also, preaching is more like a ritual, in the mosque, something like that." Just as with English, in Indonesian there isn't a single word that fully captures the concept of Da'wah, which, to Faqih, encompasses more than a discrete ritual at a place of worship. He continued: "While for me, [Da'wah] is in the mosque, in the mushalla, in the hotel, in the community, in the grassroots. In the river, in the . . . I will come and be with them." For Faqih, discrete spaces, like discrete identity labels, deny the dialogic in-between-ness of meaning-making that happens when "be[ing] with" his community. Designating separate spaces for identity labels or for Da'wah belies the continual work of *serving* Allah in all spheres.

Faqih: On Translating Da'wah

The concepts of *Tawhid,* which signifies the oneness of God, and the responsibilities that Muslims have as *khalifah*, or guardians of God's creation, interanimate how Faqih interprets and performs "Da'wah." *Tawhid* refers to the Islamic belief that there is only one God, and thus it translates roughly to how I, as a Western, non-Muslim scholar, initially interpreted "monotheism" when my research participants used the English translation of *Tawhid*. Tawhid, however, encompasses more than my initial and limited Western interpretation. The concept of Tawhid encompasses the belief in one God *and* the belief in the *indivisible oneness* of God. From an Islamic perspective, God is a unity that encompasses all of creation, or, to put it another way, all of creation *is* God. In turn, humans, according to Faqih, "are created by God to share the mandate of serving as *khalīfa*," or caretakers of creation ("*Qirā'a Mubādala*: Reciprocal Reading" 198). Assuming discrete social roles when discussing identity atomizes creation, just as relegating

Da'wah to one sphere—the mosque—denies the relationality between all aspects of creation implied by Tawhid.

This idea of relationality, which serves as a counterpoint to static colonialist dualities, interanimates Faqih's work, influencing his rhetorical orientation and thus the way he engages in translingual praxis. When I suggested in our conversation about translating Da'wah that "Maybe it's not the language that matters, it's the *actions* . . . ," Faqih interrupted me and laughingly said, "It's like *mubadalah* itself. *Mubadalah* is in-between. *Mubadalah*: the main is not language, but the message. The substance." As we'll see, mubadalah, the global movement toward gender justice that Faqih began with his graduate work, illuminates his orientation toward translingual praxis; namely, it is not the linguistic *origins* but the substance and the message relayed to his intended audiences—and the way *they* move that message into action—that matters.

Faqih:
Mubadalah
Is
In-Between

Although, as will be discussed below, Faqih's understanding of mubadalah as "in-between" prioritizes his intended audience's interpretive action, this relational in-betweenness, which decolonial and feminist scholars might term "border thinking," also occurs in the ways Faqih activates the voices in his citational repertoire who precede and thus interanimate the work of mubadalah. Faqih's work draws from English-medium feminist theory *and* from Islamic jurisprudence. However, when I asked him if he considered himself an "Islamic feminist," he replied:

Faqih: On
Feminist
Products
vs. Feminist
Performance

Let's say most Muslim feminists are doing academic product. Only circulated among them. Not come to the earth. How to be more practical and visible. So my role is how to interpret, of course, by my own way, my own language, my own understanding, my experience, but in general, in substance, I agree with feminism. In the substance if not the details.

In addition to foreshadowing his belief that action is more important than product, Faqih once again takes to task the notion of "separate spheres," this time when it comes to the separation between the discursive and the material planes in scholarly circles— with scholars only talking among themselves— a symptom of the rational/embodied duality promoted by coloniality. In general, however, Faqih agrees with the *substance* of feminism, if not of the siloing of Islamic feminist work from its *doing*.

Though Faqih may draw from the tenets of feminism, whether he chooses to use the word "feminism" itself depends on the context and *who* is interpreting. Foreshadowing his desire to *serve* his intended audiences, he admitted that he defended the term "Islamic feminism" in his dissertation, that he has published in books like *Being a Muslim Feminist in Indonesia*, and that he recently contributed to a webinar called "Do Indonesian people still need feminism?" However, he explained that for him, when it comes to naming his identity, "It is much more comfortable to say 'Muslim.'" For Faqih, gender justice *is* the substance of Islam, and thus the term "Muslim" should suffice.

Faqih: To Be Muslim Is to Be Feminist

When it comes to what *others* call him, however, he cedes control: "To have people say I'm a feminist, it's up to them. I will not reject, I will not say no, no, no; it's up to their definition." For Faqih, the *substance,* which again is created "in-between" through the dialogic interaction between himself and self and the interpretations of those *with whom* he circulates knowledge, is much more important than the terminology itself. Rewriting the mind/body duality so that scholarly and activist work coexist *on the same plane* rather than in opposition—a reconfiguration Faqih hints at when he says his identity is "in-between activist, kyai, scholar"—makes it easy for him to cede control to his audience when it comes to naming, provided socially just *action* ensues from the interaction.

Faqih: On Others Calling Him Feminist

That's not to say, of course, that Faqih is unaware of existing power relationships and of the fact that the term "feminist" originated in English and thus is correlated with Western thought. He explained:

> When I talk feminism, [my Indonesian community] say[s], "What is feminism?!? It is very Western." . . . Yeah: you belong to Western when you talk about feminism. But I think it's not important the word, the term, but the substance, and the message. Of course, in some cases, or in some public, we should say "feminism" in order to block, or to keep people

Faqih: On the Term "Feminism" and Its Western Legacy

from Western-phobia. We need it. But not always. Not always. Because some people associate this message as Western. If I always refer to "feminism" . . . they'll say that our agenda is UN agenda, is Western agenda, is CIDA [Canadian International Development Agency] agenda. Because my language, that language, is Western language. (2022 interview)

Faqih once again emphasizes that the message, rather than language itself, is what matters, so he feels little friction code-switching to reach his audiences; that said, his careful discussion of when a scholar-activist might want to use the term for different intended audiences, or not, shows that he is aware of the English term's ties to Western thought—a linkage he has long grappled with. Notably, Faqih's current orientation toward *what* he studies and performs— Islamic gender justice, or mubadalah— intersects with the ways his orientation toward English has evolved over the course of thirteen years, highlighting the importance of linking translinguality to broader, nonlinguistic orientations toward knowledge itself.

REWRITING ENGLISH TO SERVE
AN INTIMATE AUDIENCE

As evidenced by his careful negotiation with the word "feminism," it is clear that despite the unity implied by his religious ideals, Faqih is aware of the politics linked to English language use. This has long been the case. When I asked Faqih in 2010 why he chose to apply to the English-medium ICRS, he pointed to issues of access and accusations of Western imperialism. Faqih explained that he already had a BA in Islamic Law from Damascus University in Syria and an MA in Islamic Law from the International Islamic University Malaysia. Therefore, he took a colleague's advice and decided to apply to PhD programs in Western countries "to have another point of view and to have a new methodology." He explained,

Because my first and second degree are in theological point of view, so I want a different point of view—an anthropological one. I want much knowledge about how to understand religious context, so I can understand religions not only from the text itself, as theology does, but also from people and how they understand the text.

Faqih wished to add new voices to the Arabic-medium theological voices he negotiated with for his BA and MA. To gain an anthropological understanding of religion, he must engage with English as most texts of that sort are published in English—a testament to what Robert Phillipson and others dub "linguistic imperialism." Thus, he explained, it seemed "natural" for him to apply to programs in the West to access these conversations.

However, other religious colleagues, hearing about his decision to go West, warned him against it:

> The problem is my colleagues, especially the Muslim and religious people suggested me not to go to Western country, because of my position. Because when you go to Western country, you may lose your religious position because it will be difficult to accept for political reasons, so they said if you want to take a program in English, it would be better to take it here in Indonesia. (2010 interview)

Fears that his religious identity would be misinterpreted because of religious "politics" drew Faqih in 2009 to ICRS, a program that would give him access to English-medium research but within an Indonesian context where he could continue to serve his Indonesian community.

Indeed, foreshadowing his belief that scholarly work should catalyze material action, Faqih emphasized that studying at an English-medium institution in Indonesia allowed him to "spread his understanding" of religion locally. When I asked him, in his 2010 interview, "What audience do you imagine most often when you write?" he pointed to his local community as his primary audience:

> Actually my imagination is only my Indonesian English-speaking friends and my English friends who don't know Indonesian well at ICRS, so not farther than here. So it's local. But foreigners also; foreigners here. I don't have any

imagination to talk to American people or Australian people over there. I feel difficult to write when I imagine Western people because I don't know their context. Because my life is to serve people in Indonesia, so intimate audience makes it easier and more comfortable to write down.

When asked *for whom* he generally imagines writing his English texts, Faqih points to the importance of his immediate, or local, audience—and to the ways that the audience at ICRS, despite being a mix of Indonesian and Western English-users, is also "local" in many regards, especially in relation to the abstract Americans and Australians he imagines as geographically "over there." He attributes the fact that he most often imagines such an "intimate audience"—even when writing in English—to his desire to "serve people in Indonesia." In our increasingly interconnected world, audiences are rarely discrete entities, and, importantly, knowledge can be delinked from its original language and geographical location and resignified for local, non-Western purposes. *For whom* Faqih addresses his texts and *from whom* he draws this knowledge at particular moments in time is very much tied to *with whom* he sees his knowledge circulating in the material world—a multivocal audience, this chapter will show, that exceeds the English-medium texts he produces. As we trace his linguistic negotiations from his first year in graduate school to his postdoctoral life, we can see his evolving understanding of English's ties to Western culture.

"WHERE IS GOD IN MY WRITING?"

Achieving his rhetorical purposes, for Faqih, involves critical negotiation with competing interpretive lenses across different knowledge traditions and languages, a diachronic and dialogic process that points to ways textual assimilation might result from translingual praxis. We can turn to a critical literacy narrative assignment and an end-of-semester writer's reflection that Faqih wrote in my PhD-level academic writing class for his own descriptions of what this negotiation looked like.[31] These texts, in turn, point to an orientation toward knowledge and audience that circulates into his future dissertation and activist interventions.

The critical literacy narrative prompt I crafted for students' first assignment asked them to analyze their rhetorical practices in at least two different discourse communities and then to reflect on how this negotiation might influence their negotiations with English. To theorize his approach to the English language, Faqih chose to analyze the writing styles of two of his Indonesian communities—his Muslim community and his feminist activist community.

He begins his literacy narrative by discussing a central question that guides his rhetorical practices: "Where is God in my writing?" He explains:

> To apply the question, I quote what God have said to human being. That is the written words in the Holy Book the Qur'an. Many Muslims recite the Qur'an every day and refer to it for many matters of their lives. Sometimes I flourish my writing with abundance of verses of the Qur'an. I put them along in my introduction, in the middle of my writing and also in the end [. . .] I also put that there are always the "hands of God" at work within human efforts, especially in the context that people should have hopes that God will solve their problems.

Faqih begins his literacy narrative with his Islamic faith, highlighting its importance in his literacy life, emphasizing how, for a deeply religious man, invoking the Qur'an—a text that Muslims believe is God's word made real—might be the default when trying to persuade a local audience toward action.

However, Faqih then contrasts this religious writing style to his practices when working with a local feminist NGO for which he writes. Initially, it seems, bringing God into his texts got him into trouble with his activist editor:

> When I sent my first writing to a magazine circulated among social activists in 2000, its editor replied with comments that my writing was too flourished with "hands of God." She found the ideas wonderful, but it was too general and was covered mostly by religious texts. It had too many "flowers," as she said in her reply. She suggested that I rewrite the article and replace "hands of God" with "what people can do now, practically."

Since receiving this feedback, Faqih explains, he has chosen to lessen the number of textual references to God from his writing, instead invoking the "human" when writing to local activist audiences. He explains his reasoning this way: "As problems come from human factors, I should reveal them and exhibit them in my writing. [T] o empower community is to make them realize their own capacity to solve their problems. I was assigned to empower a marginalized community and my writing is one of forces to do so." Faqih writes to *serve* his audiences.

Notably, it is directly after this statement where Faqih inserts the "customers are king" metaphor with which this chapter began, where, once again, he asserts that "if I do serve a community with my writing, I should please them by changing my style of writing." When it comes to serving activist audiences, he has no problem removing God from his actual texts; in fact, with his "customer as king" metaphor, he implies that what his texts *do* for his community matters more than what they look like. Foreshadowing a question he would return to at the end of the semester, and throughout the thirteen years we worked together, assimilating to his audience's needs and removing God from his *texts* does not erase God from his citational repertoire—Faqih's religious identity is tied not to textual choice but rather to the ways he might serve his community through extratextual action. God exists *in process*, in this case, not in the written product.

To end this first essay, Faqih draws from his experience navigating his dueling Muslim and feminist discourses to hypothesize that moving between them has prepared him for writing in English:

> I think my experience above seems to be similar to what I will experience with English writing academic skills. All that should be done before any step in developing English skills is to know and be aware enough of what is so called as Western "academic." The awareness then should be applied in my writing.

Although he is aware of English's ties to Western ideology, Faqih implies here that in his desire to serve he will assimilate to English norms. He believes that as long as he learns the appropriate "rules," he will be able to shift identities without sacrificing his ideals—just as he does when he moves between his other discourse communities.

From this first essay we can see that writing, for Faqih, isn't necessarily about empowering himself through the assertion of his voice; rather, Faqih views writing as a means to empower his *audience* through the knowledge he conveys. Which past voice—God or human—he chooses to bring into his texts is less important than what his texts can *do* in the hands of the audiences with whom he communicates. Taking up a positionality deeply tied to his religious identity—and, as we'll see later, to his academic leanings—when it comes to the knowledge he transmits, Faqih positions himself as a conduit between past and future interpretations rather than as the sole originator of knowledge. Given his desire to serve, he foresees feeling little friction assimilating to English writing norms.

Despite his initial optimism, in his end-of-semester writer's reflection Faqih reported increasing tensions when it came to assimilating to English rules. He sought to understand this unanticipated friction by delving deeper into his evolving interpretations of his faith and the tension involved with reading "the text as it actually is" amid competing theological and feminist interpretations. Faqih's habits of mind—what Jerry Fodor terms "language of thought" (qtd. in Li Wei 19)—commingle and enmesh, regardless of originating language, transcending one discursive field—in this case, Arabic-medium religious inquiry—to illuminate another, his English literacy practices.

Once again, Faqih begins his text with a discussion of his religious identity, writing, "Fifteen years ago, when I was a first rank student of Islamic theology, I was bound closely by religious norms. [The Qur'an] was a text strictly to be followed. It should be implemented 'actually as it is.'" When he became a feminist activist and delved deeper into his scholarship, however, things changed:

> Ten years later, I realized that there is no "actually as it is." It is not only because I joined a group advocating women experiences, but also I was faced by many opinions conflicting one with the other, even coming from the same Islamic school,

due to variety of experiences. In my mind then, experience is very important in determining the so called "text as actually as it is."

We can imagine the struggle Faqih, as a deeply religious man, must have had when realizing that God's "rules" were open to interpretation based on the differing experiences of worshipers—that, in fact, God's word[32] might be followed differently depending on these interpretations. Faqih even goes so far as to ask in his reflection, "Is the text already dead in my mind? Or is its author really dead?" These questions highlight his discomfort with the postmodern suggestion that, because of myriad interpretations, authorial intention and thus the author—in this case, God—might be dead.

Faqih comes to no definitive answer to these difficult questions about God as author and his word. Instead, Faqih writes, "I am really not sure, since structuralism is now whispering to me that 'freedom is an illusion.' Am I really free from 'the language'?" Faqih does answer *this* question, implying that the author, in this case God, is not dead despite the freedom to interpret his language: "I am aware enough now, that I will be free only within these rules." Faqih can interpret, but God's word transcends and thus dictates the form that his interpretation takes, which once again positions Faqih as a conduit between God and the audience he intends to serve.

Faqih applies this same theoretical lens to reflect on the tensions he feels when writing in English. Notably, English takes the place of God in his previous metaphor:

> My writing is now a bit different too. English academic writing, to some extent, its rules are burdening me more. My mind is not free enough to articulate in English like it is in Indonesian. It is my problem, being surrounded by two poles: "rules of the text" and "freedom of expressing experiences."

He sees the same tension between the written word and the multiple interpretations of "truth" he negotiates in his religious tradition in the way he negotiates as an Indonesian with Western English norms. He continues:

> On the one hand, I like to know rules of grammar, nice flow of sentences, proper structure, the proper discourse community to whom I should address my thought, theories of thinking that I should refer to, etc. I like them all as I like my religion. It is the text that should be followed. On the other hand, those English rules disturb me when articulating my thought. I need to express freely my voice, my mind, and especially my Indonesian experiences. Is it possible to articulate out of the English rules? How?

Faqih asks pressing questions: Can the English language ever represent his Indonesian experience and thus his Indonesian voice? Is it possible to challenge English writing "rules" to better relate his Indonesian interpretations? Harking back to the desire to serve that he discusses in his first essay—and to his relationship with the Qur'an—his answer to the last question is "no":

> Of course, it is impossible to write outside English rules or I will be excluded from the community . . . . No rules, no community. I should like "the rules of writing" at least as I like the text of religion or the religion itself. It is the way I am trying to pass on English problems little by little. I know that I will, with God's willingness of course, be successful in terms of passing the problems.

This last passage points to the powerful role religion plays in Faqih's literate identity and how his Arabic-medium religious negotiations might influence his orientations to English, regardless of whether the Arabic shows up in the written text itself. Significantly, Faqih brings into his text the phrase "God's willingness"—an English translation of a common Muslim supplication, "Inshallah," from its original Arabic. By translating "God's willingness," or "Inshallah," into English, he performs the very assimilation he describes. This rhetorical move works performatively to emphasize the point of his closing paragraph. Despite his "problems" negotiating Indonesian experience with Western textual forms, his religion—regardless of the language in which it appears—helps him negotiate the writing *process*. When placed in the context of the content of this essay, it is clear that his choice to assimilate through translation is deliberate and a means to show how English and Islamic belief—even if divorced from its original Arabic—can coexist within the same text. He moves the knowledge derived from his faith, not the Arabic language itself, which to Faqih doesn't dilute its meaning, provided his words *serve* his intended audience. Just as with his activist literacy practices, it's not the language itself but what precedes and proceeds from his language that matters.

A purely text-based study of Faqih's genre-conforming essays might lead one to assume uncritical assimilation rather than translingual praxis on Faqih's part. Looking at these texts in relation to his larger dialogical rhetorical process paints a different picture, however. If we broaden our understanding of translingual negotiation to encompass the ways a writer like Faqih intentionally negotiates and then translates past voices prior to textual production—and then focus on how he meshes seemingly dissonant *knowledge traditions* into a single text—then assimilation can be the product of translingual praxis, no matter how linguistically "uniform" the final text looks. It's not the textual features that are meshed if we look at Faqih's portfolio, but the content, with much of the translingual work happening extratextually as Faqih seeks to serve his audiences by moving knowledge originally conveyed in Arabic, Indonesian, and English into new forms—albeit ones that *seem* to conform when concretized.

FROM THE TECHNICAL TURN TO RELATIONAL WISDOM

Faqih's writing *process*, then, has long emphasized his ability to delink language from originating culture to reach new audiences. However, how Faqih views the relationships between seemingly disparate cultures and their associated languages has shifted from dualistic to relational over the past thirteen years. When I asked Faqih in 2014 whether he still viewed English as imperialist, he pointed to how the global Muslim diaspora has begun to delink language from culture to adopt English as their own:

Actually to me now English is not anymore an imperialist language because now many Muslims are using the language for communication. The problem is, we used to see and perceive that because of education; we have been educated that all that belongs to the West is bad and imperialist. And language is part of that, because language is connected to culture, etc. But there's been a technical turn, when many Muslim are now using the language. Even now OIC, the Organization of Islamic Countries, English is the first language before Arabic. So I think less people who now see language itself—not culture—but language as imperialist. (2014 interview)

Here Faqih emphasizes that language *does* represent culture, but that it can also be appropriated from its originating context and resignified to serve Muslim purposes.

Though Faqih's work very much emphasizes this delinking from the "West," in 2022 Faqih drew from his Islamic faith to complicate this notion of English's "technical turn" and the discrete "cultures" suggested by the West and his Muslim community. Rather than a dualistic model, he forwards a *relational* model by suggesting that knowledge itself transcends language to unite humanity. When I asked Faqih whether he still viewed English as a "technical tool," capable of being adapted for Muslim purposes, he explained:

Knowledge is very important, because that will drive us to action. Knowledge is everywhere. We call it in Islam "wisdom." Wisdom is everywhere. And we can take and own, reclaim the wisdom even from outside, even from non-Muslim, even, because wisdom belongs to all of humanity. So English, in my experience, in my faith, is a means to have more wisdom. More knowledge. Because experience is very important and we need many experience from other people. And when global people write their experience and their knowledge in English, it means we should read English. We should use English. So of course I refer many times to English books, but not only written by Western people, but also by Muslim,

Faqih: On
Hikmah and
Engaging
with English

by Asian. It's about the wisdom, about the knowledge, about the experience.

In 2022, Faqih links English to shared experiences, rewriting the technical tool metaphor to emphasize shared "wisdom" and a shared humanity despite difference. Once again Faqih also chooses to translate an Arabic term, this time "wisdom," into English, which evidences the importance he places on communicating the message itself, regardless of language, as well as his desire to serve his audience—in this case, me as his interviewer.

Curious as to the original Arabic term for "wisdom" and how it might relate to Faqih's views of English, I did some internet searching (in a rather performative manner), and landed on the term *hikmah* as the most likely Islamic terminology for "wisdom," and from there, this Hadith by Abū Huraira: "The word of wisdom is the lost property of the believer. Wherever he finds it, he is most deserving of it." When I WhatsApped Faqih to ask whether *hikmah* was the term and whether Abū Huraira fairly represented what it means in an Islamic context, he confirmed.

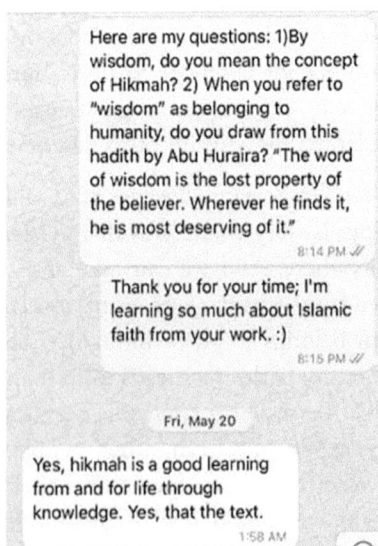

> Here are my questions: 1)By wisdom, do you mean the concept of Hikmah? 2) When you refer to "wisdom" as belonging to humanity, do you draw from this hadith by Abu Huraira? "The word of wisdom is the lost property of the believer. Wherever he finds it, he is most deserving of it."
>
> 8:14 PM
>
> Thank you for your time; I'm learning so much about Islamic faith from your work. :)
>
> 8:15 PM

Fri, May 20

> Yes, hikmah is a good learning from and for life through knowledge. Yes, that the text.
>
> 1:58 AM

Notably, Abū Huraira's Hadith emphasizes that wisdom preexists the faithful, a formulation which points to Tawhid, or the oneness of God, who created all things. Wisdom is not created by a *singular* human being, as Western interpretations often assume because of the "rational mind" ontology of colonialism, but rather it is *found* by interacting with the world, "wherever" a believer chooses to look. For Faqih, wisdom, or hikmah, given by God, transcends notions of "inside" and "outside" to unite humanity, provided one takes action to look for it and then *acts* upon it. Assuming the role of khalifah may involve engaging with English to understand human experience more broadly.

By positioning wisdom as exceeding linguistic and cultural borders and linking it to human *experiences* rather than to how specifically these experiences are communicated, Faqih rewrites colonial dualities that assume immutable difference rather than the relational connection of "in-between." Faqih's evolving understanding of language and culture and the way he moves from static duality between "cultures" to relationality through shared human *experience* is central to how he envisions gender-based equality from within an Islamic framework. As we focus in on how Faqih theorizes mubadalah on the discursive plane and then performs it in the world, we can see how deeply enmeshed his linguistic orientations are with his broader orientations toward religion, religious study, and activism, *seemingly* disparate interventions he would, of course, just call "Da'wah."

[CON]TEXTUALIZING ISLAM

In addition to understanding how Faqih interprets the central *concepts* of Islam as a way into understanding how he performs translingual praxis, it is also important to understand the central *texts* that shape Islamic faith to map the overlapping discourses that interanimate Faqih's work toward mubadalah. Given the relative dearth of conversation in English-medium writing studies scholarship when it comes to Islamic faith (see Lynch and Miller), a brief overview of the texts that dictate Islamic practice might be valuable for some people in my audience.

We can turn to Faqih's own work to begin. In the writer's reflection discussed above, Faqih describes being "surrounded by two poles; 'rules of the text' and 'freedom of expressing experiences,'" which he then applies to his negotiations with English. Importantly, this tension exists within Islam itself—Faqih brings this habit of mind, likely initially fostered by his religious practice, into the way he negotiates language. One "pole" of Islam—and the most important—is the Qur'an, which Faqih also refers to as "the text as it is." Muslims believe that the Qur'an is literally God's word as transmitted through the Prophet Muhammad, who directly transcribed these revelations into the Arabic-medium Qur'an. It is important to note that Muhammad is called "the announcer," the "prophet," "servant of God," and other names that portray him as a neutral conveyer of God's word. God's word, in Arabic, moves through Muhammad; he is not the author of the Qur'an—he's merely a conduit between God and the world. Therefore, the Qur'an, and the "rules of the text" therein, should be read "as it is" because it is God's word made real.

Even though it's the central text, the Qur'an does not stand alone in Islamic religious practice. The other "pole" of Islam Faqih refers to are the written exegeses, or interpretations (Sunnah) of the Qur'an, which detail how to *practice* what is laid out in the Qur'an. These exegeses, called Hadith, are accounts of the Prophet's lived experiences, words, and actions as reported by his Companions, often posthumously, which are meant to teach Muslims how to perform God's law as set forth in the Qur'an. In this case, the Prophet Muhammad *is* an agent in these texts, though the accounts of his actions are conveyed through the varying perspectives of his Companions. Thus, as Faqih implies, the Hadith "express experiences" outside of "the text as it is."

Notably, in response to the variability of second-hand knowledge, the rhetorical structure of the Hadith requires each narrative be linked back to Muhammad, a citational move that makes quite concrete the Bakhtinian notion that each utterance is tied to a dialogical chain of signification comprising "echoes and reverberations of other utterances to which it is related by the communality of the sphere of speech communication" ("The

Problem of Speech Genres" 91). The Hadith are composed of two parts, the *matn*, or the main narrative detailing the Prophet Muhammad's teachings and actions, and the *isnad*, a written account of the chain of narrators who related the matn through time, from one generation to the next—a rhetorical device meant to establish the Hadith's legitimacy and authenticity by linking the report back to people with direct contact with the Prophet Muhammad. Despite this citational practice, as Faqih mentions in his final writer's reflection, the Hadith are full of ideas "conflicting one with the other, even coming from the same Islamic school, due to variety of experiences." Riddled with contradictions, the Hadith have been followed selectively, discounted entirely, and, importantly for Faqih's scholarship, subjected to rigorous interpretive inquiry in the field of Islamic jurisprudence.

THEORIZING MUBADALAH

Just as the Hadith are riddled with seemingly "conflicting" voices, so too is Faqih's English-medium dissertation, *Interpretation of Hadith for Equality between Women and Men.* Not only is his dissertation composed of knowledge translated from Arabic by him and others into English, it is also composed of knowledge originating in English that stays in English; of knowledge produced in Indonesian academic circles that Faqih moves into English; and even of published translations from German into English, in the case of philosopher Hans-Georg Gadamer. And with this "spiral" of languages comes the competing knowledge traditions they bring with them, which inevitably intersect, affect, and reflect Faqih's meaning-making process, no matter what form the final text takes. How Faqih approaches seemingly dissonant *content* in his dissertation mirrors how he negotiates competing *languages* associated with this content. Faqih's willingness to look past the knowledge's origin to what audiences can *do* with the knowledge that erupts at the contact zone between competing traditions also applies to the way he negotiates English's imperialist past with his Indonesian present.

Faqih's dissertation, which spurred the concept of mubadalah, explores the jurisprudence work of Egyptian Muslim scholar Abū Shuqqa and his Arabic-medium *The Liberation of Women at the*

Time of the Prophecy,[33] which Faqih often shortens to *Tahrīr,* a text which has yet to be translated into English, thus requiring Faqih to translate it himself (Abdul Kodir 31). In this text, originally published in 1990, Abū Shuqqa compiled in one place "a huge number of hadith related to women's issues" (8). Abū Shuqqa's purpose, as Faqih writes, was to reinterpret the Hadith "that influence many conservative Muslims, especially those who are known as 'the Islamists' to hold more friendly interpretations of women" (8). Mirroring the citational chains that occur in the isnad, Faqih's dissertation work interprets the interpretive processes that precede Abū Shuqqa's interpretation of the Hadith. Faqih explains his niche in this way: "The work of Abū Shuqqa that relates in particular to ways of interpreting the Hadith has not been sufficiently studied yet" aside from "one work of . . . conservative scholarship that attempts to bring back the hadiths as source of traditional discriminative interpretations" (16). Much of the other scholarship, he explains, consists of "descriptive articles written [by progressive Muslims] simply to appreciate Abū Shuqqa's ideas on the liberation of women in Islam" (17). Though he too is appreciative of Abū Shuqqa's work, Faqih wants to move past discussions of *content* alone: "[My research] fills the gap neglected by both conservative and progressive Muslims concerning the actual interpretive processes involved with Abū Shuqqa's rereading the hadiths for Islamic gender equality" (17). Faqih focuses on *process* as opposed to just the product—on the hermeneutics that led to and thus can proceed from the text Abū Shuqqa produced as opposed to just the "text as it is."

Both Abū Shuqqa and Faqih himself perform "border thinking" when it comes to negotiating seemingly dissonant voices in their citational repertoire. Faqih emphasizes that "to [Abū Shuqqa], Muslims should follow the ancestors in principal things to maintain the originality (*asala*), and then take advantages of any civilization, including from the West, in all contemporary aspects (*mu'asara*)" (83). Echoing Leila Ahmed's argument to focus on *merit* of ideas rather than on *origin,* Faqih emphasizes that Abū Shuqqa is less concerned with defending Islam against "Western invasion" and more concerned with promoting gender justice from within an Islamic framework (43), an orientation toward knowledge that Faqih shares.

In fact, German philosopher Gadamer's work on dialogical hermeneutics is one of the central theories Faqih invokes from his citational repertoire to frame his interpretation. Faqih explains Gadamer's methodology this way: "[I]nterpreting a text always involves two perspectives, i.e. 'two horizons,' in Gadamer's terms. Here, understanding becomes a fusion of horizons; the horizon of the past (the text) and horizon of the present (the interpreter)" (27). Faqih continues, emphasizing the crucial role that the intended audience—rather than the original writer—plays in the production of meaning:

> When meaning is written through fixed form, it detaches itself from the intention of the author and gains its ideal character in this form. The meaning will come out again in the surface through mediation of interpretation by its reader. This does not mean that meaning belongs to the reader alone; it also belongs to the text since interpretation is an ongoing dialogue between the text and its reader. It is a living conversation between the past and the present. Since the meaning of the text is mediated through its interpretations, every reading becomes more or less a part of uninterrupted spiral of all the processes involved with finding the truth from a text. In other words, every reading becomes a pre-text or fore-conception (prejudice in the term of Gadamer's hermeneutics) for the following reading. (28)

Meaning-making exists in the relationship between a "text and its reader" and as a "living conversation between the past and present." Just as the isnad of the Hadith cite the "spiral" of interpretation from the author of the matn back to the Prophet Muhammad, so, too, does Faqih, as audience to Abū Shuqqa's text, contribute to the "ongoing dialogue." That said, once his work is concretized in text, in keeping with Gadamer's theory Faqih makes it clear that it is in his audience's hands to interpret. Indeed, what distinguishes Faqih's approach to interpreting the Hadith from other scholars, he declares, is the way his "study utilizes the conversational hermeneutics that impugns authorial intention and its methodological approach" (35). The religious and scholarly audiences in Faqih's citational repertoire intersect in theory and practice, in excess of their originating languages and associated cultures, and, when viewed relationally, likely explain his willingness to relinquish authorial control to serve his intended audiences.

In keeping with his desire to serve, in the methodology section of his dissertation Faqih asserts that he interpreted Abū Shuqqa's work as both "a scholar and an activist" (30), which spurred him to move past mere interpretation of the work to develop a heuristic for rereading the Hadith toward gender justice for his own audiences. He has since termed this heuristic "reciprocal reading," or *mubadalah*. He details this heuristic at length in his Indonesian-medium book *Qirā'ah Mubādalah: Tafsir Progresif untuk Keadilan Gender*, and in English, in his forthcoming chapters, "*Qirā'a Mubādala*: Reciprocal Reading of Hadith on Marital Relationships" and "Abū Shuqqa's Approach to the Hadith: Towards an Egalitarian Islamic Gender Ethics." In keeping with the holistic and dialogic nature of mubadalah itself, I'll put theoretical knowledge outlined from Faqih's two most recent English-medium chapters in conversation with his earlier dissertation work, which will ultimately emphasize that Faqih's linguistic negotiations with English and other languages—and thus his approach to translingual praxis— can be read by analogy through the lens of mubadalah.

In "*Qirā'a Mubādala*: Reciprocal Reading of Hadith on Marital Relationships," Faqih defines the central assumptions behind mubadalah as follows:

> With the *Qirā' a Mubādalah* method, all people are addressed and are equal subjects of the conversation in all texts. Therefore, this method assumes that the underlying message of any text—whether general, addressed to men only or women only—is applicable to all people. This assumption is based on three basic premises: (1) that Islam is for all humanity, so its texts should address everyone regardless of sex; (2) that

the Qur'anic principle of human relations is cooperation and reciprocity, not hegemony and power; and (3) that Islamic texts are open for reinterpretation to allow the previous two premises to be reflected in every interpretative effort. (*Qiraa'a*, 210)

These assumptions undergird the two central methodological approaches he recommends to reinterpret the Hadith toward gender justice.

The first overarching method to reread the Hadith, for Abū Shuqqa as well as Faqih, is to move from an atomized reading of the Hadith in isolation from the Qur'an, which has long been the practice of Islamic jurisprudence, to a reading that views these two texts as *relational*, with Tawhid, or the oneness of God, the guiding principle. In "Abū Shuqqa's Approach to the Hadith," Faqih explains, "Abū Shuqqa recognizes the prevalent argument in the Islamic legal theory (*usūl al-fiqh*) about the certainty of Qur'an and probability of Hadith, but he does not polarize these two sources. Rather, he brings both together to figure out the truth about the equality between women and men" (9). The veracity of the Qur'an, as God's word made real, is a certainty, and the Hadith, which relay the experiences and messages of the Prophet, merely probable; however, rather than discarding one text and focusing solely on the other, one can find truth at their *intersections* through the interpretive process.

To ground his interpretation of the Hadith in the Qur'an, in his article "*Qirā'a Mubādala*" Faqih cites amina wadud's hermeneutical reading of the Qur'an to emphasize that Tawhid, or the oneness of God, promises gender equality and reciprocal relations between men and women, because placing primacy of one sex over the other—in the case of patriarchy, putting men in the position of power over women—equates to engaging in an act of *shirk*, or recognizing a God other than Allah. In Faqih's words, "Since humans are meant to have vertical relations only with God, the relations between men and women need to be horizontal, with both parties equal" (204). Faqih, citing Indonesian scholar Nur Rofia, also emphasizes that from the perspective of Tawhid "the quality of human beings is not determined by their biological sex, but by their *taqwā* (God-consciousness) and the deeds they do to benefit human beings and the universe" (205). All humans should be caretakers, or khalifah, of God's creations, which includes one another. The central tenet of the Qur'an, and the very practices required to be a good Muslim, call into question the hierarchical atomization of the patriarchy, suggesting instead relationality, which Faqih terms "gender-based reciprocity," or mubadalah, because such caretaking requires active "in-betweenness."

Faqih then goes on to cite multiple verses in the Qur'an that forward reciprocity, rather than unequal relations, and that, importantly for his rereading of Hadith, include the Arabic words for men *and* women (*Qirā'a* 207). For example, he cites verse 9:71: "The believers, both men and women, support each other; they order what is right and forbid what is wrong; they keep up the prayer and pay the prescribed alms; they obey God and His Messenger. God will give His mercy to such people: God is almighty and wise." This verse, which comes directly from Allah through Muhammad according to Islamic faith, emphasizes that men *and* women must support each other in their worship, which suggests a reciprocal relationship between men and women rather than a model that positions men as morally superior to women.

The Qur'an also discusses what makes a good marriage—a relationship that Abū Shuqqa and Faqih place primacy on in their move to reread the Hadith for gender justice. To emphasize "the beauty of sexual intimacy between husband and wife" (*Qirā'a* 207), for example, Faqih cites verse 4:21: "How can you take it away after each one has enjoyed the other, and they have taken a firm covenant from you?" In this case, "it" refers to the covenant of marriage. Embedded within this verse about divorce, however, is the assumption that "each one has enjoyed the other," which indicates that both men *and* women should sexually please each other within the sacrament of marriage. The male-centric interpretation of this verse focuses solely on the admonishment of a husband who wants to leave his wife, which positions the woman as a passive object, whereas a reciprocal reading would add another layer to the meaning by also focusing on a woman's role as an active participant in marital pleasure.

The second overarching interpretive method Faqih recommends is employing *usūl al-fiqh*, which is an already-established method of extracting Islamic law from "limited source texts" and applying them to "an ever-expanding and infinite reality" (*Qirā'a* 207). Employing usūl al-fiqh when it comes to mubadalah involves interpreting through analogy. Essentially, this interpretive practice entails making what is absent from the text, but assumed, present when interpreting, which could involve rereading the Hadith themselves with the assumption of reciprocity or, conversely, rereading problematic jurisprudence drawn from partial readings to forward reciprocity. One of the central ways of rereading the Hadith, then, is to move away from "partial reading, in which only a sentence or a phrase from the text is used as the normative basis of an interpretation without considering broader principles of Islamic teachings such as mercy, noble character, or the *objectives* of the Sharia" (*Qirā'a* 207, my emphasis). Calling forth, through the action of interpretation, the values forwarded by the Qur'an and the overall *purpose* of sharia,[34] or that which exists *in excess of the specific terminology* used in the Hadith, can help challenge misogynistic messages drawn from partial, and isolated, readings of the texts themselves.

Faqih's dissertation offers many historical examples of this type of partial reading and their derogatory effects on current gender relations. Faqih explains, for example, that Abū Shuqqa chooses to reinterpret all other Hadith through the Arabic phrase "al-nisa shaqa 'iq al-rijal," or "women are full sisters of men" (212), a phrase which can be found in the canonical Hadith collections *Sunan Abū Dawud* and *Sunan al-Turmudhi*. Despite its presence, the phrase is ignored in the latter authors' interpretations. Faqih explains the context of this phrase as follows: "This saying is uttered by the Prophet to answer a question raised by a woman about whether she should take a bath when she had a wet dream and found moisture

expectations. When it comes to the way he performs translingual praxis—both in his willingness to assimilate to written norms he's uncomfortable with and in his willingness to relinquish authorial control to his audiences—form matters less than the actions, both discursive and material, that precede and proceed from the language itself.

PERFORMING MUBADALAH

Given Faqih's description of what it means to perform Da'wah, it is not surprising that he has since moved the theory he developed on the discursive plane into his community to take material action when it comes to gender justice. Faqih's activism did not begin with his scholarly study, however, but instead has worked in tandem with it, emphasizing the mutually transformative, rather than dualistic, relationship between scholarship and embodied action that permeates Faqih's life.

History Page: Fahmina Institute

In 2000, Faqih was a cofounder of the Fahmina Institute in Cirebon, which holds as its "core belief that Islam or 'Islamicness' must take shape within a framework of social justice." Through contextual study of Islamic texts and training workshops linking Islam to Indonesian reality, the program seeks to use Islam as a starting point for pluralism, social justice through community democracy, and gender equality. In training workshops with feminist activists as well as religious leaders, Fahmina "historiciz[es] and contextualiz[es] the discriminatory rulings on women that have become part of Islamic law, showing that they are neither manifestations of divine will nor immutable, but rather that they are juristic constructs that are shaped by, reflect, and can change with time and place." One such juristic intervention will be discussed in more detail in the next chapter, in Nina's portrait, when she discusses her research on minority women's agency in the oppressed Ahmadiyya Muslim Indonesian community.

Though Faqih stepped back a bit from the Fahmina Institute as the mubadalah movement took off,[35] the clear link between his scholarship and his social action continues. The last sentence of his dissertation foreshadows both his desire to relinquish control of interpretation and a call to action that has since materialized:

In this study, I have shared horizons of Abū Shuqqa, the author of the book *Taḥrīr al-Marʾa fī Aṣr al-Risāla*. I have shared my own horizons as an activist of gender justice within Islamic perspective in Indonesia. Then I leave all of these to the readers to make their own conversation. Especially, the religious leader are recommended to listen and learn from lived realities of women, and all Muslim women, all of them, are encouraged to read and interpret religious texts based upon their lived experiences.

Faqih ends his manuscript by turning to his own intended audience, emphasizing *for whom* he created this knowledge, and with that, *with whom*, on the material plane, he wants his knowledge to circulate: with religious leaders and women and, importantly, religious leaders who *are* women.

Since finishing his English-medium dissertation and publishing it in the Indonesian-medium *Qirāʾah Mubādalah: Tafsir Progresif untuk Keadilan Gender*, Faqih's theory has reached audiences both within Indonesia and beyond, emphasizing his translingual fluency on both the discursive and the material planes. By tracing how Faqih moves knowledge and, just as importantly, by tracing how Faqih's intended audiences put his knowledge into practice once Faqih relinquishes authorial control—we can see the relational, rather than atomized, understanding of knowledge creation that Faqih emphasizes when he describes the search for *hikmah*.

Emphasizing the reciprocal rather than the dualistic relationship between discursive and material action that animates Faqih's translingual work, Faqih's theory of mubadalah has been concretized in the material world with an official headquarters in Cirebon, which I visited in 2022. As I entered the Mubadalah compound after a long, hot train ride from Jakarta, I was greeted in a lush garden by a group of young activists, mostly female, wearing jilbabs and gracious smiles. After Faqih introduced me to each community member, he invited me to take off my shoes and sit in a circle with them in a traditional Javanese outdoor meeting space, with a thatched roof and open-air walls, all overlooked by the official mubadalah logo, pictured here. In a nod to border thinking, this logo meshes the

Chinese symbol for yin and yang with the traditional batik design local to Cirebon, which they call *mega mendung*, or cloud batik. The mega mendung design, in turn, is a meshing of traditional Javanese patterning and patterns the Chinese ethnic community brought with them when they came to the bustling seaport long ago. It seems fitting, then, that it was under this symbol that we discussed intersections between our respective projects.

As I snacked on *salak* (Indonesian snake fruit) and sipped Fanta,[36] the mubadalah activists asked me to discuss my scholarship about language in relation to mubadalah on video so they could share our dialogic interaction digitally with their mubadalah community. We discussed in particular how my work with translingualism and feminist rhetoric intersects with their work toward gender justice and mubadalah, and how the dynamic sharing of power suggested by mubadalah links to reciprocal listening—both to "nonstandard" English and to knowledge long subjugated by coloniality. In the middle of our discussion, I looked up and realized that Faqih had exited the circle so that I could engage directly with the women with whom he works, emphasizing, once again, the way he helps creates space for dialogic interaction—for mubadalah— and then relinquishes control.

Amber's Dialogue with Mubadalah Activists

Not surprisingly, then, Faqih credited the voices of Muslim women like those whom I met at the Mubadalah compound for spreading the message of mubadalah. When I asked him to discuss the trajectory of mubadalah, he explained that the movement began in 2016 on a personal blog he created to sound out his ideas as he was working on his dissertation, but then it was transformed into a vehicle to serve:

> Actually, mubadalah firstly, initially, was my blog. I write down my own knowledge, my experience, my travel, something like that. And then people inspired from this, and they say they want send me similar content. "So please send, you can send!" And then maybe so many people write like mine, and then it becomes public. So I, it's not . . . at this time, my writing become very few, because now that it become public more than 300 contributor, mostly women. About 90 percent that write about this issue, using mubadalah perspective. (2022 interview)

Faqih: On the Origin of the Mubadalah Movement

Since our 2022 interview, the number of contributors has jumped to four hundred, with two-thirds of them women and one-third men. Not surprisingly given Faqih's desire to serve, what started out as a personal blog space dominated by his own voice soon became a website, *Mubadalah.id,* that works to amplify the voices of others, and in particular women, who add their experiences to the spiral of interpretation mubadalah emphasizes. Though Faqih did initially create the blog and then the Mubadalah.id website, and though he does post some articles, his own voice is subdued when compared to the voices and interpretations of Indonesian women that his site amplifies. Once again, it's not himself as originating author that matters but the action his theory can foster in the hands of others, and in particular women.

A glimpse at the Indonesian-medium *Mubadalah.id* [37] showcases posts on topics that span religious exegesis, the environment, politics, family, and gender, all from the perspective of mubadalah. For example, there is an article by female Islamic jurisprudence scholar Nur Rofia, whom Faqih cites regularly in his academic work, in support of the passage of Indonesia's first sexual violence bill.[38] In this January 17, 2022 article, Rofia argues that the passage of this bill—of which Ninik, Chapter 8's case study, was a legislative initiator and that has since been passed into law—is an apostolic duty. Rofia writes:

> The Apostolic mission is to fight injustice in any form on the basis of monotheism or faith in Allah as the only God. Any nation that endeavors to build a legal system to prevent sexual violence on the basis of one Godhead is a nation that is also carrying out an apostolic mission. ("Urgensi")

Referring with the phrase "one Godhead" to both the Indonesian nation-state's founding document, Pancasila—which premises unity under one God but doesn't name a religion to ensure religious plurality—and Tawhid, which is specific to Islam, Rofia draws from the Islamic faith to argue that passing a bill preventing sexual violence against women is the duty of the Indonesian government.

Notably, Rofia continues by citing KUPI, or the Congress of Indonesian Women Ulama, in her argument, stating that this coalition of women religious leaders "has issued the Results of a Religious Deliberation which confirms that committing sexual violence, both inside and outside of marriage, is *haram!*" With its reference to marital rape, it is likely KUPI drew from the mubadalah-focused reinterpretation of the Hadith described above, which seems to justify the practice unless read through mubadalah; likewise, Chapter 8's case study, Ninik, also alludes to this reinterpretation in her interview with me when discussing her own escape from violence and the sexual violence bill she helped pass as legislator.

ACTIVATING KUPI

That KUPI and Mubadalah.id are citationally linked is no surprise considering that Faqih helped cocreate the KUPI initiative in concert with activists from the Fahmina Institute, which, as mentioned above, Faqih also helped cofound before he began graduate studies. According to *Kupipedia,* a website developed by Faqih and maintained by mubadalah activist Nurul Bahrul Ulum, the first KUPI conference took place in Cirebon in 2017. In keeping with the final call of Faqih's dissertation that more women's interpretations of Islamic texts be added to the conversation, the purpose of this conference was to amplify the voices of female *ulama*, or religious leaders, by gathering them into one space for dialogic interaction (a network that Kupipedia also seeks to mirror, albeit in digital form). As proclaimed on the Kupipedia website:

> It is time for female ulamas to consolidate themselves to strengthen their clerical capacity, meet each other, and then move together to build Islamic civilization, nation and humanity together with male clerics, the state, and all other elements of civil society. ("Women Scholars")

During my 2022 visit to Cirebon, Faqih and Nurul took me to the site of this first KUPI conference. Emphasizing the dialogic, as opposed to dualistic, interaction between religion and education in Indonesia, the first KUPI conference was held at Kebon Jambu al-Islami Pesantren, an Islamic boarding school, which was chosen because it is headed by female cleric Ibu Nyai Hj. Masriyah Amva, who has long advocated for Islamic gender justice both in her community and in scholarly publications focused on literature, gender equality, and pluralism.

On our drive through the darkened streets of Cirebon to the pesantren, Faqih and Nurul relayed an anecdote about Ibu Nyai Amva to explain why her school was chosen for the first conference. Apparently, prior to the first KUPI, the conference organizers had a heated conversation about whether to use the term "feminist" in their proceedings, and eventually they decided to avoid the term because they feared its origins might call the locality of their purposes into question. When Ibu Nyai Amva, pictured on the next page, took the stage to open the conference, however, she began her speech with the phrase "I am a feminist," and then proceeded to discuss how Islam and gender justice intersect. Not surprisingly, the unifying theme of her Islamic boarding school—and the pedagogy therein—is Islamic Family Law and Gender, with mubadalah as an organizing principle.

After entering the pesantren's large tree-lined courtyard and being greeted by male students preparing for an evening event to celebrate Idul Adha, I was welcomed by Ibu Nyai Amva and other faculty with a delicious student-prepared Javanese meal and conversation about the history of the school and KUPI. After dinner, I was invited to meet the hundreds of female students being educated there, and we had an impromptu question-and-answer session, with Nurul translating, where questions ranged from the purpose of my visit (most had never met a person from the United States) to a final question about how to become a professor when they were older. I was then invited to witness a beautiful student-choreographed light show in celebration of Idul Adha.

A Video of the Idul Adha Light Show

This group of children I was privileged to meet, led by this powerful female ulama, will likely circulate the concept of gender reciprocity into their community, adding to the spiral of interpretation toward gender justice Faqih imagined in his dissertation. Indeed, in a press release, the mubadalah website reported that just after I left Cirebon thousands of children from twenty-seven pesantren participated in the Second Halaqah Muda Pre-Congress of Indonesian Women Ulama, a hybrid religious gathering for young people led by Nur Rofia, which was meant to introduce them to the principles to be discussed in the second KUPI in the fall of 2022 (Redaksi).

Press Release About Kupi Youth Conference

Though (by his own design) Faqih's participation in codeveloping KUPI is muted on the Mubadalah and Kupipedia websites, he did discuss his role in our 2022 interview, when I asked him about his use of English within Indonesia. After admitting to me, "I need more time or more community of English that makes me become more comfortable" in using it, he explained:

> But actually English give me more opportunity to deliver my message. When there is KUPI, there are more than eighteen Muslim countries coming, and most of them are talking to me. I was so afraid, but it's like, there's no one other than me. Who knows the substance, the meaning, the paradigm [of mubadalah], and at the same time knows English. So at the time in our circle, there are only two people who know . . . English: me and Nur Rofia. And there is, there are guests and they need one who talk English . . . .

Faqih: On Using English at KUPI

Once again, delivering the *message* to a global audience—the knowledge itself—to serve Muslim women trumps any trepidation Faqih might feel when addressing this audiences in a language he is still not entirely comfortable with.

Faqih has also been asked to present his theory using English in places as varied as France, the Netherlands, Germany, Thailand (five times), the Philippines, Malaysia, Qatar, Hong Kong, and Bangladesh. That breaking down the discursive/embodied or signifier/signified divide when considering translingual praxis is important can be seen in the way Faqih relays an anecdote from one of these in-person trainings. He exemplified how he performs, and thus embodies, the dialogism theorized in his English-medium writing in this way:

> There is mostly clerics. And some of them reject the idea that woman can be leader or responsible for household. "It's not Islamic, blah, blah, blah." So I'm not angry. I do not reject him. I just ask him, "What do you mean by leader of family?" So he says, "Leader means one who is responsible." "What do you mean by responsible?" He says, "Maybe going to work, and coming with money to family." So I ask him, "Is there any woman who go to work and come to family with money."

"Yes!" "What do you define?" "Yeah, but it's not leader . . . "
[Faqih laughs] "How do you define the role of such kind of
woman? You think that it's good?" "Yes—it's good, but not
'leader!'" "So what's your definition of leader?" And then it
becomes, ding, ding, ding! (Faqih makes game show sound).
"OK. I agree with your idea, but I don't want to say woman
is 'leader.'" "It's up to you, as long as you appreciate the social
role of women and mention them in your religious sermons!"
(2022 interview)

Faqih:
Woman as
"Leader"
Anecdote

In the dialogic interplay of this anecdote, Faqih highlights how
language itself—in this case, applying the term "leader" to a woman—may get in the way of the *message*, in this case, that women
are equally responsible for taking care of their households, which
should allow them to work outside of the home like their male
counterparts. Performing his belief in relinquishing control to his
audience, Faqih intimates that as long as the cleric includes women
in his sermons and interprets Islamic exegesis in a way that emphasizes reciprocity and women's strength, the term the cleric uses to label a
woman who works outside of the home —provided "it is good"—is
"up to him." For Faqih, Da'wah is a relational performance that both
includes language *and* exceeds it through performative dialogism.

And sometimes language is not even a necessary prerequisite to
mubadalah. In his 2022 interview, Faqih amplified the work of his
fellow ICRS alumni, friend, and legislator, Ninik, who is showcased
in Chapter 8, when discussing representation and female leadership:

So, we need much more women to become on stage. In
politics, like Ninik Wafiroh, even if they don't talk about Islam.
But people will say, "This is example of Muslim woman." So
people will see other kyai, other ulama, male cleric, will refer
to her: "This is example of good Muslim woman." Who let's
say, who, interprets and translates the teaching into her life.
That type is also interpretation.

Faqih: On
Ninik as a
Powerful
Muslim
Woman

To clarify my interpretation of his message, I asked, "So interpretation is discursive and it's material, right? It's material actions, in
addition to texts?" Faqih replied, emphasizing by gesturing to the

space in between us, that from his perspective, interpretation bridges text and world, "Yeah. *This* is the material, *this* is the model, *this* is the world of interpretation. So interpretation not only in book." To return to the concept of Tawhid—or the oneness of creation—for Faqih, language and the body, the academic and spiritual, the rational and the felt, exist on the same plane, ready to be interpreted in the search for *hikmah*, and it's in the dialogic movement between these realms where we can rewrite the world toward gender justice, regardless of the language used. In Faqih's words, "It's about action and intertwined. Because people have minds, have wisdom, have feeling." And all of these attributes exist on the same plane rather than in opposition.

Faqih: On Interpretation as Discursive and Embodied

Faqih: On the Interrelationality of Mind and Feeling

CONCLUSIONS

Faqih's portrait highlights ways of conceptualizing rhetorical negotiation that are central to understanding how translinguality and theories of Islamic gender justice intersect. First, by asking "for whom" Faqih intends his texts, we can see how English can be appropriated to serve local, non-Western audiences, emphasizing, as Xiaoye You suggests in *Cosmopolitan English*, that language can no longer be tied to broadly perceived national borders and the audiences implied thereby. Audience is complicated when it comes to local-global language negotiations, requiring that we complicate simplistic models that link one language, or one type of language user, to a monolithic, one-dimensional intended audience (see also Canagarajah, "Toward").

In fact, Faqih's portrait shows the affordances of expanding past an isolated examination of text in relation to intended audience—the *for whom*—to instead reframe global audience negotiation as a dialogic negotiation among past, present, and future voices (Bakhtin, *Dialogic Imagination*). Tracing Faqih's audience negotiation dialogically makes it clear, for example, that assimilation to audience expectations can be a critical choice. If we were to look at Faqih's texts in isolation, their assimilative nature might point to a lack of agency when it comes to his ability to negotiate English's power. However, when we look at the translingual process that led to his final texts—to the way he negotiates the many voices in his multivocal citational repertoire and at the way he moves his knowledge across languages to reach new audiences—it becomes clear that textual assimilation can be the product of translingual praxis, depending, of course, on the writer's intentionality in relation to these choices. My ethnographic approach, with its mixed methods and longitudinal lens, allowed me to explore translingual praxis from a dialogic, spatiotemporal perspective, which, as Anis Bawarshi, Min-Zhan Lu and Bruce Horner, and Brooke Ricker Schreiber and Missy Watson argue, is central to understanding translingualism in excess of *textual* deviance.

Faqih's portrait also emphasizes the importance of mapping his "language of thought" (Fodor), which as Li Wei argues requires moving past linguistic markers to focus on enmeshed habits of mind (and body) that exist *in excess of* language ("Translanguaging" 19). One way to map this interplay, I argue, is to take the *actual content* of writers' scholarship seriously, which this study does by asking *from whom* Faqih drew his wisdom. Closely examining the theoretical lenses writers use in their advanced academic texts—even if these lenses do not address *language itself* in an explicit way—may unearth habits of mind that transcend the content of the text itself to inform their orientations toward translingual praxis. Faqih's use of Gadamer's theory to explore Abū Shuqqa's reading of the Hadith in his dissertation, for example, intersects with how he discusses his writing choices and audience negotiation in the first year of his graduate education. In his first-year literacy narratives, Faqih attributes his choice to assimilate to his desire to serve his intended audience, which shows a willingness to surrender authorial power, while in his more advanced scholarship he uses Gadamer's theory to argue that the relationship between text and audience is more important than the authorial intent of the originating author. Though the content of his first assignments focused explicitly on writing, and the content of the latter on ways of interpreting religious exegesis, Faqih exhibits the *same orientation* toward knowledge construction in both. Namely, it's not the author's voice that matters most but what an audience can *do* with the author's text. When seeking to understand translingual praxis, we mustn't view linguistic choices in isolation from the *values* they represent, which, because of the overlapping nature of discourse, inevitably transcend the equally arbitrary boundaries we create to distinguish one language from the next.

Breaking down these boundaries, in turn, is central to understanding how Faqih's work might contribute to conversations about decoloniality. Though Faqih would call his work Da'wah, and not "decolonial," his interrelational understanding of the world emphasizes that borders long constructed as "discrete" are in fact enmeshed. Faqih's scholarly work is deeply informed by Tawhid, or the oneness of creation, which, he explains, undergirds all of his actions in the world, regardless of how they're named. Imagining discrete boundaries between religious, scholarly, and activist discourses belies the possibilities that they may intertwine, interanimating one another with new resonances and possibilities. Faqih writes, "I should love English like I love the text of religion itself" in his final writer's reflection, which clearly indicates that he sees a connection between his religious literacies and his academic literacies. As we trace the theoretical trajectory of mubadalah, it becomes clear that his willingness to assimilate while simultaneously being open to interpretive dissonance is very much linked to his religious training, where the Qur'an itself might be immutable but how worshippers interpret the life of the Prophet Muhammad diverse, frictive, and generative. Just as he is able to reconcile embracing "the text as it is" while also valuing the diachronic and dialogic interpretive process that led to the dissonant voices of the Hadith, Faqih is also able to reconcile embracing English textual forms as they are, since the process that leads to his final texts is undoubtedly as frictive—and, I would add, as translingual—as the process made concrete by the chain of narrators listed in the Hadith. Locating translingual praxis requires acknowledging that religious and academic discourse—regardless of their originating languages—are meshed in ways many Western scholars trained to understand these discourses as a duality are unaccustomed to.

Locating translingual praxis also necessarily requires moving past such text-based analysis to look at *with whom* writers like Faqih circulate academic knowledge in their local communities, which requires audiences trained to view mind and body dualistically to relink these modalities and to understand them dialogically. Faqih's academic texts might assimilate, but the ways he moves knowledge created at the contact zone between competing discourses from his English-medium texts into his lived, embodied reality is undoubtedly translingual. Faqih's ultimate desire is to serve his community and to foster an environment where mubadalah—itself an amalgamation of competing discourses—can flourish in the spaces "in-between," regardless of what language this knowledge is conveyed in. This desire to foster Islamic gender justice and to serve the Indonesian community, we will see, unites all three case study portraits in this book, though the three writers' translingual engagements differ because of their differing lived experiences. It is my hope, to paraphrase Faqih's dissertation, that the next two portraits add further nuance to the "uninterrupted spiral" of interpretation when it comes to global communicative practices.

Chapter 7

"The Women, Hand in Hand, Made a Human Chain": Translanguaging to Access

We, the Ahmadiyya community, give informal education to our adolescent girls and women in mosques. They learn about religious, social, and humanitarian issues and language. A mosque for us is not only a place of worship, but also plays the role of a center of our activities, especially providing a space for women and girls. However, following Joint Ministerial Decree 2008 *on Ahmadiyya, there are attacks on them and our mosques being closed down by local authorities. Consequently, this informal education for women of my community has been largely affected. Do you think it is fair for women in my community to lose out on their opportunities because their security cannot be guaranteed??* (Dr. Nina Mariana Noor, Speech to United Nations, November 29, 2019)

Translated Joint Ministerial Decree

Video of Nina Addressing the UN

Statement in 12 Forum on Minority Issues, UN

AFGHANISTAN

second languages and inclusive education are encouraged. Our community give informal education to our Women and Girls

The excerpt above is drawn from an impassioned speech—in English—that Dr. Nina Mariani Noor made to an international audience at the United Nations Forum for Minority Issues in Geneva. Nina emphasizes the lost educational opportunities her community, and in particular women, face as conservative Muslims within Indonesia physically bar access to Ahmadi mosques because they are hostile to the Ahmadi interpretation of Islam. By making explicit the connection between faith, place, and education when addressing the diverse UN audience *with whom* she is communicating—some of whom may view rationality and religion dualistically—Nina anticipates and then rewrites narratives that falsely position social, humanitarian, and linguistic education in opposition to Islam. With her use of "we"—and with her own embodied performance for this powerful UN audience—she also emphasizes that Ahmadi women, like herself, are active participants in Islamic faith rather than passive victims to it, challenging long-held misconceptions promoted by coloniality that position Islam as inevitably oppositional to female empowerment (see Ahmed; Mahmood). For Nina, religion and gender justice are deeply intertwined. Nina uses English—one of the many languages in her repertoire—as a means of *accessing* this global UN audience, which might, in turn, have the power to influence the Indonesian government to adopt her recommendations: namely, honoring the religious harmony and pluralism promised by Pancasila so that minority women and girls can access their educational spaces. This speech serves as a microcosm for the scholarly-activist work showcased in this chapter, in which Nina strategically accesses and then helps various audiences imagine a more just world in multiple languages.

If Faqih's general orientation toward translingual praxis evidenced a desire to *serve* his audiences, Nina's translingual praxis emphasizes how women from minoritized communities might create circumstances amenable to *accessing* more powerful audiences. Enacting her Ahmadiyya Islamic community's motto, "Love for all; hatred for none," Nina's scholarly-activist work focuses on fostering interconnectivities when it comes to the global Muslim diaspora and the role women of faith might play to further social justice—provided religious communities long positioned at odds with one another, like her Ahmadi community and the dominant Sunni community in Indonesia, strive equally to connect across difference when it comes to the stories they engage with *and* the material spaces they share. Indeed, though the title of this chapter, "The Women, Hand in Hand, Made a Human Chain," is how Nina describes the *embodied* agency of the Ahmadi women she researched for her dissertation, it also serves as an apt metaphor for how Nina engages in translingual praxis as she shuttles among languages and audiences to create the means for more ethical and equitable interfaith and gender-based interconnectivities. To first access and then transform existing power relationships between herself and more dominant audiences, this work requires that Nina, as an Ahmadi woman, be a strategic player in relation to the scripts she encounters, both globally and locally, in English and otherwise.

EVEN IN DIFFERENT LANGUAGES, I'M STILL THE SAME PERSON

Understanding the intersecting voices that inform Nina's "discursive energy field," to return to Krista Ratcliffe's *Rhetorical Listening*, is crucial to understanding how she engages in translingual praxis to increase access. In 2010, when I asked Nina whether she felt any identity shifts when writing to different audiences in different languages, she alluded to the many enmeshed discourses in her repertoire and how her identities merely shifted dialogically in relation to her intended audiences:

> Even in different languages, I'm still the same person, but maybe with new ideas, with a new way of thinking, so when I write for Indonesian audience, my idea is Indonesian, and audience are Indonesian too. We have the same stories. But when I write for international audience, I think, "You are academician, I am academic also, that's fine." Identity is fluid I think. I can say I'm an Ahmadi Muslim, I'm a woman, I'm a

feminist, I'm a housewife. That's fine. To my friends, I say I'm a working studying mother. (2010 interview)

During her first year in graduate school, Nina defines her identity as intersectional, to employ Kimberle Crenshaw's term, and in so doing she intimates that she shifts identities depending on what "serious game" she encounters—a process that doesn't *negate* the silenced identities and that doesn't preclude her from drawing on different identities in the future.

Border thinking, which, as Gloria Anzaldúa, Walter Mignolo, and others argue, involves focusing on overlap between identities as opposed to imagining them as discrete, is central to understanding Nina's translingual praxis. In her 2022 interview, Nina emphasized that at the root of this identity map is her Ahmadi identity, but it is important that she also repeatedly emphasizes that this religious identity *coexists with* and interanimates her other identities. In so doing, she challenges the essentialist concept promoted by coloniality that positions practicing Muslims as entirely *subject to* an all-consuming faith that is inevitably counter to critical thinking and intellectual engagement (see Tayob). She explained: "So actually, for me as a Muslim, Islamic teachings offers all things for our life. We just can adjust it with situation, actually. So Islamic values never in conflict with other values. Good values. Ethics, for example." When I asked her in 2022 if she considered her scholarly-activist work "decolonial" because she challenges the problematic notion that religion and intellect can't coexist, she replied in the affirmative:

Nina:
Islam as
Co-Existent
with Other
Discourses

Actually, yes. I can say what I teach is decolonial. Even in my study program. It's interdisciplinary Islamic studies, so we do interdisciplinary, but we still use Islam. As a Muslim, we can't just leave our belief aside, and just be "rational." But, being rational, we also attach religion, we bring it everywhere. This is intersection.

Nina: On
Religion and
Rationality
in Teaching

Here Nina foreshadows the border-thinking pedagogy she employs while emphasizing intersectional as opposed to discrete discourse shifts when it comes to her identities. Nina's scholarly life, in fact, allows her to engage in different ways with her faith, something she views as a privilege:

> I am lucky because I can be an Ahmadi, I can write about Ahmadiyya, about my community and my faith, but still I can increase my career. [. . .] So I do activism, because in Indonesia, as a lecturer, being a lecturer in Indonesia is quite hard. [. . .] We have three dharma: first is teaching, the second, research and publication, and third is community service. So I can do it with one topic. (2022 interview)

Nina: Faith as the Root for Academic Commitments

Once again, Nina makes it clear that her Ahmadi faith is at the root of her required academic commitments, which, although *seemingly* discrete, are united—all in one—because of her faith.

It is not surprising, then, that Nina's faith—and the oppression of her community—were her primary motivations for studying interreligious dialogue at ICRS. In her 2010 interview, she put it this way:

> I'm a Muslim, but actually I'm a member of Ahmadiyya movement. It's a Muslim organization all over the world, and it has headquarters in London, where we have our caliph. But in Indonesia, Ahmadiyya is considered as non-Muslim, so some of us were attacked and even some people were killed by mainstream Muslims. So that's why I think that OK, as a woman, and as a Muslim and as Ahmadi, I have to learn about interreligious studies to reach and teach my own knowledge . . . and maybe I can do something for my community then.

As a member of a transnational religious group that is oppressed within Indonesia, over the past thirteen years Nina has been able to access knowledge through English that in turn helps her access dominant local and global audiences to "reach and teach" about Ahmadiyya—knowledge she believes might help stem the violence she and her fellow religious community members have experienced as Indonesian citizens.

Nina's grounded-in-faith—yet also fluid— understanding of her own identity also mirrors her beliefs about language. Like many

Indonesians, Nina grew up speaking Javanese and Bahasa Indonesia. She acquired English and Arabic through more formal educational channels. When I asked about her history with English in her initial 2010 interview, she explained that although English was both her favorite and best subject in school, because her father was an Arabic teacher she chose to earn her BA in Arabic literature instead. When it came to her master's degree, however, Nina's overlapping interests in English and social justice for women prompted her to apply to an English-medium Indonesia-based program in social work cosponsored by CIDA, the Canadian International Development Agency, and the Yogyakarta-based Universitas Islam Negeri, the State Islamic University. Nina applied to this English-medium international MA program, she explained in her 2010 interview, because teaching English and Arabic full-time at a community *pesantren*, or Muslim boarding school, had helped her realize that "education is part of social work":

> I was thinking about my community at the time. As you know, most of the young women are migrant workers there. And I thought, why are they becoming migrant workers? But at least if you are migrant worker, you can get better life or better way if you use English. So after they graduate from high school, they can go not to Saudi Arabia, but to Taiwan, Hong Kong if they can use English. It is better conditions for women there, I think. So my social work emphasis was I like English and I can help my community with it too.

Nina points to the stark reality that many young women from her area are forced, because of economic circumstances, to become migrant workers in more affluent nations. She believes that if they know English, they at least have a chance at working in less oppressive circumstances than those in Saudi Arabia. Here Nina foreshadows how intertwined education, religion, and social justice are in her life—and the fact that English can be appropriated to serve local audiences in support of, rather than in opposition to, these entwined discourses.

Indeed, this MA program gave her the opportunity to study and write academically in English *within* Indonesia about Indonesian female migration, emphasizing, as Faqih's portrait has also shown, how English is continually being adapted to local purposes. This scholarly experience, she explained in her 2010 interview, also affected her beliefs about the English language:

> I never think English is imperialist . . . . Maybe I differ from my friends in that. Yeah, because my experience with academic writing. I wrote for the first time in English. So maybe that's the difference . . . that's why. So maybe Ninik or Faqih, they are very good at writing in Indonesian so they feel different.

Nina reflects on her language history in relation to her friends' differing relationships to English, indicating that linguistic affiliations form in relation to individual literacy histories and not necessarily in relation to affiliations with a particular nation-state. As Xiaoye You suggests in his *Cosmopolitan English*, assuming a direct correlation between language—in this case, language affiliations— and broadly defined geopolitical borders is problematic.

Nina continued, once again showing her belief in multiplicity— this time in relationship to language, as opposed to identity:

> Writing in English doesn't mean we don't respect our Bahasa [Indonesia]. We respect it. But as a part of being international academicians, we have to admit that English is used by many people. Because in Indonesia, there are some people who think, "OK. You use English. You are like bule.[39] You are not nationalist" . . . But I do not find any difficulties in grasping English since I put myself not only as a Javanese but as a Javanese who is using English. (2010 interview)

Nina likely doesn't see the English language, or the "bule" identity it supposedly represents, as imperialist because she has long experienced it as part of her local context. Just as she can be an Ahmadi Muslim engaging in scholarship, teaching, and community activism, she can be a Javanese user who uses English. English, long used to promote Western interests, can no longer be viewed as dichotomous to non-Western meaning-making. To truly see the complex and interrelational nature of Nina's work requires challenging the seemingly immutable relationship between language and nation-state, a process that requires simultaneously acknowledging global power relationships *and* acknowledging localized agency to appropriate and resignify.

In fact, for a member of a religious minority like Nina, English has long been a way to *access* dominant local and global audiences to advocate for her Ahmadi community. When I asked her in 2022 *for whom* she most often intended her knowledge, she emphasized, "I rarely write for my [Ahmadiyya] community. It's like my job is like the *humas* . . . ambassador, yeah. So I talk more, I write more, outside. [. . .] But for my own community, sometimes I become speaker. So I speak to my community. [. . .] But mostly I speak outside my community. When my community needs a speaker for outside the community, they ask me." Nina most often communicates her knowledge to audiences she views as "external" to her Ahmadi community—a community which, rather than the Indonesian nation-state, serves as the locus for Nina's understanding of what she considers "internal" and thus "external." A look at Nina's dissertation work, and how she subsequently circulates that knowledge across languages over the course of thirteen years, emphasizes different ways Nina draws from her English-medium scholarship to reach more powerful audiences to advocate for interfaith gender justice for her community.

Nina: On Her Role as an Interfaith Ambassador

ACCESSING THE AHMADI FAITH

But first, given the monolithic understanding of Islam some folks in my own audience may be subject to, a brief description of the Ahmadi faith[40] is likely necessary to understand the power differentials Nina navigates in her scholarly-activist work. As a testament to Bakhtinian interconnectivity when it comes to knowledge-making, I can cite how Nina herself defines her faith community in her dissertation, *Ahmadi Women Resisting Fundamentalist Persecution: A Case Study on Active Group Resistance in Indonesia* (Noor). In her dissertation, Nina explains that the Ahmadi faith "was founded in 1889 in Qadiyan Punjab, India, by Mirza Ghulam Ahmad (1835–1908)." She continues, writing,

The root of conflict between the Ahmadiyya community and mainstream Muslims is on the difference in interpretation on the finality of prophethood—*khataman nabiyyin* in Qur'an 33:40, which declares "Muhammad is not the father of any of your men, but he is the Messenger of Allah, and the Seal of the Prophets." Mainstream Muslims believe that the Prophet Muhammad is *khataman nabiyyin,* meaning the "last prophet," while Ahmadiyya community considers Muhammad as the ultimate prophet, the seal of prophets, the last messenger who brings *shariah*/law. Therefore, according to Ahmadiyya there is a possibility of a coming prophet after him who does not bring new law (because he is from Muhammad's followers), but he is a Muslim who will continue teaching Islam.

The Ahmadi believe that Mirza Ghulam Ahmad was a "Promised Messiah and prophet" who came after Muhammad—one who did not add new laws to those set forth by God through Muhammad, but who was still a prophet, not just a follower, of Islam.[41] These competing interpretations of Qur'an 33:40, Nina explains, have fomented the belief in some Indonesian Muslims, the majority of whom are Sunni and thus believe that Muhammad was the last Prophet, that Ahmadiyya are heretics.

In her 2014 interview, Nina drew from a portion of her dissertation research to explain how this oppression has manifested itself in the past, and one way the Ahmadi community—and in particular, women—took agency to counter the violence:

> In West Java, near Cirebon, there is one village, and 70–80% of them are Ahmadi, so they got 9 mosques that belong to Ahmadiyya. It's the biggest Ahmadi population in Southeast Asia. So people before 2008, I think, from 2002, the local government and fundamentalist Muslims who don't like Ahmadi, always seal the mosque closed, and the community didn't do anything. So sometimes they let the mosque be sealed for two or three days. They seal with wood on the doors and windows so they cannot get inside, or do prayers

inside . . . . They are always blamed by the local government, the ulema, also the people: "You are deviant. You are heretic. That's why you cannot pray even in your own mosque."

This embodied action by conservative Muslims—physically denying her community access to their place of worship—Nina explained, was at first accepted by her community because "they didn't know that it is their legal right to defend their property."

Nina's community did not remain passive victims, however. Referring to the social-justice organization that Faqih, Chapter 6's case study, cofounded, Nina explained that in 2005 the Fahmina Institute intervened. The activists in his organization—well-versed in Indonesian law— gave this community "some knowledge about property rights and law . . . so Fahmina helped them advocate." Armed with the legal knowledge circulated by the Fahmina Institute, the Ahmadi women in this particular community took agency. Nina continued:

> When they try to seal the mosque, the women, hand in hand, made a human chain to protect the mosque. And they are first in line. Brave but crying. I think before that, people thought, "OK, because you are a woman, just stay away. Go inside." And at first they would go inside and pray, and just cry, but that changed. They started to go outside and defend their mosque physically. So they feel better now, because now, if it's sealed, they open it.

These women met threats to their physical space with an embodied agency, which was, in turn, spurred by an increased understanding of their legal rights according to Indonesian law. In essence, the discursive intervention led by the Fahmina Institute spurred them to take embodied action to protect their mosque. Tracing how knowledge moves across contexts from text to body and back again is central to reframing translingual praxis as a human-driven, rather than solely a text-centered, phenomenon. Indeed, though Nina refers to the embodied intervention described above when she explains that "the women, hand in hand, made a human chain," this phrase also serves as an apt metaphor for the way Nina herself takes agency as a scholar-activist on both the discursive and material planes.

"THEY DON'T KNOW US AS HUMANS"

By tracing the knowledge that precedes and proceeds from Nina's English-medium dissertation work, we can see how writers, like Nina, from nondominant groups, can localize English to increase access to more dominant, and potentially hostile, local audiences. Importantly, for Nina, this translingual process involves drawing from the prestige linked to English itself to establish her credibility as a scholar and then moving the knowledge garnered from her English-medium research into the material world to reach and teach non-Ahmadis using multiple languages. Similar to Faqih, the definition of agency Nina develops in her dissertation to describe Ahmadi women's agency when confronted with religious violence also mirrors the way she herself performs translingual praxis as she moves knowledge into the world both discursively and materially. Understanding the discursive and material planes interrelationally and exploring how they mutually inform each other in relation to situational power dynamics is central to understanding how writers perform translingual praxis.

Unlike Faqih, who writes from a position of power as a male Sunni religious leader, Nina writes from a positionality that might bar her access to dominant scholarly conversations within Indonesia. Nina's scholarship cannot be divorced from her own experiences as an Ahmadi woman. As Ratcliffe argues in *Rhetorical Listening*, once embodied, discourses—and how they're interpreted by the audiences *for whom* writers intend their texts—cannot be separated from existing power relationships, a fact that Nina is quite aware of. As an Ahmadi woman researching Ahmadi women, for Nina, "the personal is political" (Hanisch 204)—a situation that presents both affordances and constraints when it comes to her scholarly work.

When it comes to affordances, the fact that Nina is Ahmadi herself gives her access to new ways of interpreting past knowledge—or the scholars that precede, and thus are audience to, her work. In her words, "There are research about Ahmadiyya, but not by an insider like me, an Ahmadi and a woman. So maybe I'm the first to see it and write about it from an Ahmadi female perspective. Because actually my research is also a continuation of my friend's research on Ahmadi women" (2014 interview). By citing her female colleague here, rather than dismissing her because she is not Ahmadi, Nina emphasizes the way she works "hand in hand" on the discursive plane with a previously published scholar who is external to her community, foreshadowing the type of strategic networking she and her community do when it comes to the non-Ahmadi audiences *with whom* they wish to connect. To me, this invitational, rather than exclusionary, approach to citation performs what Ratcliffe terms "feminist rhetorical listening" (*Rhetorical Listening*).

Despite the insider access Nina is privy to as an Ahmadi woman, she is *also* cognizant of the danger involved with performing this "personal as political" scholarly position, particularly as a member of a maligned group. The audience *for whom* Nina addresses her work is very much mediated by her desire to access non-Ahmadi audiences for the sake of social justice, which requires critical awareness of how she might be "read" as an Ahmadi scholar. This critical praxis resulted in Nina's choice to address her scholarship to a non-Ahmadi, *English-using* Indonesian academic audience—a choice, we will see, that does not preclude her from accessing different audiences in the future. When I asked in 2014 whom she hoped her dissertation scholarship would reach, she emphasized that she wanted to reach Indonesian academics:

> So for academics, when they read an article, they will use their brain, not only their heart. Brain and heart. Not only their gut feeling. And not just theological thing, either. So academicians see many different perspectives, not just theology, so they won't stop reading once they see I'm Ahmadi because they think I'm a liar. So I hope that people will see that my work is based on good academic research, but also on narrative.

Nina believes that an academic register lends her scholarship as an Ahmadi woman legitimacy. To return to Bakhtin, *for whom* Nina addresses her words is mediated by her experiences negotiating past voices—who have viewed her as a "liar" because of her faith—which in turn informs her understanding of how they will read her work in the future, thus informing her rhetorical choices. When I asked her in this 2014 interview why she chose a narrative methodology to reach this audience, she put it this way:

> Because of social justice, that's why I use narrative. The purpose of narrative is to get social justice. So sometimes conflict is a problem for our community, but maybe mainstream Muslims haven't heard from women. Maybe they have from interview on TV or radio, but only one person, so they will not be heard. But when they become like a communal voice, if together they speak out their voices, it's easier to get social justice. And sometimes I understand why people accuse us as being alien—and why they can kill us. Because they don't understand. That's why it's our duty to make them understand. It's like, I think the conflict is happening because they don't know us as humans.

Nina points to the dangers of individualizing systemic oppression (see Hesford and Schell 462); focusing on one woman's story, as opposed to the pattern of oppression experienced by the broader community, makes it easier for conservative Muslims to justify that person's story as "exceptional" and to continue to dehumanize the majority of Ahmadi people. Accordingly, as the next section will explore, Nina's scholarship both tells the stories of individual women and then charts broader trends when it comes to the ways they—and she—can collaboratively take agency against oppression, hand in hand, with audiences both internal and external.

Nina's abilities with English, in turn, helped her forge the interconnectivities necessary to access more powerful audiences, like the English-using Indonesian audience for whom she writes her dissertation. When I asked her in 2014 how she thought other Indonesians interpreted her abilities to use English in her scholarship, she said, "I think [non-Ahmadi Muslims] respect me. They need to . . . because they think 'Oh, you already go abroad and you speak English as well. And you're Ahmadi?' At least they will see another side of Ahmadiyya community." Nina's capacity with the global language of power, she believes, makes her non-Ahmadi Indonesian audience members more receptive when it comes to her scholarship and the stories it conveys. Nina localizes English when writing her dissertation, leveraging English's status as the global language of power to encourage dominant Indonesian audiences to view her community as fully "human"—a discursive intervention that, she hopes, affects their actions in the material world when confronted with religious difference.

INTERRELATED AGENCIES

Importantly, the *content* of Nina's scholarship—and the way she defines female agency—also mirrors the way she herself performs translingual praxis as she moves from one limit-situation to the next. Nina's translingual rhetorical work emphasizes the transformative possibilities of epistemological border work and a dialogic, rather than dualistic, relationship between linguistic agency and academic content as well as between scholarship and engagement with the world.

In her dissertation, Nina uses narrative methodology to explore how women in three different Indonesian locations collaboratively take agency from within Lajnah Imaillah, an organization in the Ahmadiyya faith community devoted specifically to women's religious empowerment. All Ahmadi women, once they reach the age of fifteen, take part in this organization, which, according to Nina's dissertation, "provides women a structure to train and develop and enhance their religious and academic knowledge, to acquire health and fitness skills, manage trade and business affairs, and develop their financial abilities" (91). This women-run organization, though subject to the Khalifah's overarching vision, provides Ahmadi women agency in a larger religious system that is patriarchal. Nina, who has been president twice in the Yogyakarta branch and currently serves in the national branch as secretary, explained in her 2022 interview that "Yes, in Islam, as always, the highest leader is man. But for women, it's fine, we have our organization. We

Nina's
Dissertation
in Published
Form

can extend and exercise our capacity in our organization. Even in my research, as you have read my dissertation, I found that mostly women are initiators in all programs." Here Nina foreshadows her understanding of female agency as simultaneously a collective endeavor and one that is subject to situational power relations. This statement also foreshadows the way she herself, as a woman, initiates external programs to gain access to more dominant audiences.

Nina: On Women's Agency Within Lajnah Imaillah

As a testament to the way that the past voices who populate a writer's repertoire interanimate one another despite linguistic and cultural differences, in her dissertation Nina puts into conversation the narratives of Ahmadi women, which she translates into English, the definition of agency developed by US anthropologist Sherry Ortner, and the concept of "hidden transcripts" developed by US-based scholar James Scott to map what female agency looks like from within Lajnah Imaillah. From this scholarly border work emerges Nina's definition of female agency:

> As agents playing serious games, Ahmadi women are not free agents, but rather they pick up a cultural script and then decide how to play it. Therefore, they are neither passive recipients of a predetermined role nor a mirror for societal rules. These women are playing as strategic participants in social life. (27)

Referring to Ortner's metaphor of "serious games," Nina acknowledges existing power relationships that Ahmadi women like herself face and the fact that performances may shift, depending on the script, which requires a more expansive understanding of Ahmadi female agency than that offered by the powerful/powerless binary.

Nina's research highlights three major ways the Ahmadi women she studied took agency when faced with oppression. The first Nina describes as "docile agency," or remaining passive when confronted with violence and discrimination, a choice she attributes to her faith's belief in nonviolence and the mandate to start with "reasons and explanations to people who do not agree to their faith" before resorting to more active resistance (153). Notably, acquiescence to power *is* a form of agency for Nina, as the women made choices in relation to the "cultural script" they were confronted with, and in this case women chose to remain silent when publicly shamed; they chose to flee their communities, becoming internally displaced persons; and they chose to rationalize their trauma. They also chose to code-switch when it came to how they discussed their faith. Nina writes that "In order to observe their religious activities, Ahmadi women used general terms that are usually used by other Muslims, such as changing terms *'muawwanah'* (monthly religious meeting for members) into *'pengajian'*" (159). The latter term translates to "study," though she herself does not translate *pengajian* in her dissertation, which points to her Indonesian audience. This passive form of agency, Nina argues, though it did not disrupt the larger system, allowed women to maintain and to continue practicing their faith "internally."

The second type of agency Nina describes Ahmadi women taking is more active, albeit *reactive*, and was prompted by a greater understanding of their "rights as Indonesian citizens" and their "legal standing" (159). She explains that Ahmadi women, when educated about their legal rights, moved from being passive victims to "active victims" (160). This type of agency involved accepting invitations from NGOs and governmental organizations to discuss their experiences with violence; reporting their stories to the press after the violence happened (166); and, as described above, physically protecting their mosques, hand in hand, as "life barriers," in reaction to anticipated physical violence (162).

The third type of agency Nina points to in her research resulted, she explained, from the Lajnah Imaillah community's critical reflection on both the personal and systemic levels about how they might more explicitly communicate their Ahmadi identities when engaging with non-Ahmadi Indonesians. One way that women within Lajnah Imaillah seek to fulfill the social-justice aims of their faith and to increase acceptance is by engaging in social-justice work—for example, through blood drives and organ donation drives, which benefit *all* Indonesians—and by taking part in other extracurricular activities, like sports, with non-Ahmadi women in their communities (175). This type of agency—which emphasizes a preemptive "rewriting" of existing relationships so potentially hostile audiences have access to the Ahmadi community as *humans*, not just as faceless Ahmadiyya—is more proactive than the "active victim" form of agency, which generally manifested itself after threats of violence or violence itself.

This community-building work, however, was not enough to stop oppression, Nina found, because often Ahmadi women hid their Ahmadi faith "because they thought that people have already known about them and their Ahmadi identity . . . so that there was not a need to talk about their identity, or because they were afraid of revealing their identity" (173). After much reflection within Lajnah Imaillah, the Ahmadi women whom Nina researched began to explicitly name their identities when engaging with non-Ahmadis, drawing strength from their collective identity as members of Lajnah Imaillah. Nina points to the efficacy of programs she terms "programmed *rabtah*," or programs *explicitly* sponsored by Lajnah Imaillah that were meant to "[develop] good affiliation with others" (181). One example she writes about is a parenting workshop led by Ahmadi experts in the field. "In these workshop and training activities," Nina explains, "Ahmadi women open up their identity as Lajnah Imaillah Indonesia with the hope that people will recognize them as Ahmadi." Foreshadowing her own strategic games when accessing potentially hostile audiences, Nina explains that "based on my observation the materials that they give in parenting workshop mostly are Islamic values in educating children from Qur'an and *hadits* that are similar to other Muslims' teaching" (182). By explicitly naming their religious faith and emphasizing religious commonality despite difference, Nina argues that the women in Lajnah Imaillah are more effective in stemming violence bred from misunderstanding.

By exploring the ways her Ahmadi community engages in strategic games when presented with new scripts, which might at different points in time involve taking docile agency; or engaging as "active victims"; or making explicit Ahmadi identity and then connecting across difference through community engagement,

Nina emphasizes that indeed women in her community are capable of negotiating with power to increase access—whether that access means being able to worship within their community or using programming to increase access for external audiences to their community.

To return to the questions that interanimate *my own* text, it is important to note that Nina herself is an Ahmadi woman and that she sees language work as a means of fostering social change, which suggested to me that the models she develops to understand the agency of Ahmadi women in her community might also apply to the way she takes agency as a writer and language user. In our 2022 interview, I asked her if this was true, and she replied:

> So in writing, yeah, I always bring my identity as Ahmadi woman, so that's why when I make proposal in my university, I always take the position of minority, and my identity as an Ahmadi Muslim, and woman. This is not only proactive; it's more than that. So not only preventative, but also now, facing the conflict itself.

Nina: On Explicitly Naming Ahmadi Identity in Her Writing

Echoing her assertion that her faith is the bedrock, and intersects with, all of the identities she performs—as a scholar, an activist, and a teacher—Nina almost always explicitly names her female Ahmadi identity in her writing, just as the women in Lajnah Imaillah with whom she studies and worships have begun to do in their community outreach.

In so doing, Nina challenges the border that separates *knowledge* that is written about—in this case, the types of embodied agency she sees women performing for interfaith justice in her research—and how she herself *writes* to transform the world. By linking what's written about with how she herself communicates in this way, she connects material action to discursive action and what's lived to how she communicates. Furthermore, this naming happens regardless of for whom she writes or what language she uses, whether that audience is her Indonesian university or, as the opening excerpt indicates, a global audience and regardless of whether she is writing in Indonesian or English. As we trace how Nina moves knowledge from her research into the world, we can see how her Ahmadi faith transcends long-held rhetorical and linguistic "borders," serving as the impetus for the ways she works toward access and, with that, more equitable relations.

FEMINISTS BY TRAINING AND FEMINISTS BY DOING

Nina's choice to self-identify as an Ahmadi woman is intimately tied to her belief that her religious advocacy work can foster gender justice for women in her own community and beyond. Like Faqih, her work challenges the long-held colonial duality that positions Islam and female agency as incommensurate. Although the Ahmadi identity she calls forth to engage in this work remains constant, the *language* she chooses to label this activist work toward faith-based gender justice is dependent upon situational power dynamics. In some limit-situations, by delinking action itself, or the doing, from the originating knowledge-base, or the "training," Nina is able to strategically access audiences she may not otherwise be able to—a move that, if we view language and action from a spatiotemporal perspective and as dialogically intertwined on the *same continuum* rather than in opposition, doesn't obviate different action in the future.

When I asked Nina in 2022 about how she saw her Ahmadi identity and her activist goals intersecting with her use of English, she explained:

> I speak up about women, not only my own community, but minority women in general, so it is my activism . . . . So I use [English] in my activism, and I also still speak up in my academic writing. Even in my class, I always say to my students that I'm an Ahmadi. Because even in an Islamic university, there are different kinds of Islam. And they can accept me.

Nina: On Speaking Up in English Across Multiple Contexts

Here we can see that English, for Nina, is intimately tied to "speaking up" not just for Ahmadi women but for all minority women. In addition, she once again suggests that her Ahmadi identity transcends linguistic borders to inform *all* of her work, whether she's trying to reach and teach an activist audience or her Indonesian students about gender justice.

When I asked her whether she would call this type of speaking up "Islamic feminism," she replied, "There are different types of feminists: feminists by training; feminists by doing." Actions themselves can be feminist without labeling them as such. She continued, referring to Faqih's work as a lens into her own:

> Most feminists in Indonesia, they rarely use the term "feminist," because if we use the term feminist, usually they accuse us "OK you are imperialist; you study abroad, so you got westernized." That's why Faqih does this using the term *mubadalah*; actually it is feminist, but he choose a term that is already familiar for Muslims. So I use "feminism" only in academic area.

Here Nina points to code-switching as a means of promoting feminist ideals without the impediment of the term's links to Western feminism. To return to the theoretical lenses Nina develops in her own scholarship, she might deem this type of linguistic action "passive agency." Just as the Ahmadi women with whom she researched chose to code-switch what they called their religious meetings when faced with the options of worshipping or not worshipping, so, too, might people *perform* what in some circles might be called "feminism" without labeling it as such to achieve their ends. In this case, the desired action trumps the terminology. Breaking down the mind/body duality and focusing on action helps us see this code-switching as more than just a linguistic capitulation to power.

Nina puts theory to action as a professor of minority and gender studies and interdisciplinary Islamic Studies at the Graduate School UIN Sunan Kalijaga. In her multilingual pedagogy, Nina places in conversation Western (purportedly secular) theory and Islamic scholarship, ultimately preferring to focus on the "doing" of feminism in order to help her students better access local audiences. In 2022, she discussed one of her graduate courses, "Gender and

Nina: On Feminists by Training and Feminists by Doing

On Code-Switching the Term "Feminism"

Feminism," at length with me. Given the way she has long localized English to reach Indonesian audiences, I asked her if she ever translated knowledge she drew from English-medium research into Indonesian and vice versa. She explained:

> I teach in Bahasa, because it's not an international program, but I always give my students reading in English. Because they are graduate students. It's a requirement in Indonesia, you know, that even if you don't want to study abroad, the requirement the TOEFL score is 450. I and my colleagues usually give readings in English. Even in my program, it's inter-Islamic program . . . . Of course, most of us refer to what we call Western theory. So they learn Bordieu, they learn Foucault . . . . We want them to go right to the source, the firsthand source.

Nina: On Assigning English-Medium Theory in Her Gender and Feminism Course

Here she points to the predominance of Western English-medium theory globally and to the role English plays in global academic thought, regardless of locale—a symptom of coloniality and Western imperialism, but one that does not keep her from localizing this knowledge through performance. She continued, pointing to how her students come from all over Indonesia, "with different level of English and academic life," which causes some friction when it comes to whether and how she should translate (or not):

Nina: On Differential Access to English

> So for translation, maybe sometimes I can't translate from English to Indonesian. Because if, as you know, translations, there are maybe some changes in meaning. So that's why we use it just as it is, and then explain what it is in Bahasa.

Nina: On Translating English-Medium Texts

Nina assigns English-medium texts, but then, rather than doing direct translation of terms themselves, during class time she explains what they mean in Bahasa Indonesia, resignifying the signifier with Indonesian meanings, even as the terms remain "intact," which emphasizes the importance of locating translingual praxis and its border-thinking possibilities both in text *and* in process.

If we look at the syllabus for Nina's "Gender and Feminism" class, we can see that it also exemplifies border thinking both linguistically and epistemologically. It's simultaneously multilingual, with English-medium texts like bell hooks's "Gangsta Culture: A Piece of the Action" put in conversation with Indonesian-medium texts like Faqih Mansur's "Analisis Gender dan Transformasi Sosial," *and* epistemologically meshed with content long positioned as mutually exclusive by the colonial matrix of power put in conversation. Returning to her choice to use "feminism" in limited contexts, Nina explained the content of her course in this way:

> So I use "feminism" only in academic area, so for example, now I teach gender and feminism, but then I want my students later, when they graduate from our school, so they can also do gender mainstreaming through their community, but of course with their own language. That's why in the syllabus, we use three parts. So first is on "What is feminist? What is gender?" It's theoretical. And the second one we relate Islam and feminism. And then the third part, because in my interdisciplinary Islamic school, in my school, there are several concentrations, so like Hermeneutic Koran, Islamic Psychology, so for the third part we try to give them more relating gender and their concentration. (2022 interview)

Nina's course challenges long-held dualities in form and content as a means of fostering local social justice, all the while emphasizing that the "doing" of gender mainstreaming is more important to her than the terminology students use to define their work. Though the course begins with defining terms, ultimately it's not the language that matters; it's the *action* that matters when these seemingly discrete published texts are put in conversation.

Nina's choice to avoid using "feminist" in some contexts should not imply that she does not see commonality despite difference when it comes to beliefs about gender justice, a nondualistic orientation we can also see in her research on the ways Ahmadi women forge interfaith connection. As further testament to the need to move past originating language to explore overlap in epistemological orientations toward *knowledge itself*, how Nina interprets the strategic relationship-building between Ahmadi and Sunni faiths in her own research mirrors the way she describes Islamic feminism and its relationship to what she terms Western feminism (because of its more secular nature). Nina explained in 2022:

> Actually, we [Western and Islamic feminists] struggle on the same purpose, I think, on the same point, but because of the different culture, different aspect, and different society . . . but actually the social construction is almost the same for women everywhere. But maybe because in religion, in religious community, mostly people prefer using Islamic teaching. So how we struggle is *also* using religious teaching.

The past voices Islamic feminists and secularized feminists draw from when working for gender justice might be different, but Nina emphasizes that the struggle is the same: ending patriarchal oppression. Similarly, Nina's research itself suggests that the women in Lajnah Imaillah pave the ground for interfaith understanding despite difference by focusing on the shared action of ethical parenting from an Islamic perspective as a common goal of Muslim women—whether they are Ahmadi or Sunni. This commonality, fostered through shared *purpose*, lays the groundwork for a more receptive understanding of religious difference.

Nina: On Women's Shared Struggle, with Religion as a Resource.

Rather than flattening difference, or collapsing feminisms or faiths into the same, Nina takes a pluriversal perspective by focusing on *shared action* despite the differing voices, religious or otherwise, that catalyze this action. When it comes to feminisms and faiths, Nina's focus on *doing* is, to my mind, one way to construct what Ratcliffe calls a "shared atmosphere," a space that allows communicants to simultaneously identify *and* disidentify with the discourses that move through the rhetorical situation as they work toward a shared goal (*Rhetorical Listening* 71). For Nina, the work of gender justice and interfaith dialogue is deeply intertwined, both in substance *and* in performance, and one does not obviate the other.

"TO BE RELIGIOUS IS TO BE INTERRELIGIOUS": LOCALIZING ENGLISH-MEDIUM KNOWLEDGE

Focusing on *performance* allows us to see how Nina translates knowledge—and her orientation toward communicative action—from her English-medium scholarship into her community to foster more just relationships. By focusing on two "moments" Nina highlighted in her 2022 interview, we can see how she establishes a "shared atmosphere" to access potentially hostile audiences, a process that involves—as she recommends in her dissertation—explicitly, yet also strategically, naming her Ahmadi identity to reach the non-Ahmadi Indonesian audiences *with whom* she wishes to connect.

When I asked Nina in 2022 whether and how she had translated her English-medium dissertation work into local community activism, she pointed to how her dissertation research had unearthed overt discrimination in Manis Luar, where Indonesian civil officers had repeatedly barred Ahmadis from officially registering their marriages. She explained that in 2017, she wrote a handbook in Bahasa Indonesia for civil servants on the illegality of this practice and that in 2022 she was invited to do a workshop with these officers. She described an interaction with a local official at the workshop this way:

> At the time, one of the officers said, because my writing is about Ahmadi, he said, "What I heard is that Ahmadiyya is not Muslim, blah, blah, blah." OK. It's a good question. "I hear their shahadah,[42] they are different from other Muslims." And then I just smile and answer, "OK, sir, you heard me when I did assalamualaikum?[43] And after assalamualaikum, I recite shahadah? Is it different from your shahadah? It is the same, right?" And then [I say] "I'm an Ahmadi."

Nina: On Performing a Shared Muslim Identity at a Civil Servant Workshop

She explained to me that "This is my way to show my agency as an Ahmadi, and 'OK you are Muslim.' I use my identity to make people understand, and to tell what I *do* as Muslim." Here Nina puts her English-medium research on Ahmadi female agency into action, albeit strategically, for a local Indonesian audience. First, she established "shared atmosphere" by performing assalamualaikum and shahada—a shared religious practice that links Ahmadi and Sunni Muslims. Only then did she make explicit her Ahmadi faith through explicit naming. Nina is a strategic player when it comes to accessing dominant Muslim audiences; she forges shared connections between her own "discursive energy field" (Ratcliffe, *Rhetorical Listening* 70) and theirs, before moving to difference.

Nina's joint collaboration with an Indonesian women's organization, Srikandi Lintas Iman, which translates to "Cross-Faith Heroine," and another NGO, toleransi.id, showcases the systemic connections women from Lajnah Imaillah, like Nina, seek to foster with other Indonesian women's organizations while also, once again, showing how Nina engages in strategic identity work when it comes to presenting her Ahmadi identity to the broader Indonesian public. Nina describes the Srikandi Lintas Iman organization as follows:

Srikandi
Lintas Iman
Facebook
Page

> It consists of women—different kinds of women, from students and lecturers and housewives—and from religions of different kinds, from Islam, from Christianity, and from Hindu, several. And this community, Srikandi, is very active. And we got a donor, several donor, and also sometimes we got it not as in terms of money, but in terms of activities. So for example, a training on writing on pluralism for women and education for women, because our focus is on women and kids. (2022 interview)

Nina's
Description
of Srikandi
Lintas Iman
Collabora-
tion

These women work "hand in hand" across perceived difference to promote interfaith harmony and the promise of Pancasila. One of the donors, toleransi.id, sponsored a workshop on how to write about pluralism for the women in the organization. This spurred a young woman to want to create a comic strip promoting interfaith understanding, and she asked Nina to be the main character, because, she said, in Nina's words, "You're Ahmadi and also you're active in interfaith, not only academic but also in my real life." This collaboration, which Nina took a very active part in, resulted in a comic strip to post on social media that detailed Nina's story "from when I was a kid. How my neighborhood, how my parents raised me, what identity I bring, that I'm Ahmadi, and my first contact

Nina as
Interfaith
Activist in
Theory and
Practice

Nina's
Framing of
"Breaking
the Fast
with Nuns"
Comic

with non-Muslim, to do interfaith dialogue, but in daily places"
(2022 interview).

A close reading of the rhetorical moves in "Berbuka Puasa
Bersama Biarawati," which translates to "Breaking the Fast with
Nuns," shows how Nina and her collaborator strategically navigate
introducing Nina's Ahmadi identity to potentially hostile audiences
(for the full comic and my English translation of it, please follow
the QR code here).

Amber's
Translation
of Inter-
religious
Comic

The Indonesian-medium comic strip begins with Nina the
narrator immediately introducing herself in this way: "Hello, I
am Nina. I was born in a family of Ahmadiyya. / And I lived in
a community that was majority Muslim. / When I was a child I
almost never met followers of other religions. / So I was afraid of
them." In this first panel, Nina the narrator leads with her Ahmadi
identity and establishes without question that she is part of a
Muslim community by emphasizing that she was afraid of "other
religions."

The second panel then works to further establish Nina's Muslim identity by contrasting it with the beliefs of her Catholic schoolmate: "My first non-Muslim introduction was in senior high school. / My seatmate was Catholic." Nina the narrator explains that this encounter with someone from another faith "unblocked my eyes to other religions. / We often chatted about religion with each other. / Without prejudice, without embellishment, just because we were interested." This experience, she explained, led her to join Srikandi Lintas Iman when she got older.

By introducing Nina's Ahmadi faith explicitly, then having her admit that she herself fears other religions, and then establishing what actual religious difference looks like by defining Nina's Muslim faith against that of her Catholic peer, Nina and her comic strip collaborator play a strategic game in order to access an audience potentially hostile to the Ahmadi faith: first, by emphasizing that Nina herself is subject to the same fear when it comes to religious difference, they ameliorate any guilt non-Ahmadi audience members might feel for having had similar fears about Ahmadi; and second, they establish—through contrast—that in fact Ahmadi and Sunni Muslims share more in common than they do with those practicing the Catholic faith.

Nina and her collaborator then work, of course, to show how Muslims and Catholics can also connect across difference through interfaith dialogue, in this case by showing how Nina and friends from Srikandi Lintas Iman broke their Ramadan fast in a Catholic monastery, where, in keeping with Muslim tradition, the Catholic nuns presented their Muslim friends with a delicious feast at *iftar*, the sunset meal when Muslims break their daily Ramadan fast.

Notably, in the second-to-last panel (featured on the next page), which depicts the nuns and their Muslim friends breaking fast together, Nina and her collaborator inserted the English phrase, "To Be Religious Is to Be Interreligious." Curious as to why they had chosen to insert this one English phrase into the otherwise Indonesian-medium comic strip, I asked Nina about her rhetorical purpose. She explained that she liked the rhythmic nature of the phrase, that it couldn't be easily translated into Indonesian, and "Maybe because of my background also; I usually use English, and I find that this is the best way to say what I want to say." For Nina, English is a language very much tied to her identity as an Ahmadi Indonesian and her work to connect across difference to simultaneously promote interfaith understanding and female empowerment.

Nina: English
Says It Best

By tracing how Nina translates *knowledge* garnered from her English-medium dissertation into local activism on both the material and discursive planes, whether by training civil servants or by disseminating her story via a social-media comic strip, we can see the strategic games Nina plays as she engages in translingual praxis to access audiences within Indonesia who may not be able to access her English-medium scholarship.

TO BE RELIGIOUS IS TO BE INTERRELIGIOUS

BAGI SAYA, TOLERANSI ADALAH KETIKA KITA BISA MENERIMA PERBEDAAN DALAM HAL APAPUN.

ENGLISH IS MY SWORD: REWRITING *WITH WHOM*

Nina's engagement with external audiences also extends past this more localized negotiation, as the UN speech which began this chapter suggests. Though much of Nina's motivation *is* local to Indonesia, Nina's scholarly-activist access work also extends well past the Indonesian nation-state. If at the local level she unlinks *knowledge* from originating language by translating her English-medium research into Indonesian for the public, at the global level she uses English itself to increase access to resources on both the material and discursive planes. This English use benefits the larger Ahmadi community, which extends well beyond Indonesian borders, as well as non-Ahmadi audiences in Indonesia and elsewhere. Each time Nina circulates knowledge and resources across traditional "borders" using English, she in turn rewrites notions of "internal" and "external," suggesting the importance of understanding English-medium audiences in excess of the geopolitical nation-state.

Nina, as mentioned above, does acknowledge that English is a way to increase her own credibility in the eyes of audiences who may discount her words because of her religious faith. In her 2022 interview, however, she emphasized that her desire to use English extends past this need for personal recognition. When I asked her what role English played in her Ahmadi community, she emphasized: "English is not only *for me*, but it's my sword, it's my weapon. So this for organizationally, and discussion for internal and external [audiences]." Nina, who has never viewed English as imperialist, sees it instead as a sword she can use to foster access for her Ahmadi organization and beyond.

Nina: English
is my sword

As mentioned above, Nina views her scholarship as a means of "reaching and teaching" non-Ahmadis about her faith. For scholarship to be transformative, however, audiences, whether local or global, must have access to it in the first place. As a graduate student, Nina's goal to "reach and teach" others about her community was mediated by material inequality when it came to literate resources about her faith. As Chapter 4 explains, ICRS works to challenge unequal access to published resources by fostering strategic alliances with academic institutions in the Global North so that their students might take a semester abroad to use better-equipped libraries. This opportunity very much shaped Nina's scholarship and, later, her activist work.

Nina's academic work within Indonesia was at first curbed by the unavailability of published sources on Ahmadi women, both because of limited access to academic databases in general and because she chose to study a religious group long silenced by dominant Indonesian discourse. Studying abroad at Boston University, alongside Ninik (next chapter's case study) gave her access to resources not available in Indonesia. She explained,

As you know, in Indonesia, sometimes we find it difficult to find resources in libraries, but over there in Boston, I even found a book about Ahmadiyya in the library that I couldn't get in Indonesia. Not even in my own community. So it is very useful for me to add more sources to my dissertation. (2014 interview)

Studying abroad—and the ability to access English-medium scholarship—gave her access to new voices to add to her repertoire, which she could then bring back to Indonesia to share with the audience of her dissertation *and* with her "own [Ahmadi] community."

Furthermore, as a testament to how linguistic communities are continually being redefined in ways that are separate from the nation-state, Nina's experience in the United States and her ability with English also helped her forge connections with the *global* Ahmadiyya community, which opened up further resources for her Indonesian community. She explained:

Because of my ability in English, I can also get resource from Ahmadi community from all over the world. So I connect them. We connect each other. When I go to Boston, I contacted the Ahmadi community, and they accepted me as we are sisters and brothers, so now they know more about Indonesian Ahmadiyya. (2014 interview)

Nina's experience abroad and the English language helped her share her Indonesian community's stories with her global religious community. This connection also benefitted her Indonesian Ahmadiyya community. She continued,

And now of course, I get knowledge from [global Ahmadiyya community] also. I learn that in Boston—I learn that they have newsletter—an electronic newsletter—because you know in the US, everyone has their own email. So all activities are announced through email in English. So now I see this newsletter and try to implement it in Indonesia. (2014 interview)

Nina's connection with her English-using global faith community highlighted for her how digital literacy might foster a more cohesive faith community *within* Indonesia. In graduate school, Nina harnessed her ability to move between languages to increase access across the information divide, in the process increasing access to Ahmadi knowledge across national borders.

This experience navigating the information divide also likely shaped Nina's activist work with Globethics.net, which is a legal, open-access, multilingual online library focused on sharing global research in ethics across the information divide. As Chapter 5 explains, with funding help from powerful literacy sponsors (Brandt) in the Global North, Globethics has developed partnerships with academic institutions in Switzerland, China, India, East and Francophone Africa, Russia, Argentina, Turkey, and Indonesia, where ICRS directs its open-source Islamic Ethics library, with Nina at the helm (*Ethics*). Nina emphasized that her work with this library increased digital access to literate resources not just for Indonesians but also for non-Indonesians who might not have access to published information written by Indonesians. Nina put it this way in her 2014 interview: "We don't have money, so that's why Globethics was started. And also so the North knows what's happening in the South." She went on to explain how Globethics gives Indonesian scholars the chance to engage in digital writing practices meant to spread Indonesian knowledge abroad: "Every year, we have a peer-reviewed essay competition for Indonesian scholars to get published, so we hope that some [submissions] are in English, so the wider world knows more about Indonesia and Islamic ethics from an Indonesian perspective." Nina's dissertation, in fact, was published in monograph form on this site.

Although Nina's dissertation is English-medium, submissions do not *need* to be written in English. Nina explained in 2014 that in the database, "Some of the articles are in English, but some also in Indonesian. It's multilingual, so many languages." Part of her job, in fact, was to contact researchers around the world to gather "resources related to Islamic ethics, whether in Indonesian, English or Arabic." She then "approache[s] small universities in rural areas far from Yogyakarta or Jakarta [more privileged educational epicenters] so they will post our link in their website. And they give information to their students that it's a free, online library that they can access at any time, anywhere you go. And many resources are [written] in Indonesian." In this way, Nina helped connect writers and potential academic audiences across the information divide.

As a testament to her translingual fluency, Nina's work moved beyond increasing access to *academic* resources through the database itself. In her 2014 interview, she described translating news items pertaining to Islamic ethics that were posted on the website from English into Indonesian for a wider Indonesian audience. She explained,

> So it seems like all the news is in English, so it's my part to translate it into Indonesian. So I have access to translate as an administrator, so I just open with the same password as other program executives around the world, so if there's new news, I just translate it into Indonesian. And I share it through Facebook, through other social media, too.

Nina translated and reentextualized (Schreiber) news originally published in English for the Indonesian public, increasing their access to global perspectives and possibly laying the groundwork for a more ethical understanding of religious beliefs—like Nina's own Ahmadi faith—that are different from their own.

Although Nina has recently stepped back a bit from her work with Globethics because of organizational shifts, she has continued to work toward global interconnectivity in other contexts, using English as her sword. Nina explained in 2022 that in addition to being invited by the Office of the United Nations High Commissioner for Human Rights to talk in Geneva about her experience as a minority woman in Indonesia, she was also asked by her global Ahmadiyya organization to represent their community in Germany. Nina explained that because of her abilities with English and her academic expertise, "I see myself as an ambassador, not an official one, but an ambassador. I think because of my expertise on Ahmadi, I think the Ahmadiyya organization sees

Nina: On Representing the Ahmadi Organization

Nina: On Serving as Ahmadi Ambassador in Germany

me as a representative that can speak about Ahmadiyya." As an example, she pointed out how in 2018 the president of the Ahmadi community in Germany had close relationships with government officials, and "the government is doing interfaith dialogue, all over the world and Asia, so the government asked permission from him and he suggested we should invite Ahmadi . . . from India or Asia, but it should be a woman." Eventually, the Indonesian Ahmadi president contacted Indonesia's Lajnah Imaillah, and Nina's cohorts secured her the opportunity to visit Germany to foster interfaith harmony and gender justice, using English.

From a global perspective, Nina's ability to use English as a "sword" helps her access and then redefine relationships between herself as an Indonesian Ahmadi and the various audiences for whom and with whom she wishes to communicate. When it comes to increasing access to literate resources through Globethics, for example, the audiences *with whom* she networks are defined in geopolitically recognized says; she uses English to access more privileged global audiences, creating the means to move digital resources between Western countries and Indonesia, a translingual process that benefits her Ahmadi community, the broader Indonesian public, and those in Western communities who don't have access to Indonesian knowledge. However, she also rewrites the Western/Indonesian, external/internal duality by using English to access the broader global Ahmadi community, which then helps her reach non-Ahmadi audiences. In so doing, the meaning of internal audience shifts to represent her global religious community, with non-Ahmadi audiences, like the German government or the UN and even non-Ahmadi Indonesians positioned as "external" audiences. With each new "script" she encounters, Nina rewrites her position in relation to her intended audiences—a testament to the dialogic relationship between social script and audience and to the importance of challenging the one-language-equals-one-nation-state model when it comes to global English use.

CONCLUSIONS

How Nina performs translingual praxis, then, is intimately tied to establishing a shared atmosphere with more powerful audiences, to return to Ratcliffe's term. Each time Nina engages in translingual praxis to access her intended audiences, she rewrites notions of internal and external, challenging, in turn, the seemingly immutable links between language and nation-state that *still* prop up the colonial matrix of power. What anchors her amid all this movement is her Ahmadi identity, which, as she explains, remains constant, regardless of what "script" she is working with, *for whom* she intends her texts, and *with whom* she sees her knowledge circulating. Rather than *subsuming* her identities as a scholar, a teacher, and an activist, her religious faith works in concert with these identities, serving as a foundation for all of her access work, regardless of language. Although the colonial matrix of power has long painted Islam in opposition to the mind and to female empowerment, Nina's work shows how these discourses can interanimate, rather than obviate, each other. By acknowledging that the rational and the spiritual, language and the thought that precedes language, the mind and the body and the training and the doing coexist dialogically *on the same plane*, rather than in opposition, we can better understand that emphasizing one facet at a particular moment in time does not *negate* the other facets, despite existing power relationships.

To truly listen for how writers like Nina negotiate with the many past voices who are audience to their written work, and, from there, for how they translate this knowledge into action on both the discursive and the material planes as they engage in translingual praxis requires moving past problematic colonial dualities. Understanding *from whom* scholarly-activists like Nina draw their knowledge and how the diverse voices in writers' citational repertoires, regardless of origin, might *intersect* is central to forging access across difference. Border thinking requires understanding how values themselves, despite springing from seemingly discrete language traditions, might interanimate one another. As Nina's work suggests, Western feminism and the work of Islamic gender justice can coexist and inform each other, despite the differing voices that populate these traditions, though how she names her scholarly-activist work from one moment to the next shifts depending on the audience *for whom* she writes or *with whom* she wishes to forge access. In the academic context, she explicitly names her work "feminist," despite its Western origins, while in other contexts, Nina chooses to focus on the "doing" of gender justice rather than on what it is called. Similarly, in some contexts she *immediately* names her Ahmadi identity—which again, informs *all* of her work—while at other times she chooses to *perform* aspects of the Muslim faith she shares with her Sunni counterparts *before* naming herself Ahmadi. By challenging the mind/body duality that isolates "training" (in this case, as an Islamic feminist or as an Ahmadi practitioner) from the "doing" and reimagining word and action as dialogically interconnected rather than in opposition, we can see how writers like Nina, who are first and foremost invested in *accessing* dominant audiences, might emphasize one move depending on the "script" and with whom they wish to connect, which doesn't preclude a different move in the future.

And finally, by viewing the body and the mind interrelationally, we can see intersections between how Nina *herself* takes agency in her lived world to increase access and how she describes Ahmadi female agency in her English-medium research—as existing on a spectrum of possible moves depending on power relationships and, most important, as a collective endeavor. Indeed, no matter what language she uses and regardless of perceived difference, Nina works to create a "shared atmosphere" when it comes to those *with whom* she engages. To cite the words with which Nina ended our 2022 interview: "We will be stronger if we collaborate. Now is the time for collaborating. Now is not the time for competition, but for collaboration. Because women, we need many hands to work as one." Indeed, this type of border work is crucial if we want to collaboratively challenge longstanding injustices linked to the colonial matrix of power, whether religious, gender-based, economic, or a combination of all three. Working toward access should be a collective endeavor.

Nina:
Women
Need Many
Hands to
Work as
One

Chapter 8

"Social Justice Is Not about Language; It's about Humanity": Translanguaging to Cultivate*

Belief . . . is like on a mountain, there is water, the water is coming down and the water becomes in the bottles or in the sea or in the cup. This is just only the package. The essence, the soul, is still water. So the religion is just the water. It becomes Muslim, Islam, something like that. But it is just the package.

Ninik's Interrelational Water Metaphor

---

*Portions of this chapter were published in "The 'Hands of God' at Work: Negotiating between Western and Religious Sponsorship in Indonesia." *College English* 76.4 (2014): 292–314.

THIS METAPHOR CAME UP IN MY 2022 interview with Dr. Hj. Nihayatul Wafiroh (Ninik), whom I first met in 2009 in my academic writing class at ICRS and who is currently a two-term legislator in Indonesia's House of Representatives (DPR). Ninik used this metaphor, which she told me she drew from Frithjof Schuon's *Islam and the Perennial Philosophy,* to explain that, to her, different religions share the same *essence,* even if they are packaged differently. Ninik's orientation toward religion—that there *are* differences between a cup, a bottle, and the sea, but that the water itself, or the soul, is the same—reflects a broader orientation toward knowledge itself and, with that, language, that is simultaneously border-aware *and* cosmopolitan.

To apply this metaphor to the way Ninik performs translingual praxis, the linguistic "containers" she draws from—and at times exceeds with the fluidity of her rhetorical practices—hail from both Indonesian and Western discourse communities, across the Indonesian, English, and Arabic languages and their attendant audiences. In this way, her literacy practices align with those of Faqih and Nina. However, unlike Faqih, who relinquishes authorial agency to *serve* his local Indonesian audiences, and Nina, who works to *access* dominant audiences from a nondominant positionality, Ninik draws from her experiences studying and networking in Indonesia and the United States to carefully *cultivate* audiences both local *and* global to create more socially just cross-cultural connections. Her ability to cultivate audiences—to quite strategically "prune" *for whom* her words are intended and *from whom* she draws her knowledge in order to forge connections with audiences *with whom* she might work to foster social justice—requires strategic border thinking.

Indeed, though Ninik embraces a distinctly cosmopolitan identity, the ways she performs translingual praxis is mediated by the discursive and material "borders" she negotiates when navigating dialogically between and among these sometimes-competing audiences. Discursively, Ninik must navigate the socially constructed borders traditionally drawn between languages that position them as discrete entities solely capable of reaching discrete audiences, and, on a more macro level, the socially constructed borders that link one language to one nation-state in the broader cultural imagination. When it comes to material borders, because of global economic inequality, she must navigate unequal access to published resources and thus the border between the haves and the have-nots, which involves moving herself and the literacy resources she accumulates across national borders. To complicate matters, as Ninik shifts between her academic and political identities over the course of time, so too do the power relationships she must navigate and leverage to achieve her social-justice goals. Though her cosmopolitan *ideals* remain the same, the translingual path she takes to reach them depends on the power relationships she sees in particular situations. Ninik performs translingual praxis by acknowledging, negotiating, and at times leveraging existing borders to achieve localized social justice while *still* striving for cosmopolitan connection.

THEORIZING COSMOPOLITAN CONNECTION

As established in previous chapters, effective global rhetorical connection requires that the relationships between writer and audience be reimagined as dialogical, mutually constitutive, and constantly shifting. Given the cosmopolitan ethos Ninik constructs with her rhetorical acts and the complex, local-global rhetorical situations she navigates, Xiaoye You's scholarship in *Cosmopolitan English* is particularly salient. For You, reimagining English through the lens of cosmopolitanism, with Standard English being one variety of cosmopolitan English (14), involves acknowledging the "historicity, artificiality, and rhetoricity of . . . cultural categories" (6) so "we can cease defining English along the lines of birthright, nation, ethnicity, or region, and we can instead understand it as a multiplicity of local practices constantly converging and intermingling with other linguistic and cultural forces" (19). Drawing from translingual theory, You argues against the theoretical notion that "languages are discrete systems that a speaker or writer can move between and draw elements from" (18), though he acknowledges that in practice it may sometimes *appear* that languages are discrete systems. He explains:

While CE [cosmopolitan English] is full of instances of such language uses, it does not embrace the view of language as a discrete system typically defined by nation or ethnicity. Instead, based on their assessment of the rhetorical situation, CE users marshal the available resources from their repertoires to realize different designs in speech or writing, including potentially forming identifications with the Other. (17)

Here You highlights the cosmopolitan-English user's rhetorical agency, emphasizing that different designs are possible in a translingual world. Echoing Lu and Horner and Bawarshi ("Beyond") that assimilation can evidence translingual agency, You implies that a writer may in fact choose to portray their languages as "discrete" in some "instances," reflecting and perhaps reinforcing the ideological link between language and nation-state/ethnicity that cosmopolitan theory seeks to challenge, whereas at other times they might seek to write across traditional discursive borders.

In a claim central to understanding Ninik's rhetorical choices, You also points to the role that translation plays in cosmopolitan communication: he argues that a writer may at times "form ideas and feelings in other languages first and translate them into spoken or written English" (18). However, a writer might just as well code-switch or code-mesh, "refus[ing] to translate in order to legitimize a certain type of text" or to achieve a certain rhetorical purpose (18). If we accept that writers should be able to and in fact *do* draw from the full range of languages in their literacy repertoire, we must also acknowledge that they might use different means to "[form] identifications with the Other" (17) depending on their intended audience, purpose, and rhetorical context.

A cosmopolitan orientation toward language also challenges traditional assumptions regarding audience, which often rest on dated understandings of the relationship between language and a bounded nation-state or discrete identity grouping (see Canagarajah, "Toward"). You emphasizes that "when writing in English, a writer may need to communicate with an audience that cannot be easily pinned down to a single language or single culture. It might be a cosmopolitan audience, who, like the writer, has crossed the arbitrary lines demarcating languages and cultures" (141). Or, as You suggests above, a writer might translate knowledge from one language to another to craft cosmopolitan connections between voices in their citational repertoire and their intended audiences that aren't yet there but could be. Or, alternatively, given the cosmopolitan possibilities English opens up, a non-Western writer may choose to use English to communicate with local, non-Western audiences, temporarily rewriting traditional linkages between geopolitical borders and language by localizing English, as the portraits in this book emphasize. Ninik, we will see, cultivates—and in so doing, redefines—cosmopolitan audience connection in all of these ways.

Importantly, though, these choices are very much dependent upon the power dynamics Ninik navigates in particular situations. Although You acknowledges power repeatedly, and the fact that cultural contact zones, and thus borders, do exist (11), he argues that overall, rather than implying "rupture," the "conflicts, contradictions, and paradoxes generated as cultures initially collide and entangle will in general give rise to, if not be resolved" as language users "negotiate the tensions" to move "toward cultural synthesis" (34). Echoing You's research, at times Ninik does use her translingual praxis to work toward synthesis between once-disparate audiences, redrawing traditional borders between languages, religious beliefs, and the audiences long associated with them.

Cross-cultural synthesis, however, is not always possible or desirable. In Ryuko Kubota's "Multi/Plural Turn," she asserts that calls for linguistic borderlessness could reflect and promote neoliberal ideology if not framed in relation to existing power structures. Neoliberal ideology, which promotes notions of "individual agency, difference blindness, and elitist cosmopolitanism" (14), ignores existing class stratifications within nation-states, and, with that, issues of unequal access to literate resources—an argument reinforced by the research of Theresa Lillis and Mary Jane Curry, John Trimbur, and James Ferguson, as well as my own research here and elsewhere (see "Resources Are Power"). Ninik, we will see, is continually confronted by stratifications linked to the information divide discussed in Chapter 4, which render equitable synthesis impossible.

Just as celebrating borderlessness might make it easier to ignore unequal access, it might also obscure the desire by less-powerful linguistic groups to *maintain* linguistic borders. Cultural synthesis is not always desired, Scott Lyons, Kubota, and others suggest. Though discourses coexist, are permeable, and thus cannot by nature be discrete, existing power relations *do* bleed into language mixes, often to the detriment of the least powerful language. Hybridity doesn't imply an egalitarian relationship between discourses, as Indigenous peoples, who have a vested interest in asserting borders to maintain their languages, know. In Lyon's words, sovereignty "is not something that is easily meshed. If anything, sovereignty requires the making of a fence, not to keep things out, but to keep important things in" (77). Maintaining linguistic borders, Ninik's portrait also shows, can be a way to unify against more powerful interests to achieve social justice for oppressed communities.

This tension between cultural synthesis and protective exclusion can be ameliorated by understanding Ninik's work toward cosmopolitan connection—and the translingual praxis linked to it—as a form of critical border thinking and as inevitably provisional because of the spatiotemporal nature of discursive action (see Horner and Alvarez). Rather than *ignoring* borders with the aim of reducing difference, border thinkers like Ninik dwell at the interstices of self/other to forge connections, not with the aim to *unify* but with the aim of reaching toward localized pluriversality (see Anzaldúa; Mignolo, "Border Thinking"; Mignolo and Walsh). By tracing how Ninik momentarily defines and then exceeds the diverse limit-situations she encounters, this chapter emphasizes the ongoing work of crafting cosmopolitan connection in language and action despite and in relation to shifting power dynamics. Ninik, we will see, moves between synthesis and exclusion to perform her ongoing commitment to creating a more gender-just world as time and the contexts she navigates shift around her. This process involves silencing some voices in her repertoire while amplifying others, depending on the limit-situation. To return to Bakhtin, *from whom* she draws her knowledge in any given moment and *to whom* she addresses her words is contingent upon *with whom* she seeks to make real-world, cosmopolitan connections. These dialogic audience negotiations are in turn mediated by the limit-situations she is confronted with and seeks to define amid the competing discourses in her life. At times, she may use her language to work toward cross-cultural synthesis while at others she might choose temporary exclusion. To return to Paulo Freire, Ninik is engaged in a continual process of working toward her ideals, "in word, in work, in action-reflection" (*Pedagogy of the Oppressed* 88), and underlying each intervention is her steadfast belief that working toward justice is, in essence, what it means to be human.

CULTIVATING A COSMOPOLITAN IDENTITY

Over the past thirteen years, Ninik has consistently demonstrated a border-aware yet cosmopolitan orientation when it comes to working toward social justice. This belief in connecting across difference was undoubtedly fostered by her transnational experiences and the discourse communities that shaped her—from her Muslim faith to her advanced academic scholarship in English and Indonesian both in the United States and in Indonesia. However, she is careful to avoid mapping her own experiences and belief systems onto others who may approach social justice differently, a crucial means of establishing connection despite difference, as Krista Ratcliffe argues in *Rhetorical Listening*, and a central means of transcending, or at least redefining for the time being, existing borders.

To Ninik, this desire to work toward social justice should—and does—transcend linguistic and religious borders: shared humanity should be the impetus for change. When I asked in her 2014 interview whether she used the knowledge she garnered from English scholarship to effect social change, her answer was decidedly cosmopolitan in orientation. She replied,

> Social justice is not about language; it's about humanity. Probably different people define English differently, but you already know that English is something for me, like a tool. Right now we can see that it is imperialist and political in

academic circles, but I think it's not English as itself. And right now many people use English. For me, it's like a tool. We can talk about social justice in any language.

Though Ninik admits here and elsewhere in her interviews that the preponderance of academic research in English and the requirement that Indonesian scholars publish in English is symptomatic of linguistic imperialism, she also points to the fact that it's not the English language itself but the humans using it that leads to such inequity. Given the right circumstances, English, like any language, can be used for social justice. We need to move past the text itself—or the language system being used—and focus on what we might *do*. It's not the language itself but the *action* that matters.

Ninik also pointed in this same interview to two overlapping discourses in her repertoire—often situated at odds in dominant Western discourse— that she believes responsible for fostering this "human" desire for social justice. She continues:

> For me, my motivation [for social justice] is mostly about what I see and what I read. And mostly right now most of what I read is two types: firstly, religious, about Qur'an, and, second, academic books and articles in English. Everything like that is in English. But I think when thinking about social justice, you shouldn't think about religion, the country, the color of their skin, your language—you should think about what you see and talk about it with what's in your heart. As a human. (2014 interview)

By naming these two audiences in her repertoire as her prime motivators, Ninik challenges existing (and problematic) borders in dominant Western academic thought: between religious and academic discourses and between Islam and progressive social justice (see the essays collected in DePalma and Ringer; Stenberg). These discourses, and the languages and values associated with them, coexist and interanimate each other in Ninik's discursive repertoire. Regardless of her own influences, though, she believes that global citizens need to move beyond the clear boundaries drawn around religion, country, race, or language to achieve social equity—a decidedly cosmopolitan belief.

Indeed, in her 2022 interview, Ninik, whom I and others might describe as a devout Muslim, as an academic, as an Islamic feminist, and as a two-term Indonesian legislator, once again pointed to being human as the prime motivator for the social-justice work she does. When I asked her whether she views herself as an Islamic feminist, she explained:

> I am a human being, actually, right? It means that what I'm doing is just human. I have to do. I cannot say that I'm a "feminist" because if you are not feminist, you cannot do like this. No: we have to do like this because we are *human*. Because we're humans. So if people said, "Oh, because you are having experience as victim of violence, so you do like that?" No. Even if I am not the victim, I have to do like this, because I am a human . . . .

Ninik: On Being Human

Ninik acknowledges here that identity labels like "feminist" *do* exist—and that they work, in turn, to create borders between those who identify as feminist and those who do not. Foreshadowing legislative action I'll discuss below, she also alludes to her own experience as a survivor of domestic violence, which, she argues, motivates her personally but that shouldn't preclude nonsurvivors from challenging gender-based violence. Focusing too much on borders when it comes to the naming of identity categories—or, to return to the opening metaphor, focusing too much on the bottle, the cup, and the sea, rather than on the water itself—can absolve those who don't identify in socially inscribed ways from their responsibility as *humans* to care for each other. For Ninik, the many roles she and others play may be "packaged" differently, requiring different performances depending on shifting power dynamics, but the water itself—our shared humanity—is, or should be, the same.

AT HOME WITH ENGLISH

Ninik's transnational educational history and the languages associated with it have deeply informed the way she performs cosmopolitan border thinking as a human being, an academic, and a legislator. In her 2014 interview, as she was finishing her doctoral work and just after she was elected to the national parliament,

Ninik used a metaphor to explain to me the relationship between her academic and legislative identities:

> [Being] a politician is about the outside of me . . . . Academic is already inside of me. This is like if you have bricks. I've already arranged the bricks, one by one, from the bottom, in academics. I don't want to start over. I have to make this a house. But for politics, it's like the outside. On the outside of the house, there's a garden. I don't want to throw out the garden, but I still want to keep establishing the house. It would be very nice if there was a house and a good garden.

This metaphor illuminated, for me, how central education has been to Ninik's literacy practices, spurring my decision to choose the term "cultivate" to describe her careful cosmopolitan rhetorical work as she tends to her academic house and political gardens. The house and the garden are human-constructed spaces that, though separate, are deeply interrelated and central to the concept of "home" for many people.

Indeed, if we look to Ninik's literacy history, educational spaces and "home" have long been closely linked. Ninik's family, in fact, runs a powerful *pesantren*, or Islamic boarding school, which serves approximately five thousand Muslim students in her home town of Banyuwangi, a connection that has informed her deep religious faith, her advanced academic work, her border work as a politician, and her relationship to English. Though Ninik is now at "home" with English, initially, her experience moving to a pesantren from a secular school influenced her relationship to the language. In her 2010 interview, Ninik explained it this way: "In junior high school I love English. My grades were the best. But after that I continue to high school, and I am not in secular school, but in the religious school, and the percentage is 70 percent religious courses and only 30 percent secular courses, like biology, geography, and English." Her "focus," she explained, shifted at the point when English was separated from her religious education, and it wasn't until she "got a C" in an English course in college that she looked back and reflected on her lost passion for English. To return to her metaphor, some of the "bricks" Ninik used to arrange her academic identity were undoubtedly religious in nature, but because of the long-established divide between English as a Western language and Islam, her relationship to English suffered.

That said, the literate resources available for Ninik's academic house diversified when she was accepted to the Ford Foundation's International Fellowship Program, which eventually enabled her to earn her MA in Asian Studies in the United States at the English-medium University of Hawai'i at Manoa. Notably, her English-medium thesis focused on pesantren, a topic that she returned to for her English-medium dissertation, which she wrote in Indonesia. English, once divided from her religious education, was—and still is—an integral part of her "home." Because of Ninik's experiences border hopping between Indonesia and Hawaii, when she returned to Indonesia, she knew she wanted to apply to an English-medium PhD program in Indonesia, which led to her acceptance at ICRS. When I asked her in 2010 why she chose to apply to ICRS, she explained that her primary motivation was to continue "my experience in international networking using English." ICRS, as an English-medium institution, allowed her to keep using English *within* Indonesia where she could be near her family and, given that all ICRS students are required to study abroad, pretty much ensured that she would use her English in non-Indonesian contexts, too. Bringing English "home" allowed her to continue her cosmopolitan border work.

That English is localized for Ninik, and intimately tied to her lived experiences as an Indonesian woman, can be seen in the way she compares academic writing in English to academic writing in Indonesian. Since I first met her, she has emphasized that she values English academic "style" because there is space for writers to embed the personal—a testament to the feminist scholarly community she engages with, in which "the personal is political" (Hanisch). Back in 2010, she explained that she enjoyed writing in English more than in Indonesian because Western rhetorical conventions allowed her to ground her topics close to home. Such is not the case, she explained, when writing to Indonesian academic audiences:

It's very rarely we find Indonesians writing in their thesis or article, something like "I love this topic because when I was an undergrad, my boyfriend or girlfriend introduced me to this idea" . . . something like that.

Ninik views Indonesian writing as more distant and less welcome to discussing personal motivations or exigency. To explain the difference between her Indonesian and English writing voice, she expanded:

I love English style because even if we discuss about a very difficult topic, about philosophy, women in philosophy or something like that, actually this topic I already understand from my own experiences, so I think OK, this is very, very philosophical, but also a personal story and I can write about that.

Rather than being antithetical to her Indonesian experiences, English opens up avenues for Ninik to draw from the personal. In so doing, she localizes a language long linked to Western experience—a rhetorical move that serves her well, we will see, as she cultivates various English-medium audiences, both within Indonesia and beyond, to work toward her cosmopolitan ideals.

Not surprisingly, Ninik's cosmopolitan experiences and worldview affect the audiences *for whom* she writes. Unlike Faqih and Nina, who most often imagine local Indonesian audiences for their scholarly writing regardless of the language, for Ninik, it depends on the situation. When I asked in her 2010 interview which audiences she most often imagined for her texts, she explained,

Actually, I don't think about audience at first, particularly in class papers. I just follow the topic in class, what is interesting, but I always think about what topic in each class I can relate to women issues. Then, after I'm done, I revise for different audiences I think would like my writing.

The way Ninik describes her process when it comes to audience here hints at the cosmopolitan orientation she still takes when considering audience: rather than choosing a discrete audience for her texts, she begins with the content, with social justice for women a prime motivator. Only after she writes her text does she revise for different audiences. In keeping with her own cosmopolitan literacy history, these audiences are both local-to-Indonesia *and* Western and sometimes a mix of the two, as she strategically moves academic knowledge itself from one language and audience to the next to achieve her purposes. For whom she writes, as the next sections will show, is dependent upon what voices in her existing repertoire she wishes to share and what her intended audiences need to know, choices that depend on situational power dynamics related to access and its corollary, disconnect. Though she argues for a world that looks past arbitrary identity categories and the borders that construct them, at times Ninik is forced to rely on the very same borders she wants to deconstruct to negotiate competing discourses and achieve her social-justice aims. By tracing her literacy practices through time, however, we can see how an exclusionary audience choice at one point does not preclude a move toward synthesis at another. Examining various limit-situations Ninik encounters and the way she moves between synthesis and exclusion as she cultivates audiences offers up new ways of understanding translingual praxis, and with that, how we might, as humans, strive for cosmopolitan connection despite and in relation to power.

CULTIVATING A COSMOPOLITAN INDONESIAN CONVERSATION

That achieving her ideal cosmopolitan connection was complicated by Ninik's lived experiences became quite clear in the way she engaged with assignments in our academic writing class her first year in graduate school. Depending on the rhetorical situation she imagined for her texts, Ninik at times used English to deconstruct traditional cross-cultural borders for her projected audiences; at other times, however, she *leveraged* rhetorical borders to achieve her purposes. Just as importantly, through the content of her academic work, she continually highlighted material divides Indonesians must navigate to engage with global literacies. This discursive border work in her academic life foreshadows, in turn, the way she now navigates borders to achieve social justice as a citizen and a legislator.

In the first text Ninik constructed for my class, a critical literacy narrative, she wrote her cosmopolitan ethos into the narrative *and* performed it by directly addressing an audience of Indonesian peers. *For whom* she writes her text is localized to the peers *with whom* she learns. By sharing her experiences studying abroad with an audience she assumes will also study abroad—but hasn't yet— she works to alleviate cross-cultural friction they, as people who have different experiences with global literacies, might feel. In this one text, she works toward helping others transcend borders more smoothly while also pointing to the types of borders, material and discursive, she and her Indonesian peers must navigate as they engage in global academic literacy.

Ninik begins her literacy narrative by first establishing connection with her audience and then constructing her cosmopolitan iden- tity: "Although, as with other people, I have many discourse communities, for this paper, I would only like to address two discourse communities, which are my existence as a student in Hawaii and in Yogyakarta." She then makes both her purpose and her Indonesian peer audience quite clear:

> I know not only I have problems with cultural shock. Many students who just come back from abroad and continue their studies in Indonesia will face the same problems. Right now, I am still trying to solve my cultural shock even though I have been in ICRS for one month. For those of you who will have the same position as me, I have many suggestions.

She draws these suggestions for coping with "cultural shock" from her own experiences navigating the borders between her Hawaiian and Indonesian educational contexts. To explore the friction, she moves on to interrogate differing cross-cultural audience expectations when it comes to her English ability:

> Although I am a pure Indonesian, I still got culture shock when I began studying in ICRS . . . . When in Hawaii, I was considered as an international student, I could get excuses, if

my English was not perfect. The program supported me to express myself freely. The main point when I talked in classes was my ideas. As long as my classmates and professor could catch my point, it was enough. Perfect English was not really important because it is only a tool to communicate my ideas.

Because she was considered an "international student" in Hawaii, people were more lenient of her nonstandard language use, which emphasized to her the notion that communication across borders should emphasize content and connection over dominant English "standards."

That said, when she returned to Indonesia after two years in Hawaii, she felt her Indonesian cohorts had very different expectations of her English:

Unlike in Hawaii, in ICRS my English should be perfect since I graduated from America. Actually, nobody speaks directly about that to me. However, I am able to feel it when I talk to some people. One of my friends said, "Your English must be advanced." It indicates they put my English skill higher than theirs. It really makes me uncomfortable. I am aware about my ability in English. Although I am a US alumna, it does not mean that my English skill is better than students who only study in country.

Because of these shifting expectations of her language abilities, Ninik feels friction as she works to construct an English-using identity at ICRS. She uses her literacy narrative to educate her peers, challenging assumptions they might have that English use in "native"-speaker contexts is always standard while also implicitly encouraging them as audience members to be amenable to her non-Standard English. Foreshadowing a theme she returned to repeatedly throughout the thirteen years of this project, in this first assignment, through performance and content, Ninik points to English's cosmopolitan possibilities, suggesting the possibility that *all* English-using audiences learn to listen across borders and linguistic difference.

At times, however, as an academic Ninik relied on the fact that rhetorical borders *do* exist when it comes to knowledge traditions, despite English's increasingly cosmopolitan scope. She pointed out in her literacy narrative that exigent religious topics in the United States may be "old news" to Indonesian audiences:

> The topic of research [in the United States] is also, in my view, quite dissimilar. I remember one day my Indonesian friend asking me about my Hawaiian MA capstone's title. He gave me an unpleasant comment, "Why do you discuss about pesantren? Open your eyes, a thousand people already wrote about pesantren. You have to find another topic." It really made me disappointed. I realize that the topic of pesantren is a "common" topic in Indonesia. Pesantren from many different ways is already examined. However, for Hawaiian or Western scholars, in fact, this topic is still saleable. We can not take for granted that all people in West know about pesantren . . . . They really want to know what happens in Eastern countries, so pesantren, which is associated with Eastern countries, is still interesting for them.

Not only does Ninik highlight tensions having to do with differing perceptions of "common knowledge" across national borders, but she also points to the important role English plays in spreading Islamic religious knowledge to the West, a move that works toward cosmopolitan connection.

Interestingly, the fact that there *is* a border between Western and Indonesian knowledge traditions is an affordance for Ninik; this border allows her to translate knowledge garnered from the Indonesian voices in her repertoire to educate Western audiences for whom Indonesian knowledge is not readily available—a translingual maneuver that allows her to perform the cosmopolitan ethos she cultivates. In turn, by writing about this friction in her literacy narrative, she uses English to encourage her Indonesian peer audience to do the same. English, Ninik both argues and shows, can educate Western *and* local audiences, though *how* particular content is received varies depending upon existing knowledge "borders."

In addition to discursive divides, Ninik also points to borders created by material inequality. She writes that despite having the same "standards" when it comes to academic performance, the material conditions under which she works in Indonesia are very different from those in Hawaii, making it "hard to adjust":

> Students in Hawaii are free to access library from anywhere as long as they have Internet access . . . . Online journals can be downloaded freely by using students' ID . . . . Internet is an essential tool that students are able to use anywhere in campus with high speed. The complete facility, for sure, will support students to focus more on study.

Ninik contrasts this experience with her Indonesian literacy context, where the library has "limited hours," the internet connection is always "broken," and "recent academic articles are difficult to get." In this particular limit-situation, Ninik sees her ability to use English effectively for research circumscribed by economic inequality. Despite English's increasingly cosmopolitan role, the material context in which the language is used mediates any literate action, including actions that work toward cosmopolitan connection.

Ninik ends her literacy narrative with a section she titles "If You Are in My Position," where she uses direct address to give her Indonesian peer audience advice. She begins by encouraging her peers to make local connections when they return to Indonesia: "If you feel disappointed and angry about this condition, share with your friends who have the same experiences as you. It can help you to feel that you are not alone, and some time your friends will give you good advice to solve your problem . . . ." Here, Ninik performs through her writing the very connection to her Indonesian peers she recommends, again signaling the performative nature of her literacy narrative. By conflating *for whom* and *with whom* and writing to an audience of peers, she opens up the possibility that they might respond with "good advice" in real time. In so doing, she strategically cultivates her audience.

Ninik then moves from "local" to "global," pointing to how students' Western literacy sponsors (see Brandt, "Sponsors of

Literacy") can continue to help them transcend borders when it comes to accessing literate resources:

> Keep in touch with your colleagues from your previous university. It will help you to find sources that you need. In fact, Western universities usually have more open and complete sources. It is good ways not only to find sources but also to maintain networking. I believe networking always gain good things for us in the future.

This advice came from a place of experience. As will be discussed in more detail later, although there is a knowledge divide when it comes to academic sources, networking across languages and borders does help her "gain good things" for herself and others as a citizen and a politician.

From a spatiotemporal perspective, this close reading of Ninik's literacy narrative in relation to content and audience negotiation foreshadows her future literacy interventions. Over the course of eleven years, Ninik continually returned to the themes she concretizes in her literacy narrative, in word and action. She repeatedly returned to her argument that audiences should learn to listen across difference—linguistic, religious, or otherwise—and to the importance of networking across national borders to synthesize knowledge communities and work toward social justice. Though these themes recur, Ninik's translingual rhetorical approach is mediated by situational power dynamics linked to existing societal borders, both discursive and material: as we trace her literacy practices, we can see how she uses the various languages in her translingual repertoire to move back and forth between inclusion and exclusion while also extending the themes she highlighted here in new directions.

CULTIVATING A DIVERSE LOCAL AUDIENCE

How Ninik constructs her cosmopolitan ethos to reach audiences within Indonesian borders differs depending on what she is writing about and how. The literacy narrative described above is meant for an Indonesian English-using peer audience, which points to the cosmopolitan nature of the English language itself but without challenging the traditional assumption that her "local" audience is made up solely of native Indonesians. However, in an op-ed assignment sequence, Ninik shows another way cosmopolitan synthesis might be performed, this time by expanding the borders of what we might assume a "local" Indonesian audience looks like. In doing so, she once again returns to her argument that writer *and* audience should be equally willing to listen across difference, although this time her focus is on Indonesian *content* rather than linguistic difference itself.

The op-ed Ninik composed encapsulates how deeply how deeply personal English is for Ninik while also showing how she "cultivates" a distinctly cosmopolitan, albeit local, Indonesian audience. In addition, it foreshadows the social-justice legislative work she now engages in, emphasizing the importance of understanding translingual praxis as exceeding textual interventions. As I mentioned in Chapter 5, at the midyear point the PhD students with whom I worked expressed a desire to learn genres that would help them mobilize their academic knowledge to reach local civic audiences. To help them do so, I asked them to translate an academic question they were working on into editorials they might submit, if they chose, for wider circulation. So that they made conscious choices when moving between academic and civic audiences, I also asked them to submit cover letters with their editorials, outlining to me their rhetorical choices in relation to the audience for whom they imagined their texts.

For this assignment, Ninik chose to discuss a topic close to her heart: prenatal care in Indonesia. She begins her reflective cover letter by writing, "For my editorial, I think I hope some groups that can read it are Indonesian women, activists, doctors and the government. People who read the *Jakarta Post*." She signals here a local Indonesian English-using audience, which is not surprising given the *Jakarta Post*'s readership.

However, her cover letter also signals that she does have another audience in mind: me, a white woman from the United States who lives in Indonesia. Challenging the notion that local audiences are necessarily limited to citizens of the nation-state, Ninik uses her cover letter to make a direct request that I try to interpret from the perspective of her Indonesian audience:

> When you read my editorial, please put yourself as an Indonesian woman since if you just think from the side of an American woman you will find it difficult to feel what I want to deliver to my audiences.

Interestingly, Ninik emphasizes that it is only by grounding my own identity within her Indonesian context that her opinion piece will be effective for me as a "local" reader. She encourages me to move past the notion that because I'm a native speaker of English her linguistic choices must necessarily cater to me; rather, in order to be included, I, too, as audience member must work toward cultural synthesis in my interpretive practices. In doing so, she challenges the notion that just because she is using English, she is writing to readers in Western locales, while also emphasizing that navigating across borders is a two-way street.

Indeed, throughout her editorial, Ninik synthesizes Indonesian examples, and even Indonesian languages, with the Western rhetorical appeals I introduced in class to reach this hybrid "local" audience. A "typical" American audience, for instance, may "find it difficult to feel" the type of pathos Ninik wishes to engage in with her opening example because we are interpreting from vastly different social contexts. She begins her editorial as follows:

> The day was January 14, 2010. I sat on the bus with my sister, traveling from Jombang to Surabaya. As it was a full bus, there were some people who had to stand. The weather was hot, because the bus did not have AC. Suddenly a pregnant mother was standing next to me. I spontaneously stood up and gave my seat to her, but she who maybe was in her early thirties waved her hand as a sign of quiet refusal, and she said, "Matur nuwun ya, Saya mau ngamen (Thank you, I want to sing to beg)." I was surprised, then smiled to this beautiful woman and sat back. Not so long amid the smell of stinging sweat in a bus full of passengers, this mother was singing a

song and using an instrument made of a series of bottle caps on a piece of wood.

Ninik paints a powerful image of a pregnant woman busking on a crowded, hot bus. That she is writing to an audience within Indonesia is clear by her reference to Jombang and Surabaya—Javanese cities that most people reading from a non-Indonesian context would be unaware of—and by her use of code-meshing when relating the pregnant woman's words. Though Ninik translates the Bahasa Indonesia into English, the English, rather than the Bahasa Indonesia, is in parentheses, most likely indicating an audience that gravitates toward the Indonesian language first and English second. Furthermore, that Ninik merely "smiles" and "sits back," signaling her acceptance of the woman's begging, might give someone interpreting from an American context—where beggars are sometimes seen as "lazy" rather than "needy"—pause. Ninik, however, grew up in a culture where begging is, if not accepted entirely by governmental agencies, a fact of life for many Indonesians, many of whom feel it is their Muslim duty to donate small change to those less fortunate.

Ninik, rather than condemning the mother for her decision to beg, continues: "[T]he burden of life has forced her to do this. Of course, she gathered the coins. Coins from passengers are to continue her life. They could be for childbirth preparation. Sacrifice makes truly a wonderful mother." Ninik successfully portrays the discomfort the woman must feel on the crowded bus and the poverty that forced her to such a situation. This allows her to interpret the mother's begging as "sacrifice" rather than "endangerment" of an unborn child, as unsympathetic people interpreting from a different context might. Ninik was probably quite aware of this cross-cultural difference concerning begging because of her time in the United States, which likely spurred her request that I read her text as she and her native-to-Indonesian audience would.

Ninik then steps back from pathos to acknowledge that the mother's actions were "risky" and to make her argument that reproductive health needs to be addressed in Indonesia:

What this mother did is not without risk. Economic ability is the main reason that she is doing it. Besides that, there is also the possibility she did not have enough knowledge of the risks. Here in Indonesia, reproductive health does not include in the ranks of importance in household budgets, particularly for middle- to lower-class families. The need to eat, and school for our children is more important than the funds which are allocated to reproductive health. In addition, access to health services in Indonesia is very limited. In one village, there is usually only one health service, but not all villages have this service.

With her phrases "here in Indonesia" and "our children," Ninik emphasizes that English can be used to convey local issues, challenging the traditional linkage between English and Western interests; furthermore, since these facts are likely obvious to Indonesian audiences, one could argue that Ninik is invoking a mixed audience of Indonesians and people, like me, who might be reading from Indonesian soil but without context regarding Indonesian household budgets and where priorities rest when it comes to women's health.

Ninik then moves on to an example from her own life, where, because of faulty prenatal care, her aunt died needlessly during childbirth. Her aunt had preeclampsia, or high blood pressure, she explains. When her aunt went into labor, she was scheduled for a Cesarean section, but, because of a lack of doctors, her aunt was forced to wait for four hours for the doctor to come. Her aunt—with the nurses' permission, because they lacked knowledge concerning the condition—made the choice to have a natural birth despite the fact that "Medically a person with high blood pressure is 'Forbidden' from giving childbirth naturally." Ninik's aunt eventually died. As Ninik explains in her editorial, "Finally, God gave the best way for her. On Friday, January 15, 2010, at 9:20, God called this mother to a peaceful end. Innalillahi wa Innalillahi rojiun." Ninik draws upon God in ways audiences from the United States, like me, might consider strange in an opinion piece for a national newspaper—if, that is, that audience wasn't reading with a cosmopolitan, translingual orientation. Appeals to religion are only unconvincing to those used to interpreting from a nonreligious context when reading national newspapers.

Ninik's choice to code-mesh Arabic into her English text without translation further indicates that her audience is (or should be) comfortable with and willing to understand Islamic religious references. She explained the phrase's meaning to me in her postcourse interview:

> Usually if we have sad tragedies, we always say it. It means that everything is from God and everything goes back to God. This is very common in Indonesia, so even if I publish it in the *Jakarta Post*, it's OK.

Ninik implies that even though the *Jakarta Post* is an English-medium newspaper, it is still Indonesian and thus accepting of common religious references. For this particular text, she assumes a mixed local audience that includes Muslim Indonesians and those, like me, who are willing to put in the work necessary to learn the Arabic phrase's meaning.

As further evidence of her translingual orientation, she signals that her rhetorical choices in this particular piece do not preclude her making different choices when moving content across contexts and genres. In fact, in her postcourse 2010 interview, she explained that she had sent in her editorial, but she wasn't worried about rejection because she had already circulated her knowledge elsewhere:

> I already sent it to the *Jakarta Post*. I can wait three weeks usually and then if it is not published, no problem. Because actually I have three stories in my editorial that I can share other places. I rewrote it in Indonesian on Facebook, but I didn't give any logos. Only pathos. Just giving the stories. I got many comments. But I hope through writing everybody here can accept this reality. They never realize this is important until they read it on Facebook.

Ninik highlights her belief that the *action* her words catalyze, whether in English or in Indonesian, is what matters most; whether on Facebook or in the *Jakarta Post*, she can spread social awareness through deliberate rhetorical choices, which might include using mostly English but localized content to reach a diverse "local" audience with occasional code-meshing between English and Arabic or in the case of her Facebook post, removing the logos and translating the information from English to Indonesian. By tracing how Ninik circulates the same knowledge in different limit-situations, we can see how a writer might move between synthesis and exclusion while still maintaining, overall, a cosmopolitan orientation when it comes to knowledge circulation.

Given linguistic divides, discursive borders *do* exist; however, in this particular assignment, Ninik successfully negotiates these divides to reach her local English-using audience, provided, of course, that her English-using audience members, regardless of their national origin, are receptive to her choices. In turn, by subsequently translating the knowledge from her English-medium opinion piece into Indonesian, she is able to bridge the linguistic divide for those without access to English. When viewed from a spatiotemporal perspective, her rhetorical choices indicate an awareness of situational power dynamics and an ability to perform translingual praxis accordingly.

SYNTHESIZING ACADEMIC BORDERS

Ninik's strategic border play continued past these first-year assignments into her advanced academic work and beyond. Unlike with the previous two texts, in which Ninik rewrites boundaries when it comes to our perceptions of "local" audiences and which languages can serve what communities, in her advanced academic work Ninik chooses most often to write toward traditional Western academic audiences in an effort to expand our understandings of Muslim Indonesian women's agency. Even though she still maintains the traditional link between the English language and a bounded Western identity group, her *process itself* is cosmopolitan because she seeks to create synthesis between the Indonesian knowledge in her repertoire and the Western audiences for whom this knowledge might be new.

Ninik's dissertation puts in conversation Pierre Bourdieu's theory of social capital, Sherry Ortner's theory of feminist agency, and the scholarship of Lila Abu-Lughod to explore Muslim Indonesian women's agency as they negotiate their arranged marriages within pesantren. As Ninik writes, "[E]ach woman has own way to 'play'" her agency. The structure limits women's agency, but women can also find ways to enact their agency secretly or openly" (40). Overall, she finds that women with more social capital, like her, have more leverage when negotiating their marriages. Here we can see that, like Nina, Ninik is quite aware of societal power dynamics but she also acknowledges the many ways women can and do traverse the power-ridden borders they encounter.

This topic was—and still is—deeply personal for Ninik, though the reasons have shifted. In addition to locating her research participants in pesantren, spaces she had access to because of her family connections, she herself also took part in the arranged marriage process when she was eighteen. She is now, however, healing from a divorce from her first husband—and from gender-based violence. The divorce she is willing to talk about in *any* language given that, as she says, "For me, when I was, I am a politician. Everyone can access my information, my data, even like many years ago. When I type in Google, do you know what the more people want to know about me? Nihayatul Wafiroh? Try . . . 'Nihayatul Wafiroh divorce.'" Her divorce is old news in Indonesia; her personal experience with gender-based violence in this previous marriage, however, she is only willing to talk about *in English* (more on that below).

Google "Nihayatul Wafiroh Divorce"

Although Ninik was uncomfortable discussing her actual data, if we look to the way Ninik discusses *theory* in her dissertation, the audience she chooses to reach, and her writing process, we can still see that Ninik's border-thinking cosmopolitanism continued into her more advanced academic writing, which in turn influences the way she performs translingual praxis as a legislator. Indeed, when I asked her in our 2022 interview about whether the theory of agency she developed in her dissertation transcended academia into her real-world interventions, she replied:

So I think that for me, right now, I have multi-agency. The multi-agency makes me have boundaries. But all the agency is the same thing, is that I am a woman. And I am a human. Sometimes I become a wife, become legislator, become daughter-in-law, become a boss of my staff, become part of the society, become leader in my community, become teacher. But the thing that cannot be changed out of all my agency is two: I am a woman, and I am human. So all the agency have to be built with these two values. With these two values. So this means that with all the situations, when I have to make a decision, I have to establish this decision using these two reasons. I am human and I am woman.

Ninik: I Am a Woman and I Am Human

Once again, Ninik emphasizes that identity boundaries *do* exist, requiring different types of agency, but the essence of what she stands for as a woman and a human being remains the same. Her performance just shifts accordingly.

This understanding of agency relates to the way she views audience. Given her dissertation's focus on female agency and Ninik's interest in promoting the public good, her project had the potential of benefitting multiple audiences. When I asked her in 2014 what contribution she wanted her dissertation to make, either academically or publicly, she explained that she had just been discussing this with one of her dissertation advisors, an American academic:

[My American advisor] asked me whether I was doing anthropology or activism. If you are doing activism, she said, from your dissertation you have to change something to contribute to change reality to be better, but if you want to be anthropologist, you have to explain this is the reality that is happening. Just tell the story. I choose the second one.

Ninik's advisor draws a clear border between the activist sphere and the academic sphere, in the process implying that anthropological writing for academic audiences need not "change reality to be better." Ninik chose the descriptive, as opposed to the activist, intervention.

However, when I asked her to elaborate, Ninik complicated the binary her dissertation advisor set up between activism and scholarly work by referring to an important voice from her dissertation:

> I just want to show Western academics, like Lila Abu-Lughod does, that actually we cannot say that Muslim women are always suffering. That women have agency and that they are actually doing something that people never think they are. We do agency and negotiation.

Ninik points to Lila Abu-Lughod's work as central to her understanding of Muslim women's agency. As Ninik writes in her dissertation, Abu-Lughod critiques "how some Western feminists identify the term liberalism, secularism and human rights from their own stand. From their Western views, they judge the human rights, particularly women's rights, and religions . . . forget[ting] that the contexts of politics, economy, and history exert a great deal of influence in [women's] performance [of agency]" (36). By aligning her own research with Abu-Lughod's and pointing to the way Abu-Lughod's research challenges Western academic feminists, Ninik implies in her interview that her academic work can, in fact, "change reality," at least discursively. In so doing, she challenges the boundary often placed between academic scholarship and civic change.

Ninik views her English-medium dissertation project as a means to educate a Western academic audience, which in some ways reaffirms the traditional connection between English and the Western audiences associated with it. However, by focusing on her *process*, we can see how she works toward synthesis by seeking to overcome existing ideological borders between Islamic feminism and traditional Western feminism, as well as between academic research and social-justice initiatives.

CULTIVATING AN ACTIVIST IDENTITY

Ninik's cosmopolitan orientation is evidenced in the texts she creates, and thus her language choices, but it can also be found in the ways she seeks to transcend borders in her activist work.

Focusing on Ninik's processes, as opposed to just the texts she produces, is crucial when seeking to understand how she works toward her cosmopolitan ideals by transferring resources from her academic "house" to her political "garden." She brought themes she wrote about in her academic work alive, showcasing the promise of translingual praxis and a spatiotemporal approach to tracing knowledge.

As an example, in an effort to combat the global information divide that she describes in her literacy narrative, Ninik repeatedly leveraged her relative privilege to bring literate resources from the United States and other Western countries to Indonesia. While studying for her MA in the US, Ninik capitalized on the resources that came with US sponsorship so she could start a community library in her home town, Banyuwangi. Ninik used her English networking ability to email various listservs at the University of Hawaii, explaining that many women and children in Indonesia do not have access to literate resources, and she left Hawaii with hundreds of books and multiple monetary donations. Currently, her multilingual library in Indonesia has over nine hundred books, journals, and DVDs, with four hundred fifty members. She continued bringing literate resources from the United States and other more resource-rich countries to Indonesia as a PhD student. As a first-year graduate student, she also played a central part, for example, in creating the Indonesian arm of the Swiss-based multilingual open-access digital database, Globethics.net, which was discussed in chapters 4 and 7.

Banyuwangi Community Library Webpage

This networking-toward-synthesis translated to Ninik's activist work with two NGOs, one transnational and one local, but both the beneficiaries of Ninik's aptitude for breaking down borders. In one transnational NGO, sponsored by the Canadian International Development Agency (CIDA), Ninik was tasked with synthesizing in educational contexts teaching, academic scholarship, and community outreach within Indonesia. Ninik explained that "in universities in Indonesia, there are three elements: research, community outreach, and teaching. And research and community outreach are not connected to each other. Actually, the important thing is how research can push community outreach. So I focused on community outreach." Though Ninik chooses a descriptive, anthropological approach to reach Western academic audiences in her own dissertation, through her work with this transnational English-medium NGO she helps other Indonesian scholars bridge the divide between research and real-world activism on their own soil. In doing so, she rewrites traditional demarcations by engaging with an English-medium transnational organization within Indonesia to break down perceived borders in her own community.

This border work continued, albeit differently, with Ninik's work with a local Indonesian NGO meant to empower Indonesian female legislators. She explained that when working with this NGO, "I was so surprised because not one of the female legislators have email address . . . . [I]t means that no one of them are literate in technology." She was also concerned that many of the women she interviewed were "lalu-lalu" (shy) when it came to voicing their opinions. As someone who researches female agency, Ninik was concerned by this demureness: "How about if you are talking with other people and community? How will you advocate for women in your community in the legislature?" Ninik's work with this NGO helped her spread digital literacy and encourage women to more forcefully enter the political conversation—an intervention likely fueled in part by the cosmopolitan nature of Ninik's scholarly endeavors, which gave her ample opportunities to research and perform this type of agency herself.

Ultimately, Ninik chose to run for legislative office because of a divide between activists and the political sphere that she experienced working with these NGOs. She explained in 2014:

> I have to try to run because even if in NGO I try to talk with and empower the community. If the rules and decisions . . . if in the legislature, there is no one who is aware of this problem, nothing will be done. The legislators at top and NGOs at bottom have to work together, like a sandwich. If we have the top, we have to have the bottom, too. And inside, we can put good stuff, but if there is no bottom, there is no sandwich . . . . (2014 interview)

As an example, she pointed to the United Nations program REDD [Reducing Emissions from Deforestation and Forest Degradation], explaining that they "empower community, but they only work with NGO, and don't have the networking with legislators. For example: illegal logging. The community is aware of it, but they still don't have the law. We have to put something together, bottom up and top down." Ninik once again positions herself as a conduit, capable of disseminating information to unite discrete audiences, this time within Indonesia but between activists and the Indonesian governing body.

CULTIVATING A POLITICAL GARDEN

Since Ninik has entered the public eye as an elected official, this cosmopolitan border work has become ever more complicated, though her cosmopolitan ideals and advocacy for women remain the same. At times, Ninik engages in translingual praxis as a means of working toward cultural synthesis, but at other times Ninik wants to maintain existing boundaries to achieve her social-justice aims, at least for the time being.

For some context, my first follow-up interview with Ninik occurred just after she was elected and just as the 2014 presidential election results were being counted. Ultimately, Joko Widodo, commonly referred to as Jokowi, was elected as Indonesia's seventh president post-independence and he, like Ninik, is now serving his second term. The first of Indonesia's presidents not to come from the political or military elite, Jokowi springs from working-class roots, an identity Ninik discusses later in relation to his English ability. He represents the Partai Kebangkitan Bangsa (PKB), or National Awakening Party, whose platform focuses on increasing economic opportunity in rural areas and encouraging more involvement of women in strategic sectors across the archipelago. His election to office has been credited in part to the endorsement of Megawati Sukarnoputri, Indonesia's first woman president,[44] daughter of former dictator Sukarno, and a central actor in the overthrow of Indonesia's second dictator, Suharto. Given Ninik's feminist and activist ideals, it is not surprising that she ran under the same banner as Jokowi and was elected to Indonesia's Dewan Perwakilan Rakyat, or the People's Representative Council.

Ninik emphasized in her 2014 interview that Western connections are a slippery signifier when it comes to Indonesian politics. For example, the ability—or lack thereof—to use English to network with the West was used against Jokowi during his first election campaign. Ninik explained:

> Jokowi cannot speak English as well as Probowo [his opponent], so there's been a "black campaign" that says "Can you imagine if Jokowi wants to establish networking with Western countries. How could he do that? Because he can't speak English?" It's a tool that is a bridge, but also symbolizes power and wealth and maybe Jokowi didn't have as much growing up.

Here Ninik reflects on privilege and material access, implicitly acknowledging her own while also pointing to the symbolic capital English holds and the still deep-seated link between English and the West in the global imagination.

Unlike Jokowi, whose ability to govern was questioned because of his inability to network with the West, Ninik was subject to a "black campaign" during the first election *because of* her ties to Western networking. Ninik explained that in one smear campaign, her opponent claimed she wasn't a member of Indonesia's largest Muslim organization—Nahdlatul Ulama (NU): "[My rival] made the black campaign . . . she said I am not truly Nahdlatul Ulama. This is very sensitive because in Banyuwangi we are mostly NU followers . . . . She said it is 'Because Ninik graduated from the United States.' . . . ." Ninik's opponent was able to make such accusations because of the very boundaries cosmopolitanism tries to challenge—namely that religion and nation-state exist in a one-to-one relationship, with, for example, the United States being entirely Christian and Indonesia ultimately Muslim, with little cross-pollination.

To help challenge these arbitrary borders in the minds of her Indonesian audiences, Ninik used storytelling, a process that involved translating her English-medium experiences into Bahasa Indonesia. For example, she explained that she rewrote the narrative conflating religion and nation-state in her public appearances by pointing to how NU is a global organization: "[W]hen I give the public speech to public, they ask me, 'Are you graduated from the US?' and I say, 'Yes. I graduated from the United States. And we had an NU group in Hawaii, not only from US but around the world. We not only meet in person but also on Skype in English.'" Here Ninik works to break down the link between religion and nation-state in the Indonesian public's mind while also challenging the link between language and nation-state by emphasizing that Muslims from "around the world" use English to communicate.

Ninik used a similar story from her sandwich program at Boston University to help her Indonesian audience imagine what interreligious harmony might look like from *within* the same geopolitical space:

> I always told them how during the winter I am praying. How it is difficult to pray in a public space in US. And you know in Boston, in the Commons, there is a big church, St. Paul's church. In the vestment, every Friday, they let Muslims hold Friday prayer, and two times. Because there are many people who want to pray and there's no place (2014 interview).

Just as Ninik tries to erase false borders between nation-state, language, and religion when discussing NU's global identity, through this story she shows her Indonesian audience an example of interreligious harmony and coexistence while also establishing her ethos as a devout, albeit cosmopolitan, Muslim. Storytelling, and the translingual process of translating experience from one language to another, can be a means of rewriting cultural narratives toward synthesis. As she first showcased in her literacy narrative and her op-ed, by moving content from one intended audience to the next across languages, she creates cosmopolitan connections.

CULTIVATING COMMUNICATIVE RECIPROCITY
Cosmopolitan connection, as Ninik emphasizes in her literacy narrative and the cover letter for her op-ed, is also contingent upon

the *audience's* willingness to listen, a theme she returns to as she negotiates communicative difference as a legislator. On her political website, Nihayacenter.net, Ninik uses a story from graduate school to ask her current, presumably Indonesian, public audience to be amenable to linguistic difference. In a post titled "Let's Be Learners," she writes:

Nihaya Center Homepage

> One of my friends, who is from a country where English is the second national language, once asked me, "Ninik, why are you so confident in speaking in public, even though your English is still not perfect?" Even though my friend has good language, he has never dared to speak in public, let alone become a seminar resource. At that time, I answered, "I am a graduate student, if a student has an error in giving presentation material, of course everyone will understand. Yes, it's only natural that the [student] is still in the learning stage, so if you make a mistake it can be accepted, after all, the student is in the learning stage. If you are already a professor, it's a different story, they have to be excellent." So I use this excuse as a weapon hahaha. One more, because English is not my first language and could be my fifth language, so if there are imperfections in the language, the audience will understand. In principle, I don't want to imprison my ideas just because I have to be a perfect person; as long as the audience and readers can understand the message I convey, to me, that's enough.

Article: "Let's Be Learners"

In this passage, Ninik walks her audience through her time as a graduate student into the present, where she argues for the importance of *message* as opposed to linguistic "perfection," which, she implies, "imprisons" true communication. Challenging her initial idea that professors have to be perfect, she later emphasizes, "So basically, in academia, the most important thing is the belief that is embedded in one's attitude to never stop learning, to keep reading and writing, not the problem of *perfection* in expressing or conveying ideas. If what is being pursued is perfection, a professor doesn't have to be 100 percent able to reach the point of perfection." The boundaries drawn between "perfect" English and non-Standard English obstruct communication of the message itself and thus learning from one another.

Noting this theme across our time together, in our 2022 interview, I asked Ninik about it. She first pointed to our interview itself as an example:

> So I think when people want to talk to me, communication is not only about one way. Communication is about two ways. So you listen, and you try to understand. Right now for example, my English is not perfect so you try to understand what I'm thinking, what I'm saying. So I think communication is always two ways. So I think it's like the key is if two people want to communicate, meaning that, both sides have to put in the same way. Put our mind at the table, and OK, if you don't understand, you ask. I try to understand what you say, to understand your idea. I also try. You have to try to also understand my idea.

Communication and cosmopolitan connection is a two-way street, she once again emphasizes. As with her earlier work, Ninik then moves past her argument about *linguistic* difference to focus on real-world power relationships between the humans *with whom* she engages:

> If communication is about power relationships, it's not communication. . . . OK, just put it other side, like leader and staff. Top down. The communication is between two people in the same level so everyone should try to understand. So in communication, we have to trust each other, we have to try to understand each other. There is no power relationships. For example, like in the family. Husband and wife for example, if the communication is powerful and powerless, not on same level, there is no communication.

Connecting
Communi-
cative
Reciprocity
and
Mubadalah

After I pointed out that the way she described marital relationships reminded me of Faqih's concept of mubadalah, she exclaimed, laughing, "Wow: you know about Mubadalah! It really inspire me, mubadalah." Adding to this connection I had made between mubadalah, or Islamic gender-based reciprocity, and her beliefs about communication, Ninik then applied her understanding of power relationships—which began with a discussion of *language itself*—to the relationship between Western scholars and Indonesian research participants:

> Well, actually, this is a criticism for anthropologists also, I hear one of the . . . they said that so many people came here to interview us, to learn, to do research in our place, but after they get the data, they never come back. So what we get? This is not research. This is only to fulfill your research, but this is not giving us the benefit. If you doing research on us, you have to come back to us, share what you get from us, how to make better understanding and better life for us.

Ninik: From Communicative Reciprocity to Research Reciprocity

Though it *is* important for audiences *for whom* texts are addressed to listen past *linguistic* difference, Ninik showcases here her belief that communicative relationships extend past the signifier—the originating language—to encompass the dialogic relationship between real-world communicants *with whom* she engages, whether these relationships are with staff, spouses, or researchers. As she engages in translingual praxis, Ninik challenges the discursive/embodied divide, emphasizing the importance of moving past the text to broader orientations toward knowledge itself when it comes to working toward cosmopolitan connection. It's not just the language, but the connective action, that matters.

CONSTRUCTING BORDERS: STRATEGICALLY CULTIVATING *FOR WHOM* AND *WITH WHOM*

Although much of her work is connective, Ninik also feels compelled to leverage linguistic boundaries given situational power dynamics. As someone in the public eye, Ninik also uses English, a language she has long linked to personal experience, to *construct* discursive borders to protect herself and her gender justice initiatives from potentially hostile Indonesian audiences. In fact, when I asked her whether she was okay with me including these sensitive topics in this English-medium book given her political career, she gave me permission because my audience is English-speaking.

As an example of this type of linguistic boundary work, Ninik also writes fiction, generally in Indonesian, as a means of integrating Indonesian women's stories into public discourse. In her 2014 interview, she explained:

> I am an activist; sometimes people come to me to tell me their stories. And I try to combine with my imagination and the true story and I write the fiction. Because sometimes I have something to tell, but I cannot tell with true story or opinions. I have to tell another way, through poems, stories, fiction to help with privacy.

Here she explains that she draws on generic borders between fiction and nonfiction to protect the women who come to her, which allows her to still convey their stories to public Indonesian audiences while keeping their identities private. Discursive borders—in this case between fiction and nonfiction—can work to promote connections across difference at times.

As an academic and writer, Ninik explained, she initially didn't think twice about publishing stories like these in public Indonesian venues; after all, stories can promote social change. However, once she was elected and became more of a public figure, things changed, particularly since her own religious identity was now under closer scrutiny. Synthesis across competing discourses is not always the best option when it comes to achieving one's social-justice purposes. She explained:

> One of my fictions talks about a lesbian relationship. It will be very controversial in some religious people's minds because I am Muslim. But stories humanize. Because lesbians are my friends, and they say "I love this story!" But sometimes, it will be dangerous. Because I'm connected to well-known pesantren and a politician now . . . . Because of this, I choose to translate my story from Indonesian into English.

Ninik is torn between wanting to humanize her Indonesian friends' relationships and the pressures put on her by her public identity.

To navigate this tension, Ninik chooses to translate her work from Indonesian to English, erecting a rhetorical border. Essentially, Ninik translanguages to exclude certain audiences because power relationships have shifted from one moment to the next; confronted with a new limit-situation, she translates content from one language to another to protect her friends' identities while also still working to break the silence regarding the plight of Indonesian lesbians. In this case, though the content itself works toward inclusion, the language used to convey that message works to exclude some potential audience members. To return to the opening metaphor, the water remains the same, although the linguistic packaging is different.

The need to exclude audiences also became increasingly important during Ninik's second term as she negotiated the political fallout from her divorce. In her 2022 interview, she explained to me how difficult navigating divorce had been as a Muslim woman very much in the public eye, detailing, in turn, how using English has allowed her to still share her experience and to heal from gender-based violence:

> As you know, I have experienced divorce . . . . Experiences of women is very important and sometimes, for me, when I really want to share something with others, I really want to share with English because in English . . . because if I share my experience with the English language, not all people can understand it. So, I think this is for me, is good, in one term, when I write something, this is good for me to share my experience and also good for me for my healing.

Ninik: On English as Protective and Healing

Echoing Kate Vieira's argument that writing can be a means of healing ("Writing"), Ninik explains that English has helped her cultivate a discursive space in which she can connect with others about her experiences. English, with its ability to limit access, helps Ninik to cultivate a safe space to heal from her divorce and to process her experiences with gender-based violence.

Though Ninik is only comfortable sharing her personal experience as a survivor of gender-based violence in English, she still uses the Indonesian language to catalyze public action regarding violence against women—just sans the personal exigency. Again highlighting the link between discursive and material interventions, when I asked her what type of writing she engaged in most often she explained:

> So mostly, for me right now I write about the women's experience. Usually I cannot control my argument when this is about violence against women. Because I got violence. Because I got physical violence. That's why sometimes it's very difficult for me because I was a victim, so that's why when it comes to violence against women, I cannot control myself.[45] (2022 interview)

The need to control her message to stay within the boundaries established by her political party is trumped by her desire to speak out about violence against women. Her exigency may be drawn from personal experience, but this experience is one that others needn't share to *also* speak up, as she argues above; and, importantly, Ninik does not need to make this personal motivation explicit to non-English using audiences to still advocate for gender justice.

Ninik described in her 2022 interview a particular situation she felt compelled to engage with on the national stage:

> Just recently I have a live talk show on TV. This is about a reaction of speech from very famous women artist, well actually, she was actress but she makes more force as a religious leader, religious person, something like this. And she said, actually, woman have to keep her violence, her abuse from her husband. We cannot speak to others. But if we keep this, our husband will be more loving to us. We cannot . . . this is like too bombastic if we say like this to the public. Too bombastic to say to the public. You don't need to speak up to others.

To challenge this woman's argument that survivors of violence should keep it secret, Ninik turned to Faqih's and Nur Rofia's research and the actions of the Prophet Muhammad himself. She continued, explaining:

Actually, I read this from Faqih's writing and also from Nur Rofia's writing, and some other people writing, some people writing. I said, "actually Prophet Muhammad never accept the men who doing the violence." And the first time I said that, "There is a group of women who come to the prophet Muhammad and said, 'There is still men who doing violence to the women.'" And Nabiyyin[46] said, "The person . . . the men who are doing the violence to woman, this person is not of elected men, this person not good man, something like that." And Nabiyyin, Mohammad, never said, "You cannot talk to me about this." Muhammad never said like that. And then another story. One of women come to Nabiyyin—"Nabiyyin, I got marriage proposal from this person, this person, this person." Nabih said, "This person a person, don't have enough money. The second person, he not good alternative because he is often doing the violence. You cannot choose. You have to choose the third person." So Nabiyyin not allow the women to marry with that.

Ninik Encourages Women to Report Domestic Violence

Here Ninik highlights how Faqih's research has inspired her when it comes to her personal life, and she also draws together her commitment to gender justice and her religious faith to challenge the silencing of victims of violence. Notably, in this recounting of her response to the celebrity—which was in Indonesian—she does not mention her personal experiences with violence. She reserves English for that purpose. Boundaries are sometimes necessary.

During Ramadan in 2022, Ninik also used her platform as a legislator to advocate for gender justice on national TV in a series titled "Perempuan seperti halnya laki-laki adalah khalifah di muka bumi," or "Women, like men, are caretakers of the earth." In keeping with her belief that audiences (like me) bear equal responsibility for communication, Ninik sent me both the link to her video series and the Indonesian-medium transcript of her video, which I, as audience member, then worked to translate into English using online translation tools. In this nationally televised address, which Ninik performs in a mellifluous oratorical style nearly impossible

Caretakers of the Earth Ramadan Video

to describe in text, she makes an impassioned argument that Islam positions both women and men equally as *khalifah*, or caretakers of the earth, with equal responsibility for each other. Directly addressing her viewers, she then asserts the following:

> Viewers, we must ensure that all of our spaces are free from violence. All spaces must provide benefits for all humanity; therefore, women and men must cooperate with each other, hand in hand, in calling for goodness. It is stated in Surah At-Taubah verse 71 that men and women, as Khalifah fil ardhi (keepers of the earth), must cooperate to voice good deeds, to pray, to stay away from evil, and to stay away from sinful acts, so that all people in the world can achieve benefits.

Later in the video, she then builds from this argument, which emphasizes mubadalah, or reciprocal care, to focus specifically on bodily ownership in relation to Tawhid, or the oneness of Allah:

> The Oneness implied by monotheism shows that men and women have no differences; both are servants of Allah. The body does not belong to us, the woman's body is not the property of men, the woman's body does not belong to men, our bodies belong to Allah SWT. Therefore, both men and women must use their bodies in a proper and lawful way, in a way that is good and supports the oneness of monotheism.

The human body, regardless of sex, belongs to Allah; to ensure the promise of monotheism, men must be aware that women's bodies do not belong to them but rather to Allah himself, which positions women's bodies as sacred and sacrosanct. And finally, toward the end of the video, Ninik moves from her religiously based argument against sexual violence to discuss her own Indonesian context:

> We often see many acts of domestic violence happening in Indonesia and around the world. Reports of acts of violence that occur often collide with various feelings, including doubts about acts of violence, which are often misunderstood as disgrace. Violence and shame are two different things. Disgrace is something that does not harm the body, does

not threaten the health of the body, and does not threaten a person's life. Meanwhile, violence is something that can damage oneself and can even threaten life. Therefore, if someone experiences an act of violence, it is mandatory to report it to the authorities.

By making this powerful distinction between violence and the shame caused by people doubting women's stories, Ninik emphasizes that there is a distinction to be made between feelings and material harm—that, in fact, there *is* a border that must be drawn between the fear of disgrace and the fear of physical violence in order to ensure women's bodies are safe. Echoing her critique of the woman who argued that wives should remain silent about their abuse, Ninik once again emphasizes in this video series the importance of reporting sexual violence to authorities.

This type of political advocacy—which may in part spring from her personal experience, but which Ninik chooses to keep in the religious realm when using Bahasa Indonesia—has just resulted in a major legislative move toward gender justice. In 2016, Ninik was a cosponsor of the Bill on the Elimination of Sexual Violence, which passed on Tuesday, April 12, 2022, after six years of deliberation. The law mandates fifteen-year prison sentences for sexual exploitation, four years for circulating nonconsensual sexual content, and nine years for forced marriage, including child marriage. It also requires both marital and extramarital abusers to serve up to twelve years in prison. Abusers must pay restitution to survivors, and the law stipulates that counseling also be made available for victims.

Explainer: Indonesian Bill on the Elimination of Sexual Violence

As Ninik's political website, Nihaya Center, showcases, Ninik has long used her rhetorical abilities—and research conducted across multiple languages—to advocate for many aspects of this bill, from the elimination of child marriage (which she links to maternal health, a topic she has long been interested in, as her op-d indicates), to the ending of workplace violence against women, to what constitutes sexual violence and what brought about the need for a bill in the first place—what she terms a "vortex of sexual violence in Indonesia." Notably absent from her Indonesian-medium political posts is any written mention of her *own experience* with violence.

Article: Triggering Maternal Deaths

Article: Stop Sexual Violence Against Women Workers

As she mentions in her interview, she uses *English* for that type of advocacy and self-reflection and as a means of protecting herself and healing. This self-protective linguistic boundary, however, does not preclude her advocacy work in Indonesian: the *content* may differ depending on language and audience, but the *action* can be the same. Once again, Ninik showcases that even if packaged differently, the water itself is in essence the same.

CONCLUSIONS

From her portfolio, we can see that Ninik's cosmopolitanism is an *orientation* toward knowledge that includes language itself but that also exceeds it. Just as we must locate translingual praxis both in text and in process, we must also trace how actors move knowledge and resources from one moment to the next to get a fuller picture of what cosmopolitan action might look like as power shifts around them. In some contexts, especially in the moments when Ninik uses English to reach local Indonesian audiences, she does challenge dominant ideology that has long positioned English as a Western language. She shows how English can serve local Indonesian English-using audiences, and, in turn, how English-using audiences can consist of folks from different nation-states even if they're reading from within the same geographical space—a reality that requires careful maneuvering on the writer's part, and, just as important, a willingness to listen on the audience's part. In this case, the English language itself *is* cosmopolitan.

In other contexts, however, Ninik doesn't necessarily redraw traditional borders when it comes to language itself: in her advanced academic literacy, she uses English to convey her Islamic knowledge to Western audiences, and, likewise, in her political life she uses Bahasa Indonesia to convey her stories about the United States to Indonesian audiences. These moves reaffirm, rather than challenge, traditional links between language and nation-state. In this context, it is the *content* she translates that matters when it comes to cultivating cosmopolitan connection between the voices in her repertoire and her intended audiences rather than the languages from which she draws this knowledge or in which she conveys that knowledge.

When looking at Ninik's activist work, it also becomes clear that her cosmopolitan orientation goes beyond moving knowledge across geopolitical borders and the language traditions linked to them; though Ninik does attribute her networking ability to cosmopolitan experiences made possible through English, we must look past a model that positions the English language itself as the sole impetus of her cosmopolitanism. The metaphor with which this chapter began, in which Ninik describes her religious orientation in relation to the sacred mountain to argue for a shared human "essence," could be considered cosmopolitan, pointing to how her religion informs her translingual border work. As further testament to the ways Ninik's cosmopolitanism exists in excess of the English language, we can look to the ways she transfers this orientation to contexts where she uses Bahasa Indonesia to reach other Indonesians: for example, with the feminist NGO where she works to empower female legislators so they can insert themselves more fully into the Indonesian governmental conversation and, later, as a politician straddling both the activist and the governmental realms within her home country. Cosmopolitan engagement, Ninik's portfolio shows, can be found in overt textual moves that challenge traditional divides related to language and audience, or in process, as actors transfer knowledge across existing international and intranational borders. In the case of the latter, it's not the language itself but the overall *orientation* toward humanity that evidences cosmopolitanism.

Working toward shared humanity in this way necessarily involves navigating existing power relationships. As just established, in some contexts Ninik was able to leverage her translingual resources to work toward *inclusion* and cultural synthesis, transcending existing borders, whether discursive or material. When Ninik's choices are traced over a period of time, however, we can also see how *exclusion* mediates her translingual rhetorical choices—both because of material inequality linked to unequal access and as a deliberate rhetorical choice on Ninik's part. When it comes to the involuntary exclusion related to material access, Ninik *was* able to leverage her cosmopolitan experiences to move literate resources from more affluent educational contexts to Indonesia, but issues of access still impede full and equal participation between global audiences, thus limiting true cosmopolitan synthesis. As Nina's portrait details at length, borders both linguistic and economic do still exist and impede true cross-cultural understanding. When it comes to understanding exclusion in relation to Ninik's rhetorical choices, this chapter shows that as an academic, Ninik found that the information divide between Indonesia and Western audiences actually created an affordance for her own research interests—a divide she clearly valued and in fact used to construct her cosmopolitan academic identity. As a politician, in turn, Ninik found it necessary to use English—and the linguistic divide it affords—to exclude conservative religious audiences so that she might work to connect the stories of Indonesian lesbians to broader feminist conversations. English, which Ninik associates with healing, also allows her to create a protective border while still articulating her personal experience with gender violence.

When understood in isolation from the rest of Ninik's portrait, these exclusionary moments might seem to challenge the central tenet of cosmopolitanism: working toward synthesis and mutual understanding. However, when viewed from a spatiotemporal perspective—and in relation to both the texts she creates *and* the processes she uses to transfer knowledge over the course of time— we can see that these moments of exclusion do not preclude her making different, more inclusive choices in the future. As Freire suggests, full "humanity" is constantly in the making: "Once named, the world in its turn reappears to the namers as a problem and requires of them a new naming" (*Pedagogy of the Oppressed* 88). The way Ninik engages "in word, in work, in action-reflection" (88) is dependent upon what limit-situations she encounters at any given moment, and the process is undoubtedly both continuous and translingual. To return to the opening metaphor, what connects these moments is her belief—drawn from her Islamic faith—that, though difference and power exist, underneath it all we are of the same essence. This belief flows, like water, into and out of each moment, interanimating how Ninik uses language to rewrite the world toward a more just and shared humanity.

CONCLUSIONS: LOOKING BACK TO LOOK FORWARD

SERVING, ACCESSING, CULTIVATING. These English verbs seek to describe the complex processes by which the scholarly-activists showcased here seek to bend the world toward gender justice from within an Islamic framework using the many discourses—and languages—at their disposal. By asking *for whom* each writer intends their text, *from whom* they draw their knowledge, and *with whom* they seek to circulate their knowledge on the material plane, I am able to illuminate both situational power dynamics *and* the translingual ingenuity of my research participants when faced with inequality, whether economic, religious, gender-based, or linguistic. Understanding the dynamic interplay between power and possibility in global language users' lives is central to distinguishing what I define as translingual praxis—which requires human intention, critical reflection, and often (though not always) embodied action—from translingual agency, which could just be called "agency" because it is, in fact, how language works.

Focusing on human intention when faced with inequality—on the "hands of God at work," to cite Faqih—seems necessary when seeking to dismantle systems linked to the colonial matrix of power that, though often unquestioned, were and are constructed by humans. It is my hope that by exploring the different ways Faqih, Nina, and Ninik engage in translingual praxis, this ethnographic story suggests a relational, rather than static, understanding of translinguality. From a border-thinking perspective, we need to simultaneously acknowledge that borders between discourses do have impact on the experiences of language users even if they are socially constructed, but we also need to acknowledge that these seemingly immutable borders overlap and can mutually transform how we understand the world, "in word, in work, in action-reflection," as Paulo Freire says (*Pedagogy of the Oppressed* 88).

Though ultimately, to cite Faqih, "It's up to you" what you, my own audience, take from this text, here are the contributions I see this ethnographic story making to the spiral of interpretation that preceded and I hope proceeds from this moment, organized by the heuristic with which I shaped my interpretation.

FOR WHOM?

Many studies and pedagogies that focus on audience negotiation emphasize *for whom* writers seem to be writing with their textual moves, or, when it comes to pedagogy, how students should reach particular audiences in their written texts. The question of *for whom*, though it did not stand alone, was central to this book project. As discussed in Chapter 5, during a faculty workshop at ICRS an Indonesian faculty member asked me, "But to whom do we have students write?"—a question that emphasizes how complicated audience negotiation can be as writers compose texts in local-global English-medium academic contexts like ICRS. Should the Indonesian writers at ICRS—many of whom had local motivations for getting an advanced degree in interreligious studies—address their English texts to local Indonesian audiences? To Western audiences because they're writing in English? What of those moments when seemingly discrete audiences mix and meld? As Xiaoye You argues in *Cosmopolitan English*, we can no longer assume a monolithic, geographically bounded audience for English texts.

Not surprisingly, the intended audiences whom the Indonesian writers showcased here imagined reading their texts affected the way they performed translingual praxis. Because of the local yet global identity of ICRS, the pedagogy I developed there took seriously Suresh Canagarajah's argument, drawn from the scholarly practices of Sri Lankan scholar Dr. Sivatamby, that a non-Western scholar's local audience might prompt him to completely delink English from Western genre norms: "language," Canagarajah shows, "doesn't determine the greatest difference in the texts of multilingual authors, but rather context or audience" ("Toward" 601). As Chapter 5 explores, this claim did not play out exactly as planned in the classroom; after examining my data, it became apparent how important it is to locate translanguaging both in text and in process. Though, as Zhaozhe Wang argues, texts can be seen as the "material condition where a translingual/transdisciplinary rhetoric can be operationalized" (4), the knowledge-making practices of my research participants, which transcend the bounded classroom and established academic disciplinary borders, suggest that moving past isolated texts to examine the processes that precede and proceed from writers' texts is central to understanding translingual praxis.

FROM WHOM?

In turn, asking from whom a writer draws knowledge helps illuminate the voices in their citational repertoire that precede and interanimate moments of translingual praxis. This question was central to locating translanguaging in process, to illuminating how the writers with whom I worked drew from subjugated knowledge to inform their texts, and to emphasizing inequality related to material access to published resources.

When it comes to process, asking "From whom?" of my research participants' rhetorical practices highlighted the important part translation of their multivocal repertoires played in the processes preceding moments of translingual praxis. Translation, when read in relation to the audiences my research participants imagined, can be a means of building bridges between disparate audiences across existing language divides, or, in some cases, of deliberately excluding audiences, depending on power relationships, to achieve their social-justice goals. The translation process is never a "friction-free, mechanical transfer of meaning from one language to another" (Horner and Tetreault 19) but rather involves negotiating sometimes competing discourses and their attendant values in relation to audience and situational power dynamics. As Rebecca Lorimer Leonard and Xiqiao Wang emphasize, the translation processes of my research participants signal both "fixed and frictive moments" (Lorimer Leonard 11) as they negotiated the many voices from whom they might draw to engage in translingual praxis.

Moving away from the neoliberal notion that translation is a neutral process of transmitting discrete pieces of information (see Horner and Tetrault), and asking "From whom?" of my research participants' work is also a way to move past a purely linguistic understanding of translation to instead explore how *values* might transcend the language traditions with which they're traditionally associated. As Laura Gonzales asserts in *Sites of Translation*, "Just as, due to constantly shifting rhetorical practices, translation is not culturally neutral, (effective) translation is also never a 'once and done' event. Translation processes are far from linear and involve multiple instances of negotiation and localization" (59). To understand the complex translational negotiations of my research participants required understanding how values themselves transcend originating language. My research participants' orientations toward knowledge itself—the ways they conceptualize and perform "feminist agency" in their own scholarly research, for example—often mirrors the ways they discuss their negotiations when it comes to language and power, suggesting that linguistic orientations can be linked to broader value systems that surface in their knowledge-making *processes*. As James Paul Gee emphasizes, discourses—which again represent both linguistic markers *and* the attendant values—inevitably overlap in a writer's repertoire. If indeed languages overlap and mutually transform one another in a writer's repertoire, so too do the attendant *values*, which both precede and transcend the languages with which a writer negotiates. As Li Wei argues in "Translanguaging as a Practical Theory of Language," "Human beings think beyond language . . . . We do not think in Arabic, Chinese, English, Russian, or Spanish; we think beyond the artificial boundaries of named languages in the language-of-thought" (19). Exploring values embedded in the content of writers' citational repertoires—or the voices that precede them—can help illuminate broader value systems that shape their linguistic orientations.

Furthermore, to return to the dialogic border-thinking theory that interanimates this text, understanding linguistic negotiations linked to moments of translingual praxis as interanimated by value systems that precede the texts writers compose is central to illuminating interrelation, rather than division, when it comes to epistemologies that are not often coupled in Western academic scholarship. The scholarly-activist work of the writers showcased here is deeply informed by their Islamic identities *and* by the Islamic gender justice scholarship of writers like Lila Abu-Lughod, amina wadud, Nur Rofia, and others who seek to challenge Western depictions of Muslim women, but their work is *also* informed by feminist theorists, philosophers, and theologians linked to Western academic discourse. Just as importantly, my research participants' translingual praxis is interanimated by the voices of those women in their Indonesian communities from whom they simultaneously draw their scholarly data and their motivations for grounded social justice. The stories of the writers with whom I work—and *their* stories of Indonesian women's experiences—emphasize the feminist belief that, as Cheryl Glenn articulates, "experience is a source of epistemic knowledge, as are emotions, both of them freighted with ethos and pathos, with the politicized internalized" (43). Illuminating the personal stories that precede and thus are audience to moments of translingual praxis is central to the work of my research participants, as well as to the work of moving toward what Walter Mignolo terms a body-politics of knowledge-making.

Asking "From whom?" in turn should involve more than an exploration of discursive negotiation. Asking "From whom?" also makes evident absence. Lack of material access to previously published texts mediates the possibilities my research participants see for their scholarly work to inform global academic audiences. Nina and Ninik repeatedly emphasize their lack of access to English-medium resources in Indonesia, whether it's the reliable internet necessary to get these resources or access to newly published scholarly work. As Theresa Lillis and Mary Jane Curry, Canagarajah, and Anne-Marie Pedersen have shown, despite the cosmopolitan possibilities English represents for truly inclusive global conversations, economic inequality denies scholars in developing country contexts equal access to English-medium academic resources, an issue made more pressing for my research participants, as Chapter 4 explores, because of a governmental requirement that they publish in internationally indexed journals, most of which are in English. Despite unequal access, by focusing on the "how" of translingual praxis, we can see the ways ICRS as an institution and my research participants leverage their own relative privilege to increase access to information for other Indonesians, while establishing, in turn, the means for us *all* to better connect across differences with the scholarly stories we tell.

WITH WHOM?

I emphasize *all* in the previous sentence because the labor these Indonesian scholars are doing to build these bridges, whether discursive or material, should be a collaborative endeavor. From a decolonial, feminist, *and* translingual perspective, we are all mutually responsible for transforming "power-over" relationships into "power-with" relationships (Starhawk 10*)*. Asking "With whom" writers see their work circulating gets at the responsibility audiences have for creating the connections necessary for mutual transformation on both the discursive and the material planes.

On the discursive plane, asking "With whom?" highlights the mutually transformative possibilities that moments of translingual praxis create. My research participants use various rhetorical techniques, depending on situational power dynamics, that point to their explicit awareness of audience receptivity when it comes to their translingual choices, opening up some important questions for the audiences who receive these texts—among them, us—to consider. With whom—writer or audience—does responsibility for interpretation fall, and how does this conceptualization affect translingual praxis? How can writers from a nondominant background engage in translanguaging to craft rhetorical situations in which potentially hostile audiences are receptive to their scholarship? What rhetorical techniques can writers employ to remind their readers of this mutual responsibility for communication and transformation? Throughout their portfolios, my research participants show an awareness that meaning-making is, or should be, *coconstructed* with one's audience, as scholars who study global literacies, like LuMing Mao in *Reading Chinese Fortune Cookie* and Xiaoye You in *Cosmopolitan English*; translingual theorists, like Canagarajah and Horner, Samantha NeCamp, and Christiane Donahue; and feminists like Krista Ratcliffe in *Rhetorical Listening* and Cheryl Glenn in *Rhetorical Feminisms* assert. In Victor Villanueva's words, speaking is not the same thing as being *heard* (837). For translingual praxis as I define it to be an effective tool for challenging inequality, both writer *and* audience need to critically reflect on situational power dynamics to communicate across difference.

Although audience receptivity when it comes to textual difference is a central part of asking "With whom?" the social-justice work of my research participants also suggests how important it is to move past isolated texts to focus on what their knowledge *does*. Indeed, though the writers showcased in this book may present different answers when it comes to how they conceptualize audience in global communicative contexts, they are united in their belief that writing—both the process and the product—can lead to social justice, a shared belief that they all three attribute to their intersecting religious, feminist, and scholarly identities. The way I have defined translingual praxis, I argue here, helps illuminate the intersections between the discursive and the material in my research participants' lives. The translanguaging that happens as writers move between the discursive and the material planes in turn challenges the mind/body duality long propagated by the colonial matrix of power.

We must also address the work of the very text you just read. Asking "With whom?" of my own research encouraged me to reflect on my own privilege and how to craft a more reciprocal, rather than unidirectional, relationship between my scholarship and that of my research participants. Throughout this text, I've woven in via digital means the real voices and the living projects of my research participants, which I hope helps paint a more three-dimensional picture of how our work is interconnected, despite power differences.

And, finally, though it is clear that each of these case-study chapters focuses on language, by asking "From whom?" "For whom?" and "With whom?" I also hope to emphasize that moving toward the translingual ideal is about more than *linguistic* justice and an openness to *linguistic* difference. Being receptive to language difference involves understanding from where linguistic difference comes and the discourses and attendant values that are linked to this difference; it involves understanding for whom writers intend their words, as we often make assumptions about intended audience through the lens of longstanding, problematic power relationships that assume a direct correlation between geographical location, language, and audience; and it involves understanding our own responsibility, as audience members, to truly listen, whether we are the target audience or not. It is true that such receptivity will open up space for more linguistically diverse *texts* to enter our global conversations, but more importantly, to my mind, it will open up space for *knowledge* long positioned as exterior by the colonial matrix of power to circulate in more reciprocal and mutually transformative ways. As Ninik so eloquently reminds us, "Social justice is not about language; it's about humanity."

2010 Interview Questions (approved by University of Massachusetts Amherst IRB)

Language Histories and Motivations

1. Why did you apply to a PhD religious studies program?
2. Why did you apply to one that's entirely conducted in English?
3. What are your motivations for writing about religion in English?
4. How long have you been writing in English? For what purposes?
5. What other languages do you write in? For what purposes?

Audience Questions

6. What audience do you imagine most often when you write in English? Why?
7. What audience would you like to reach that you haven't already?
8. What tensions do you feel when making decisions about whom to write to?
9. What identity shifts do you feel when writing to new audiences?
10. Have you been published before? Can you talk about that? How much of this was in English versus Indonesian? Can you compare the different writing styles to different audiences?

Discourse-Based Questions (of Portfolio from Academic Writing Class)

11. Which essay has been most difficult for you to write? Why?
12. Overall, what parts of this text do you find most successful?

13. Could you point to these places? Why are these parts successful, in your opinion?
14. What challenges did you have when creating this text?
15. Could you point to places where you had difficulty? What factors do you think contributed to your difficulty?
16. What cultural factors, if any, do you think affected your writing process or your final essay?
17. Is there anything else you would like to add?

2014 Interview Questions (approved by University of Denver IRB)

Updating Students' Understandings of English/Language Histories

1. When we talked four years ago, you explained to me [beliefs about English's imperialism]. Have your opinions changed any as you've progressed in your graduate program? And if so, how?
2. You've just studied abroad for a semester at _____ University.

   • What was your goal in choosing this institution for your sandwich program?
   • What did you learn, and how will this contribute to your work here in Indonesia?
   • How has it been transitioning back to Indonesia and ICRS?

Current Dissertation Research

3. What's your dissertation about?
4. What motivated you to study _____?
5. What contribution do you hope your dissertation makes to larger conversations about religion?
6. What audiences do you hope to reach?
7. Could you talk about some of the writing challenges and successes you've faced as you write your dissertation?

Circulation of Knowledge

8. How have you spread the knowledge you've accessed in your graduate studies so far?

   - What audiences have you reached? And how?
   - What languages did you use to reach these audiences?

9. I've read on the graduate school's website that graduate students are now required to publish in English to receive their PhDs. Before we discuss this, I just want to be careful about how you answer, as I don't want to get you in trouble with the graduate school. Are you okay discussing this? If so . . .

   - What kinds of conversations have you heard circulating about this new rule?
   - What challenges, if any, do you think this requirement poses for students working from within Indonesia?
   - What kinds of support do students receive to help them get published in English? What might be useful?
   - We've talked in the past about your past work with [activist organization]. Could you talk about why this organization was started? Does getting published through this organization fulfill the English requirement?

Religious Identity and English Writing

10. We've discussed before your close connection to your Muslim community here in Indonesia. How do you think the Indonesian public perceives you, as a Muslim, English-using religious studies scholar?

11. You mentioned in your last interview that one of the reasons you chose to get a doctorate was to help your local community. Does your religion motivate you to be interested in such social justice? If so, how?

12. In your last interview, you mentioned [question about specific social justice initiative].

   - Do you still think the knowledge you get when studying English can help further social justice for Indonesians?

- Can the knowledge you access in English help [group that exceeds Indonesian nation-state] as well?

13. How do you plan to use your degree after you graduate?
14. Is there anything else you think important to add?

2023 Interview Questions (approved by Massachusetts College of Liberal Arts IRB)

Updating Beliefs about English

1. As you know, I'm interested in your interpretation of English's role when it comes to global communication. Have your beliefs about English shifted any since 2014, when you told me "[excerpt from previous interview]"?
   - If so, why?

Tracing Knowledge Circulation

Context: As you know, I'm interested in how writers mesh English and the knowledge it conveys with other languages and knowledge traditions to make *new* meaning for different local and global audiences. The following questions will help me understand how you perceive this type of movement among language, knowledge, and audience. I'll start with questions pertaining to what kinds of writing you do for what audiences, and then we'll discuss translation.

2. What kind of writing do you do most often since we last talked? I'm thinking about "writing" quite broadly, from social-media posts, to academic writing, to workplace writing, to speech writing.

   - And in what languages?
   - And for what audiences?

3. How often do you use the English language itself in your work as an Indonesian professor/activist/politician?
   - Could you give me some examples of the types of English texts you write?
   - Could you give me some examples of when you might speak English?

- Could you give me some examples of the types of English texts you read?

4. How often do you use *knowledge* that you first read in an English source—but not English itself—in your work as an Indonesian professor/activist/politician?

  - Could you give me an example of a time when you translated *knowledge* from an English source into Indonesian, Javanese, or Arabic, for example? To reach a new audience?

5. Could you give me an example of when you have translated *knowledge* from sources that use Bahasa Indonesia, Javanese, or Arabic into English? To reach a new audience?

6. Do you ever find yourself mixing English into your non-English texts, or vice versa?

  - For what audiences are you most likely to mix different languages?
  - What effect do you think this has on your intended audience?

7. Anything else?

Defining Islamic Feminism

8. What circumstances led you to become an advocate for gender justice?

9. Do you consider yourself an "Islamic feminist"? This is obviously an English term; is there a term in Indonesian, or Javanese or Arabic that might be more appropriate to describing how you identify?

  - How would you define Islamic feminism/other term you prefer for a non-Muslim, Western audience (like me)?
  - How would you define Islamic feminism/other term you prefer for an Islamic Indonesian audience who may be unfamiliar with the term?

10. Could you describe your most recent contribution to gender justice?

11. You draw from Western knowledge in your academic work (for example, [names of authors]). Some might argue this implicates you in Orientalism and/or Western imperialism. What are your thoughts about the role Western thought plays in your own understandings of Indonesian religion and Islamic feminism?

12. In your scholarly work, you define feminist agency as "[cite dissertations]"? Do you think there are parallels between how you define feminist agency and how you understand your own linguistic agency when it comes to negotiating English norms?

13. Anything else?

Mapping Relationship among Religion, Academic Scholarship, and Activism

Context: The last set of questions has to do with looking at how religion, academic scholarship, and activism intersect in your life.

14. First, I'd like to talk about the intersections between your faith and your academic work. As you likely know, in the United States we assume that there is a clear divide between religion and academic knowledge: that religion is the opposite of scholarly, rational thought, which I, of course, don't think is true. Decolonial scholars have argued that this divide has been used to silence non-Western ways of understanding the world—of silencing Muslims, for example— and that by breaking down this boundary between religion and scholarly thought we might create new and more just ways of understanding the world. Have you considered whether your own scholarship could be considered "decolonial" in this way?

    • If so, how do you think your scholarly work, which I think does confirm that religion and scholarship can coexist, might help foster more ethical ways of understanding the world?

Context: Now let's talk about religion, scholarship, and some global organizations I know you're affiliated with: [names of organizations].

15. Could you tell me a bit about the [activist organizations] or initiatives you've been a part of since 2014? What are their goals? What were your motivations for taking part?
16. Does your activist organization have global partners? If so, could you describe their role in your organization? Has your organization's ties to non-Indonesian partners ever made others in Indonesia or elsewhere question your motivations?
17. How has your scholarly work informed your community activism since we last talked, if at all?

   • If it has, are there any theorists or theories that you continue to draw from as inspiration? Why? How?

18. How, in turn, does your Islamic faith inform your community activism, if at all?

   • If it does, are there any passages from the Qur'an/ Hadith or a religious leader that you regularly draw from for inspiration? Why? How?

19. Anything else?

NOTES

1. The opinions, findings, and conclusions stated in this book are those of the author and do not necessarily reflect those of the United States Department of State.
2. Although the "West" is, of course, a slippery social construct, I choose to use it rather than Global North/Global South or center/periphery terminology because "the West" was the term most often used by my Indonesian research participants to describe Anglo hegemony.
3. Ramadan fast-breaking.
4. Race, of course, is a construct. The fact that Nina is brown within an Indonesian context is inconsequential; however, when read from within the colonial matrix of power, which created the notion of white/nonwhite to justify oppression, her race does matter, and that's why I mention it here.
5. My purpose here is not to offer a genealogical or full-fledged exploration of the nuanced and ever-evolving field of decolonial studies but rather to highlight *specific* theories within the field that helped me, after I had collected and coded my data, to reflect upon initial blind spots.
6. Because of space restrictions, my explanation here is necessarily a brief overview of the complex historical movements that led to and from this epistemic shift. As Mignolo's "Delinking" shows, the movement from theo-logical to ego-logical played out differently in different locales at different times, depending on geopolitical specificities. For a detailed genealogy of this shift from the "theo" to the "ego," or what she calls "Man 1" to "Man 2" (269), see Sylvia Wynter's "Unsettling the Coloniality of Being/Power/Truth/Freedom: Towards the Human, After Man, Its Overrepresentation—An Argument."
7. The belief that Islam is simultaneously "irrational" and that it subsumes all other ways of knowing has been promulgated by

theories such as Peter Berger's metaphor of a "sacred canopy,"
which positions religion as static and all-encompassing and
reaffirms the rational/religious divide long used to dismiss non-
Western knowledge-making and the role that Islam plays in
knowledge-production.

8. For a look at the intersections of race and religion in the settler-
colonial context of the Americas, see Iris D. Ruiz's chapter "Race"
in *Decolonizing Rhetoric and Composition Studies*.

9. See also Judith Butler, *Bodies That Matter*; Alastair Pennycook,
Global Englishes.

10. Since I actively avoid the type of neutral, text-based analysis Gee
ascribes to "little d" discourse and wish to instead view all language
acts in relation to "big D" Discourse from now on, I will use a
lower-case "d" to refer to the recursive language-value relationship.

11. See also Karl Jaspers's *Philosophy of Existence* and Anthony
Petruzzi's "Between Conventions and Critical Thinking."

12. Rachael Shapiro's and Missy Watson's article "Translingual
Praxis: From Theorizing Language to Antiracist and Decolonial
Pedagogy" was published just as this book was about to go into
production and thus did not inform the work here. However, the
critical orientation to language they develop for the classroom, and
their argument that translingual pedagogists must focus on both
"practices and processes" *and* larger systemic oppression explicitly
and in tandem, aligns with what is presented here. One caveat:
as Chapter 5 explores, my research participants seemed to come
to the critical pedagogy I developed in 2009 *already* performing
translingual praxis, perhaps because of their already quite
translingual Indonesian context and the critical engagement with
power required of them as thinkers forced to confront English's
imperialism in a geopolitical space where English is not the de
facto norm.

13. My research was separate from my ELF duties and was in no way
sponsored by the United States Department of State, though my
position did implicate me in the very Western imperialism ICRS
points to.

14. This recursive consent process actually extended past the official
documents, especially for Ninik, who chose to share that she
is a survivor of gender-based violence. Given the duration of
time from her actual interview in 2022 and this manuscript's
going into production, I wanted to make sure she still felt
safe sharing her story, so I checked in with her separately via

WhatsApp with various options for revising the chapter if she did not feel comfortable sharing. She consented again, with slight modifications.

15. It is important to note that from 1602 to 1800, Indonesia was also a lucrative outpost of the Dutch East Indies company (VOC), which, because of its purely extractive aims, "ruled" Indonesia indirectly through already established Indonesian rulers. When the VOC went bankrupt and its assets were taken over by the Dutch government in 1800, however, the relationship between colonizer and colonized was reimagined. Tania Murray Li argues that "as Dutch emphasis on regulation, enumeration, and bureaucratic compliance increased, so did the range of fronts upon which [Indonesian] rulers were found deficient (17)," a constructed deficiency which in turn reimagined the relationship between ruler and ruled in more hierarchical, paternalistic, and oppressive terms.

16. As a testament to the difficulty of isolating discrete languages, Subhan Zein puts the count at over seven hundred languages, spoken by over six hundred different ethnicities.

17. Mark Woodward suggests that the Dutch chose Malay over Javanese—despite Java's importance to the colonial enterprise— because of the hierarchical nature of Javanese, which involves navigating multiple registers (my students explained that it's more like three different languages) depending on to whom one is talking. If colonial officials were to speak to Indonesian rulers in the honorific register, it would imply equal power positions; if they were to speak to Indonesian rulers in the register reserved for inferiors, it would make their true sentiments toward local rulers quite explicit, undermining relationships important in maintaining local acquiescence to colonial rule (23).

18. Tania Murray Li argues convincingly that these failures were due to remaining colonial structures and the persistent discourse of "improvement" that encouraged paternalistic and authoritarian intervention by the government for the people's own good. She cites Daniel Lev, who writes that "the independent state was not merely similar to the colonial state. It was the same state" (cited in Li 51).

19. It is important to note—and as case studies of my students will show—that although Bahasa Indonesia is the only official language, provisions were also made in the constitution to preserve the islands' rich linguistic diversity. Children are taught in their home languages for several years before Bahasa Indonesia

is introduced, and, during the rest of their education, classes in local languages are offered "where teaching materials and qualified teachers are available" (71). Governmental mandates for the preservation of local languages as well as the national language, Peter Lowenberg argues, encouraged the language's success while also assuring that the majority of Indonesians are multilingual (71).

20. Although important to ICRS's history, due to space limitations, I will not outline CRCS's history in detail. In brief, CRCS, founded in 2000, is the MA counterpart to ICRS, from which many of ICRS's faculty, policies, and structures were adopted.

21. As I discuss in "Writing the Local-Global," all Indonesian undergraduates must also pass the TOEFL with a score of 450 to earn their BAs, and at ICRS, the requirement is 550.

22. Globethics.net has since developed the Globethics.net Academy, which in addition to its open-source library works to provide courses in ethics for institutions across the globe. It has just been accredited by the European Agency for Higher Education and Accreditation (EAHEA) (*Ethics*).

23. English for Specific Purposes is an umbrella term for genre-based ways of teaching nonnative speakers of English. Some examples: English for Academic Purposes (EAP), English for Occupational Purposes (EOP), and English for Medical Purposes (EMP).

24. Genres I taught included texts they would be asked to write as graduate students, such as the response paper, the literature review, and the research proposal; genres that would allow them to spread their knowledge to a wider academic audience, such as the research article and the conference paper; and, given students' interest in social justice, genres that would help them reach the Indonesian public, such as the opinion piece.

25. As the most populated and powerful of Indonesia's seventeen thousand or so islands, Java was perceived by most students as having a culture distinct from the broader, more diverse national "culture" implied by Indonesia as a nation-state.

26. Given its focus on extratextual and in-process negotiation, this chapter mainly discusses the processes prior to students' final textual products; a more thorough analysis of specific students' portfolios will happen in Chapters 6 to 8.

27. My teacher's journal notes that it was an Islamic holiday that day, which accounted for the fact that four students were absent.

28. This student-generated list, as we can see, ignores the fact that audience might comprise a mixed group of people, something the initial reflective writing activity in this unit tried to address by asking them "Which country *or countries* [might your audience] come from?" Students' rather monolithic understanding of audience could be indicative of their positionalities as novice academics exploring the concept of audience for the first time; since few had taken courses explicitly devoted to writing and rhetoric—either in English or in their home languages—it was probably easier for them to imagine a monolithic audience for the time being.

29. Faqih spells this term in two different ways, depending on what language he is translating the Arabic to. In Bahasa Indonesia, he includes an "h" at the end, whereas in English he ends with the final "a." As I was first introduced to the term in Bahasa Indonesia, I will spell it with an "h" in my own text.

30. Having worked with Faqih for many years, I knew that in his desire to serve his audiences, he preferred to translate Islamic terms into English, so I didn't suggest just retaining "Da'wah" and explaining the term in his text.

31. See Chapter 5 and my "Writing the Local-Global" for a more extensive discussion of these assignments.

32. As will be discussed in more detail below, Muslims believe that God's word was transmitted through direct revelation via the archangel Gabriel to the prophet Mohammad, who is referred to as "prophet," "servant of god" "the announcer," and other names that portray him as a neutral conveyer of God's word. Thus, the Qur'an, Muslims believe, is the literal "word of God."

33. The Arabic title for this work is *Taḥrīr al-Mar'a fī 'Aṣr al-Risāla; Dirāsa 'an al-Mar'a Jāmi'a li al-Nuṣuṣ al-Qur'ān wa Ṣaḥīḥay al-Bukhārī wa Muslim.*

34. In Arabic, *sharia* translates literally to "the clear, well-trodden path to water." On a metaphorical level, sharia is the Muslim code for living as per the Qur'an and Hadith.

35. Given his involvement with Mubadalah, Faqih is now a board member, with fewer day-to-day interactions with Fahmina.

36. Most of the *mubadalah* activists were fasting for Idul Adha, but, knowing I was not Muslim, they offered me sustenance, an offer made all the more gracious given their own abstinence from eating and drinking during the day.

37. Various websites and apps can easily translate Indonesian-medium websites into English. Be aware, however, that in Bahasa Indonesia "dia" is the only personal pronoun and thus represents all genders; sadly, but not surprisingly, many translation tools automatically translate "dia" to its male he/his corollaries in English, which can muddy the translation if one doesn't understand the context.

38. Showcasing his desire to amplify the voices of female ulama (religious scholars), after Faqih read a draft of this chapter, he sent me videos depicting more of Nur Rofia's work, where she discusses reinterpreting gender relations through the Qur'anic principles of justice and equality and female genital mutilation from a biological and Qur'anic human rights perspective ("FGM" and "Musawah Webinar").

Video of Rofia Discussing Islam and Equality

Video of Rofia Discussing Female Genital Mutilation

39. "Bule" is a widely used slang term used to refer to white people in general, though it was initially used to refer to Dutch colonists.

40. The Ahmadi faith is much more complex than what is shared here, for the sake of this project. For a thorough understanding of the nuances, see Nina's dissertation (Noor, *Ahmadi Women*) and Simon Ross Valentine, *Islam and the Ahmadiyya Jama'at: History, Belief, Practice*.

41. As further testament to how problematic it is to understand Islam as monolithic, in her dissertation Nina emphasizes that in addition to the more dominant Sunni/Shia communities, there are two communities of Ahmadiyya—the community she studies and refers to here, called Jamaat Ahmadiyya, and the Lahore community, who view Mirza Ghulam Ahmad as a "reformer" rather than a prophet.

42. "There is no God but Allah, and Muhammad is his messenger." This phrase is the first of the five pillars of Islam and is recited in each daily *adhan*, or call to prayer, as well as during each worshiper's daily prayer, or *shalat*, which happens five times a day.

43. "Peace Be upon You."

44. For a fascinating look at Megawati's rhetoric, see Gregory Coles, "'What Do I Lack as a Woman?': The Rhetoric of Megawati Sukarnoputri."

45. The recursive consent process for this interview, plus further follow-up closer to production, was especially important in ensuring that Ninik felt agency when deciding both how and whether to include this moment.

46. This is another title for Muhammad; it means the "Seal of Prophets" or the Last Prophet.

WORKS CITED

Abdul Kodir, Faqihuddin. "Abū Shuqqa's Approach to the Hadith: Towards an Egalitarian Islamic Gender Ethics." *Ḥadīth and Ethics through the Lens of Interdisciplinarity*. Ed. Mutaz al-Khatib. Brill, 2022. pp. 221–47.

———. "Interpretation of Hadith for Equality between Women and Men: Reading *Taḥrīr al-Mar'a fī Aṣr al-Risāla* by 'Abd al-Ḥalīm Muḥammad Abū Shuqqa (1924–1995)." Diss. U of Gadjah Mada, 2015.

———. *Qirā'ah Mubādalah: Tafsir Progresif untuk Keadilan Gender.* Penerbit IRCiSoD, 2019.

———. "*Qirā'a Mubādala*: Reciprocal Reading of Hadith on Marital Relationships." *Justice and Beauty in Muslim Marriage: Towards Egalitarian Ethics and Laws*. Ed. Ziba Mir-Hosseini et al. Oneworld Academic, 2022. pp. 197–225.

Abu-Lughod, Lila. "Do Muslim Women Really Need Saving? Anthropological Reflections on Cultural Relativism and Its Others." *American Anthropologist* 104.3 (2002): pp. 783–90.

Ahmed, Leila. *Women and Gender in Islam:Historical Roots of a Modern Debate.* Yale UP, 2021.

Alaoui, Fatima Zahrae Chrifi. "Arabizing Vernacular Discourse: A Rhetorical Analysis of Tunisian Revolutionary Grafitti." García and Baca pp. 112–40.

Alvarez, Steven. "Rhetorical Autoethnography: Delinking English Language Learning in a Family Oral History." García and Baca pp. 85–111.

Anderson, Benedict. *Imagined Communities: Reflections on the Origin and Spread of Nationalism.* Rev. ed. Verso Books, 2006.

Anzaldúa, Gloria. *Borderlands/La Frontera: The New Mestiza.* Spinsters/Aunt Lute, 1987.

Ayash, Nancy Bou. *Toward Translingual Realities in Composition: (Re)working Local Language Representations and Practices.* UP of Colorado, 2019.

Baca, Damián. "Doing Rhetoric Elsewhere: Chicanx Indigeneities, Colonial Peripheries, and the Underside of Written Communication." Lloyd pp. 382–85.

———. *Mestiz@ Scripts, Digital Migrations, and the Territories of Writing.* Palgrave Macmillan, 2008.

Baca, Damián, and Victor Villanueva, eds. *Rhetorics of the Americas: 3114 BCE to 2012 CE.* Palgrave Macmillan, 2010.

Baddar, Maha. "From Athens (via Alexandria) to Baghdad: Hybridity as Epistemology in the Work of al-Kindi, al-Farabi, and in the Rhetorical Legacy of the Medieval Arabic Translation Movement." Diss. U of Arizona, 2010.

Bakhtin, Mikhail Mikhaïlovich. *The Dialogic Imagination: Four Essays.* Trans. Caryl Emerson and Michael Holquist. U of Texas P, 2011.

———. "The Problem of Speech Genres." *Speech Genres and Other Late Essays.* Trans. Vern W. McGee. Ed. Caryl Emerson and Michael Holquist. U of Texas P, 1986. pp. 60–102.

Barlas, Asma. *Believing Women in Islam: Unreading Patriarchal Interpretations of the Qur'an.* 2d ed. U of Texas P, 2019.

Bawarshi, Anis. "Beyond the Genre Fixation: A Translingual Perspective on Genre." *College English* 78.3 (2016): pp. 243–49.

———. *Genre and the Invention of the Writer: Reconsidering the Place of Invention in Composition.* Utah State UP, 2003.

Bazerman, Charles. "Genre and Cognitive Development: Beyond Writing to Learn." *Pratiques: Linguistique, Littérature, Didactique* 143–44 (2009): pp. 127–38.

Berger, Peter L. *The Sacred Canopy: Elements of a Sociological Theory of Religion.* Open Road Media, 2011.

Bhabha, Homi K. *The Location of Culture.* Routledge, 1994.

Blommaert, Jan. *The Sociolinguistics of Globalization.* Cambridge UP, 2010.

Bloom-Pojar, Rachel. *Translanguaging outside the Academy: Negotiating Rhetoric and Healthcare in the Spanish Caribbean.* NCTE, 2018.

Borrowman, Shane. "The Islamization of Rhetoric: Ibn Rushd and the Reintroduction of Aristotle into Medieval Europe." *Rhetoric Review* 27.4 (2008): pp. 341–60.

Brandt, Deborah. *Literacy in American Lives.* Cambridge UP, 2001.

———. "Sponsors of Literacy." *College Composition and Communication* 49.2 (1998): pp. 165–85.

Brandt, Deborah, and Katie Clinton. "Limits of the Local: Expanding Perspectives on Literacy as a Social Practice." *Journal of Literacy Research* 34.3 (2002): pp. 337–56.

Browne, Kevin Adonis. "Moving the Body: Preamble to a Theory of Vernacular Rhetoric, or How a Caribbean Rhetoric(ian) Is Composed." García and Baca pp. 196–222.

Burke, Kenneth. "Terministic Screens." *Proceedings of the American Catholic Philosophical Association* 39 (1965): pp. 87–102.

Butler, Judith. *Bodies That Matter: On the Discursive Limits of "Sex."* Taylor and Francis, 2011.

Canagarajah, A. Suresh. "Challenges in Decolonizing Linguistics: The Politics of Enregisterment and the Divergent Uptakes of Translingualism." *Educational Linguistics* 1.1 (2022): pp. 25–55.

———. "Codemeshing in Academic Writing: Identifying Teachable Strategies of Translanguaging." *Modern Language Journal* 95.3 (2011): pp. 401–17.

———. *Critical Academic Writing and Multilingual Students.* U of Michigan P, 2002.

———. *Resisting Linguistic Imperialism in English Teaching.* Oxford UP, 1999.

———. "Toward a Writing Pedagogy of Shuttling between Languages: Learning from Multilingual Writers." *College English* 68.6 (2006): pp. 589–604.

———. *Translingual Practice: Global Englishes and Cosmopolitan Relations.* Taylor and Francis, 2012.

———. "Translingual Practice as Spatial Repertoires: Expanding the Paradigm beyond Structuralist Orientations." *Applied Linguistics* 39.1 (2018): pp. 31–54.

Clark, Irene L. *Writing the Successful Thesis and Dissertation: Entering the Conversation.* Prentice Hall, 2007.

Coe, Richard M. "The New Rhetoric of Genre: Writing Political Briefs." *Genre in the Classroom: Multiple Perspectives.* Ed. Ann M. Johns. Lawrence Erlbaum, 2002. pp. 197–210.

Coles, Gregory. "'What Do I Lack as a Woman?': The Rhetoric of Megawati Sukarnoputri." *Rhetorica* 36.1 (2018): pp. 58–91.

Community Library. perpustakaankomunitas.blogspot.com/. Accessed 25 July 2022.

Connor, Ulla. "Mapping Multidimensional Aspects of Research: Reaching to Intercultural Rhetoric." *Contrastive Rhetoric: Reaching to Intercultural Rhetoric.* Ed. Connor, Ed Nagelhout, and William V. Rozycki. John Benjamins Publishing, 2008.

Cope, Bill, and Mary Kalantzis. *The Powers of Literacy: A Genre Approach to Teaching Writing*. U of Pittsburgh P, 1993.

Crenshaw, Kimberle. "Mapping the Margins: Intersectionality, Identity Politics, and Violence against Women of Color." *Stanford Law Review* 43.6 (1991): pp. 1241–99.

Crystal, David. *English as a Global Language*. 2d ed. Cambridge UP, 2003.

Cushman, Ellen. "Translingual and Decolonial Approaches to Meaning Making." *College English* 78.3 (2016): pp. 234–42.

Cushman, Ellen, Damián Baca, and Romeo García. "Delinking: Toward Pluriversal Rhetorics." *College English* 84.1 (2021): pp. 7–32.

Daniell, Beth. "Composing (as) Power." *College Composition and Communication* 45.2 (1994): pp. 238–46.

Dara Affiah, Neng. "Youth Culture and Movements: Indonesia: Fatayat-NU." *Encyclopedia of Women and Islamic Cultures*. Ed: Suad Joseph. 2009. http://dx.doi.org/10.1163/1872-5309_ewic_EWIC COM_00371

Darder, Antonia. "Freire and a Revolutionary Praxis of the Body." *Review of Education, Pedagogy, and Cultural Studies* 40.5 (2018): pp. 422–32.

de Certeau, Michel. *The Practice of Everyday Life*. Trans. Joseph Rendall. U of California P, 1984.

DePalma, Michael-John, and Jeffrey M. Ringer, eds. *Mapping Christian Rhetorics: Connecting Conversations, Charting New Territories*. Taylor and Francis, 2015.

Devitt, Amy. "Teaching Critical Genre Awareness." *Genre in a Changing World*. Ed. Charles Bazerman, Adair Bonini, and Débora de Carvalho Figueiredo. WAC Clearinghouse / Parlor Press, 2009. pp. 341–54.

Devitt, Amy, Anis Bawarshi, and Mary Jo Reiff. *Scenes of Writing: Strategies for Composing with Genres*. Longman, 2004.

Diab, Rasha. *Shades of Sulh: The Rhetorics of Arab-Islamic Reconciliation*. U of Pittsburgh P, 2016.

Engelson, Amber. "The 'Hands of God' at Work: Negotiating between Western and Religious Sponsorship in Indonesia." *College English* 76.4 (2014): pp. 292–314.

———. "'I Have No Mother Tongue': (Re)Conceptualizing Rhetorical Voice in Indonesia." pp. Lloyd 195–205.

———. "'Resources Are Power': Writing across the Global Information Divide." *Thinking Globally, Composing Locally: Rethinking Online*

Writing in the Age of the Global Internet. Ed. Rich Rice and Kirk St. Amant. UP of Colorado, 2018. pp. 161–81.

———. "'To Whom Do We Have Students Write?' Exploring Rhetorical Agency and Translanguaging in an Indonesian Graduate Writing Classroom." *Literacy in Composition Studies* 6.1 (2018): pp. 39–61.

———. "Writing the Local-Global: An Ethnography of Friction and Negotiation in an English-Using Indonesian PhD Program." Diss. U of Massachusetts Amherst, 2011.

"English Translation of Indonesian Joint Ministerial Decree (SKB) against Ahmadiyya: Joint Decree of the Minister of Religious Affairs, the Attorney General and the Minister of the Interior of the Republic of Indonesia." 9 June 2008. www.thepersecution.org/world/indonesia/docs/skb.html. Accessed 12 Oct. 2023.

Ethics at the Heart of Higher Education: Achieving Quality through Values. Globethics Annual Report 2021, www.Globethics.net. Accessed 12 Oct. 2023.

Ezzaher, Lahcen E. "Alfarabi's *Book of Rhetoric*: An Arabic-English Translation of Alfarabi's Commentary on Aristotle's *Rhetoric*." *Rhetorica* 26.4 (2008): pp. 347–91.

Fahmina Institute. fahmina.or.id/. Accessed 12 Oct. 2023.

Ferguson, James. *Global Shadows: Africa in the Neoliberal World Order.* Duke UP, 2006.

Foss, Sonja K., and Cindy L. Griffin. "Beyond Persuasion: A Proposal for an Invitational Rhetoric." *Communications Monographs* 62.1 (1995): pp. 2–18.

Fraiberg, Steven. "Reassembling Technical Communication: A Framework for Studying Multilingual and Multimodal Practices in Global Contexts." *Technical Communication Quarterly* 22.1 (2013): pp. 10–27.

Freire, Paulo. "Cultural Action and Conscientization." *Harvard Educational Review* 40.3 (1970): pp. 452–77.

———. *Education for Critical Consciousness.* Trans. Myra Bergman Ramos. Bloomsbury Publishing, 2021.

———. *Pedagogy of Freedom: Ethics, Democracy, and Civic Courage.* Trans. Patrick Clarke. Rowman and Littlefield Publishers, 1998.

———. *Pedagogy of Hope: Reliving Pedagogy of the Oppressed.* Trans. Robert R. Barr. Bloomsbury Publishing, 2021.

———. *Pedagogy of the City.* Trans. Donaldo Macedo. Continuum, 1993.

―――. *Pedagogy of the Oppressed.* 50ᵗʰ anniversary ed. Trans. Myra Bergman Ramos. Bloomsbury Academic, 2018.

García, Romeo, and Damián Baca, eds. *Rhetorics Elsewhere and Otherwise: Contested Modernities, Decolonial Visions.* NCTE, 2019.

Gee, James Paul. *An Introduction to Discourse Analysis: Theory and Method.* Routledge, 1999.

Gevers, Jeroen. "Translingualism Revisited: Language Difference and Hybridity in L2 Writing." *Journal of Second Language Writing* 40 (2018): pp. 73–83.

Gilyard, Keith. "The Rhetoric of Translingualism." *College English* 78.3 (2016): pp. 284–89.

Glenn, Cheryl. *Rhetorical Feminism and This Thing Called Hope.* Southern Illinois UP, 2018.

"Globethics.net." www.globethics.net/documents/4289936/13255613/Portrait_ShortInformation_EN.pdf/54b09132-e866-4ce9-876d-a6a8523bd064. Accessed 12 Nov. 2023.

Gonzales, Laura. "Designing for Intersectional, Interdependent Accessibility: A Case Study of Multilingual Technical Content Creation." *Communication Design Quarterly Review* 6.4 (2019): pp. 35–45.

―――. *Sites of Translation: What Multilinguals Can Teach Us about Digital Writing and Rhetoric.* U of Michigan P, 2018.

Goodburn, Amy. "It's a Question of Faith: Discourses of Fundamentalism and Critical Pedagogy in the Writing Classroom." *JAC: A Journal of Composition Theory* 18.2 (1998): pp. 333–53.

Grande, Sandy. *Red Pedagogy: Native American Social and Political Thought.* 10th anniversary ed. Rowman and Littlefield Publishers, 2015.

Halasek, Kay. *A Pedagogy of Possibility: Bakhtinian Perspectives on Composition Studies.* Southern Illinois UP, 1999.

Hanisch, Carol. "The Personal Is Political." *Notes from the Second Year: Women's Liberation, Major Writings of the Radical Feminists.* Ed. Shulamith Firestone. Radical Feminism, 1970. pp. 76–78.

Heath, Shirley Brice, and Brian V. Street. *On Ethnography: Approaches to Language and Literacy Research.* Teachers College P / National Conference on Research in Language and Literacy, 2008.

Herrington, Anne J., and Marcia Curtis. *Persons in Process: Four Stories of Writing and Personal Development in College.* NCTE, 2000.

Hesford, Wendy S., and Eileen E. Schell. "Introduction: Configurations of Transnationality: Locating Feminist Rhetorics." *College English* 70.5 (2008): pp. 461–70.

Hidalgo, Alexandra. "A Response to Cushman, Baca, and García's *College English* Introduction." *Constellations* 4 (2021).

Horner, Bruce, and Sara P. Alvarez. "Defining Translinguality." *Literacy in Composition Studies* 7.2 (2019): pp. 1–30.

Horner, Bruce, and Laura Tetreault. "Translation as (Global) Writing." *Composition Studies* 44.1 (2016): pp. 13–30.

Horner, Bruce, Samantha NeCamp, and Christiane Donahue. "Toward a Multilingual Composition Scholarship: From English Only to a Translingual Norm." *College Composition and Communication* 63.2 (2011): pp. 269–300.

Horner, Bruce, et al. "Language Difference in Writing: Toward a Translingual Approach." *College English* 73.3 (2011): pp. 303–21.

Hyland, Ken. "Genre Pedagogy: Language, Literacy, and L2 Writing Instruction." *Journal of Second Language Writing* 16 (2007): pp. 148–64.

ICRS Doctoral Handbook: PhD in Inter-Religious Studies (2020–2022). Indonesian Consortium for Religious Studies, 2022.

Introducing ICRS-Yogya: A Portrait of an International Graduate Program in Inter-Religious Studies. Indonesian Consortium for Religious Studies, 2009.

Ivanič, Roz. *Writing and Identity: The Discoursal Construction of Identity in Academic Writing.* John Benjamins, 1998.

Jaspers, Karl. *Philosophy of Existence.* Trans. and intro. by Richard F. Grabau. U of Pennsylvania P, 1971.

Jordan, Jay. "Material Translingual Ecologies." *College English* 77.4 (2015): pp. 364–82.

Kamberelis, George, and Greg Dimitriadis. *On Qualitative Inquiry: Approaches to Language and Literacy Research.* Teachers College P, 2005.

Kress, Tricia M., and Robert Lake. "Walking with Freire: Exploring the Onto-Epistemological Dimensions of Critical Pedagogy." Faculty Works: Education, Molloy U Digital Commons, 2018.

Kubota, Ryuko. "The Multi/Plural Turn, Postcolonial Theory, and Neoliberal Multiculturalism: Complicities and Implications for Applied Linguistics." *Applied Linguistics* 37.4 (2016): pp. 474–94.

Kubota, Ryuko, and Al Lehner. "Toward Critical Contrastive Rhetoric." *Journal of Second Language Writing* 13.1 (2004): pp. 7–27.

Kuhn, Anthony. "Hard-Line Muslims Test Indonesia's Tolerance." *All Things Considered.* National Public Radio. 24 May 2012.

Kupipedia: Ensyklopedi Digital KUPI. kupipedia.id/index.php. Accessed 10 Oct. 2023.

"Language Policy." *Faculty Handbook: ICRS Yogya.* Indonesian Consortium for Religious Studies, 2009.

Leonard, Rebecca Lorimer. *Writing on the Move: Migrant Women and the Value of Literacy.* U of Pittsburgh P, 2017.

Li, Tania Murray. *The Will to Improve: Governmentality, Development, and the Practice of Politics.* Duke UP, 2007.

Li Wei. "Translanguaging as a Practical Theory of Language." *Applied Linguistics* 39.1 (2018): pp. 9–30.

Lillis, Theresa M., and Mary Jane Curry. *Academic Writing in a Global Context: The Politics and Practices of Publishing in English.* Routledge, 2010.

Llewellyn, Aisyah. "Explainer: Why Is Indonesia's Sexual Violence Law So Important?" *Al Jazeera* 14 Apr. 2022. www.aljazeera.com/news/2022/4/14/explainer-why-is-indonesias-sexual-violence-law-so-important. Accessed 12 Oct. 2023.

Lloyd, Keith. *The Routledge Handbook of Comparative World Rhetorics: Studies in the History, Application, and Teaching of Rhetoric beyond Traditional Greco-Roman Contexts.* Taylor and Francis, 2020.

"Love for All, Hatred for None." Ahmadiyya Muslim Community UK, www.loveforallhatredfornone.org/about-the-ahmadiyya-muslim-community/about-love-for-all-hatred-for-none/. Accessed 12 Oct. 2023.

Lowenberg, Peter H. "Language Policy and Language Identity in Indonesia." *Journal of Asian Pacific Communication* 3.1 (1992): pp. 59–77.

Lu, Min-Zhan. "Composing Postcolonial Studies." *Crossing Borderlands: Composition and Postcolonial Studies.* Ed. Andrea A. Lunsford and Lahoucine Ouzgane. U of Pittsburgh P, 2004. pp. 9–32.

Lu, Min-Zhan, and Bruce Horner. "Translingual Literacy, Language Difference, and Matters of Agency." *College English* 75.6 (2013): pp. 582–607.

Lugones, María. "Toward a Decolonial Feminism." *Hypatia* 25.4 (2010): pp. 742–59.

Lunsford, Andrea A. "Toward a Mestiza Rhetoric: Gloria Anzaldúa on Composition and Postcoloniality." *JAC: A Journal of Composition Theory* 18.1 (1998): pp. 1–27.

Lunsford, Andrea A., John J. Ruszkiewicz, and Keith Walters. *Everything's an Argument: With Readings.* 3rd ed. Bedford / St. Martin's, 2004.

Lynch, Paul, and Matthew Miller. "Twenty-Five Years of Faith in Writing: Religion and Composition, 1992–2017." *Present Tense* 6.2 (2017): pp. 1–195.

Lyons, Scott Richard. "The Fine Art of Fencing: Nationalism, Hybridity, and the Search for a Native American Writing Pedagogy." *JAC: A Journal of Composition Theory* 29.1–2 (2009): pp. 77–105.

Mahboob, Ahmar. "English as an Islamic Language: A Case Study of Pakistani English." *World Englishes* 28.2 (2009): pp. 175–89.

Mahmood, Saba. *Politics of Piety: The Islamic Revival and the Feminist Subject.* Princeton UP, 2011.

Mao, LuMing. "Doing Comparative Rhetoric Responsibly." *Rhetoric Society Quarterly* 41.1 (2011): pp. 64–69.

———. *Reading Chinese Fortune Cookie: The Making of Chinese American Rhetoric.* Utah State UP, 2006.

———. "Reflective Encounters: Illustrating Comparative Rhetoric." *Style* 37.4 (2003): pp. 401–25.

———. "Rhetorical Borderlands: Chinese American Rhetoric in the Making." *College Composition and Communication* 56.3 (2005): pp. 426–69.

Matsuda, Paul Kei. "It's the Wild West Out There: A New Linguistic Frontier in US College Composition." *Literacy as Translingual Practice: Between Communities and Classrooms.* Ed. A. Suresh Canagarajah. Routledge, 2013. pp. 128–38.

McAdams, Mindy. "Quality in Scholarly Research in Indonesian Universities." *Jakarta Post* 12 Feb. 2012. www.thejakartapost.com/news/2012/02/18/quality-scholarly-research-indonesian-universities.html. Accessed 12 Nov. 2023.

Mifsud, Mari Lee. "A Feminist Praxis of Comparative Rhetoric." Lloyd pp. 306–14.

Mignolo, Walter D. "Border Thinking, De-Colonial Cosmopolitanism and Dialogues among Civilizations." *The Ashgate Research Companion to Cosmopolitanism.* Ed. Maria Rovisco and Magdalena Nowicka. Routledge, 2011. pp. 329–48.

———. "Delinking: The Rhetoric of Modernity, the Logic of Coloniality and the Grammar of De-Coloniality." *Cultural Studies* 21.2–3 (2007): pp. 449–514.

———. "Geopolitics of Sensing and Knowing: On (De)coloniality, Border Thinking and Epistemic Disobedience." *Confero* 1.1 (2013): pp. 129–50.

———. "What Does It Mean to Decolonize?" Mignolo and Walsh pp. 105–34.

Mignolo, Walter D., and Catherine E. Walsh. *On Decoloniality: Concepts, Analytics, Praxis*. Duke UP, 2018.

Mubadalah.id: Inspirasi Keadilan Relasi. mubadalah.id/. Accessed 12 Oct. 2023.

Nihaya Center. www.nihayahcenter.net/tentang-kami. Accessed July 25 2022.

Noor, Nina Mariani. *Ahmadi Women Resisting Fundamentalist Persecution: A Case Study on Active Group Resistance in Indonesia*. Globethics.net Theses No. 27, 2017.

———. "Berbuka Puasa Bersama Biarawati." *Facebook*, 28 Dec. 2021, 2:05 pm.

———. "Statement in Twelfth Forum on Minority Issues, United Nations." Geneva, Switzerland. 29 Nov. 2019. www.youtube.com/watch?v=L0eEsfdvkEA. Accessed 12 Oct. 2023.

Nunan, David. "Action Research in the Language Classroom." *Second Language Teacher Education*. Ed. Jack C. Richards and David Nunan. Cambridge UP, 1990. pp. 62–81.

Nuryatno, Muhammad Agus. "Education and Social Transformation: Investigating the Influence and Reception of Paulo Freire in Indonesia." Diss. McGill U, 2006.

Ortega y Gasset, José. *Man and People*. Trans. Willard R. Trask. Norton, 1957.

Ortner, Sherry B. *Making Gender: The Politics and Erotics of Culture*. Beacon Press, 1996.

Pavia, Catherine Matthews. "Taking up Faith: Ethical Methods for Studying Writing in Religious Contexts." *Written Communication* 32.4 (2015): pp. 336–67.

Pedersen, Anne-Marie. "Negotiating Cultural Identities through Language: Academic English in Jordan." *College Composition and Communication* 62.2 (2010): pp. 283–310.

Pennycook, Alastair. *The Cultural Politics of English as an International Language*. Taylor and Francis, 1994.

———. *Global Englishes and Transcultural Flows*. Taylor and Francis, 2006.

———. *Posthumanist Applied Linguistics*. Taylor and Francis, 2017.

———. "Vulgar Pragmatism, Critical Pragmatism, and EAP." *English for Specific Purposes* 16.4 (1997): pp. 253–69.

Perkins, Priscilla. "'A Radical Conversion of the Mind': Fundamentalism, Hermeneutics, and the Metanoic Classroom." *College English* 63.5 (2001): pp. 585–611.

Petruzzi, Anthony P. "Between Conventions and Critical Thinking: The Concept of 'Limit-Situations' in Critical Literacy and Pedagogy." *JAC: A Journal of Composition Theory* 18.2 (1998): pp. 309–32.

Phillipson, Robert. *Linguistic Imperialism*. Oxford UP, 1992.

Plemons, Anna. *Beyond Progress in the Prison Classroom: Options and Opportunities*. NCTE, 2019.

Prendergast, Catherine. *Buying into English: Language and Investment in the New Capitalist World*. U of Pittsburgh P, 2008.

Quijano, Aníbal. "Coloniality and Modernity/Rationality." *Cultural Studies* 21.2–3 (2007): pp. 168–78.

Ratcliffe, Krista. "Eavesdropping as Rhetorical Tactic: History, Whiteness, and Rhetoric." *JAC: A Journal of Composition Theory* 20.1 (2000): pp. 87–119.

———. *Rhetorical Listening: Identification, Gender, Whiteness*. Southern Illinois UP, 2005.

Redaksi. "27 Pesantren dan Ribuan Santri Ikuti Halaqah Muda Pra-KUPI Dua [Twenty-Seven Islamic Boarding Schools and Thousands of Santri Participate in the Pre-KUPI Dua Youth Halaqah]." 18 July 2022. *Mubadalah: Inspirasi Keadilan Relasi*. mubadalah.id/27-pesantren-dan-ribuan-santri-ikuti-halaqah-muda-pra-kupi-dua/. Accessed 1 Oct. 2023.

"Research and Projects." *Indonesian Consortium for Religious Studies*. www.icrs.or.id/research-and-project.

Ricklefs, Merle Calvin. *A History of Modern Indonesia since c. 1200*. MacMillan, 1993.

Ringer, Jeffrey M. "The Consequences of Integrating Faith into Academic Writing: Casuistic Stretching and Biblical Citation." *College English* 75.3 (2013): pp. 270–97.

Rofia, Nur. "FGM: Does Genital Cutting Violate Children's Rights? Islam's Role in Gender Norms, Peace and Security." US Mission ASEAN. www.youtube.com/watch?app=desktop&v=bjFZlzUNWvo. Accessed 12 Oct. 2023.

———. "Musawah Webinar: Approaching the Qur'an through Women's Experiences." *Musawah: A Global Movement for Equality and Justice in the Family*. www.youtube.com/watch?app=desktop&v=AVFu4USClPE. Accessed 12 Oct. 2023.

———. "Urgensi UU TPKS, dan Misi Kerasulan [The Urgency of the TPKS Law, and the Apostolic Mission]." 17 Jan. 2022. *Mubadalah: Inspirasi Keadilan Relasi*. mubadalah.id/urgensi-uu-tpks-dan-misi-kerasulan/. Accessed 12 Oct. 2023.

Ruiz, Iris D. "Race." Ruiz and Sánchez pp. 3–15.

Ruiz, Iris D., and Sonia C. Arellano. "La Cultura Nos Cura: Reclaiming Decolonial Epistemologies through Medicinal History and Quilting as Method." García and Baca pp. 141–68.

Ruiz, Iris D., and Raúl Sánchez, eds. *Decolonizing Rhetoric and Composition Studies: New Latinx Keywords for Theory and Pedagogy.* Palgrave Macmillan, 2016.

Said, Edward. *Orientalism.* Pantheon Books, 1978.

Schreiber, Brooke Ricker. "'I Am What I Am': Multilingual Identity and Digital Translanguaging." *Language Learning and Technology* 19.3 (2015): pp. 69–87.

Schreiber, Brooke Ricker, and Missy Watson. "Translingualism ≠ Code-Meshing: A Response to Gevers' 'Translingualism Revisited' (2018)." *Journal of Second Language Writing* 42 (2018): pp. 94–97.

Schuon, Frithjof. *Islam and the Perennial Philosophy.* Suhail Academy, 1985.

Shapiro, Rachael, and Missy Watson. "Translingual Praxis: From Theorizing Language to Antiracist and Decolonial Pedagogy." *College Composition and Communication* 74.2 (2022): pp. 292–321.

Sharma, Shyam. "Beyond Colonial Hegemonies: Writing Scholarship and Pedagogy with Nyāyasutra." García and Baca pp. 169–95.

Shen, Fan. "The Classroom and the Wider Culture: Identity as a Key to Learning English Composition." *College Composition and Communication* 40.4 (1989): pp. 459–66.

Shipka, Jody. "Transmodality in/and Processes of Making: Changing Dispositions and Practice." *College English* 78.3 (2016): pp. 250–57.

Skutnabb-Kangas, Tove. *Linguistic Genocide in Education—or Worldwide Diversity and Human Rights?* Routledge, 2000.

Spivak, Gayatri Chakravorty. "Can the Subaltern Speak?" *Marxism and the Interpretation of Culture.* Ed. Cary Nelson and Lawrence Grossberg. U of Illinois P, 1988. pp. 66–111.

Srikandi Lintas Iman. "Srikandi Lintas Iman–SRILI." www.facebook.com/srilijogja/?ref=page_internal. Accessed 31 July 2022.

Starhawk. *Truth or Dare: Encounters with Power, Authority, and Mystery.* Harper and Row, 1987.

Stenberg, Shari J. "Liberation Theology and Liberatory Pedagogies: Renewing the Dialogue." *College English* 68.3 (2006): pp. 271–90.

Sugiharto, Setiono. "Enacting the Locus of Enunciation as a Resistant Tactic to Confront Epistemological Racism and Decolonize Scholarly Knowledge." *Applied Linguistics* 43.1 (2022): pp. 196–202.

———. "Imposing a Publish or Perish Policy." *Jakarta Post* 25 Feb. 2012. www.thejakartapost.com/news/2012/02/25/imposing-a-publish-or-perish-policy.html.

———. "The Multilingual Turn in Applied Linguistics? A Perspective from the Periphery." *International Journal of Applied Linguistics* 25.3 (2015): pp. 414–21.

———. "Translingualism in Action: Rendering the Impossible Possible." *Journal of Asia TEFL* 12.2 (2015): pp. 125–54.

Swales, John M. *Genre Analysis: English in Academic and Research Settings.* Cambridge UP, 1990.

Swales, John M., and Christine B. Feak. *Academic Writing for Graduate Students: Essential Tasks and Skills.* 2d ed. U of Michigan P, 2009.

Tayob, Abdulkader. *Religion in Modern Islamic Discourse.* Columbia UP, 2009.

Tlostanova, Madina V., and Walter D. Mignolo. "On Pluritopic Hermeneutics, Trans-modern Thinking, and Decolonial Philosophy." *Encounters* 1.1 (2009): pp. 11–26.

Toleransi.id: Inspirasi, Aksi, Kolaborasi. toleransi.id/. Accessed 30 July 2022.

Trimbur, John. "English in a Splintered Metropolis: South Africa after Apartheid." *JAC: A Journal of Composition Theory* 29.1–2 (2009): pp. 107–37.

Tsing, Anna Lowenhaupt. *Friction: An Ethnography of Global Connection.* Princeton UP, 2005.

Tuck, Eve, and K. Wayne. "Decolonization Is Not a Metaphor." *Decolonization: Indigeneity, Education and Society* 1.1 (2012): pp. 1–40.

United States. Department of State. Bureau of Democracy, Human Rights and Labor. "Indonesia." *2021 International Religious Freedom Report.* 2 June 2022. www.state.gov/reports/2021-report-on-international-religious-freedom/.

Valentine, Simon Ross. *Islam and the Ahmadiyya Jama'at: History, Belief, Practice.* Columbia UP, 2008.

Vander Lei, Elizabeth, and Bonnie Lenore Kyburz, eds. *Negotiating Religious Faith in the Composition Classroom.* Boynton/Cook Heinemann, 2005.

Varghese, Manka M., and Bill Johnston. "Evangelical Christians and English Language Teaching." *TESOL Quarterly* 41.1 (2007): pp. 5–31.

Vieira, Kate. "Writing about Others Writing." García and Baca 49–61.

———. "Writing's Potential to Heal: Women Writing from Their Bodies." *Community Literacy Journal* 13.2 (2019): pp. 20-47.

Villanueva, Victor. "On the Rhetoric and Precedents of Racism." *Cross-Talk in Comp Theory: A Reader.* 2nd ed. Ed. Villanueva. National Council of Teachers of English, 2003. pp. 829–45.

Wadud, Amina. *Qur'an and Woman: Rereading the Sacred Text from a Woman's Perspective.* Oxford UP, 1999.

Wafiroh, Nihayatul. "Let's Be Learners." *Nihaya Center.* www.nihayah-center.net/tentang-kami. Accessed 25 July 2022.

———. "Perempuan seperti Halnya Laki-Laki Adalah Khalifah di Muka Bumi." *Muhasaba 2022.* TVRI Nasional. www.facebook.com/watch?v=428042409081794. Accessed 25 July 2022.

Walsh, Catherine E. "Part One: Decoloniality in/as Praxis." Mignolo and Walsh pp. 13–102.

Wang, Bo. "Comparative Rhetoric, Postcolonial Studies, and Transnational Feminisms: A Geopolitical Approach." *Rhetoric Society Quarterly* 43.3 (2013): pp. 226–42.

Wang, Xiqiao. "Translation as Mobile Practice." *Journal of Second Language Writing* 49 (2020): article 100733.

Wang, Zhaozhe. "Rethinking Translingual as a Transdisciplinary Rhetoric: Broadening the Dialogic Space." *Composition Forum* 40 (2018): n.p.

"Women Scholars." *Kupipedia: Ensyklopedi Digital KUPI.* kupipedia.id/index.php. Accessed 1 Aug. 2022.

Woodward, Mark. *Java, Indonesia and Islam.* Springer, 2010.

Wynter, Sylvia. "Unsettling the Coloniality of Being/Power/Truth/Freedom: Towards the Human, after Man, Its Overrepresentation—An Argument." *CR: The New Centennial Review* 3.3 (2003): pp. 257–337.

You, Xiaoye. *Cosmopolitan English and Transliteracy.* Southern Illinois UP, 2016.

———. *Writing in the Devil's Tongue: A History of English Composition in China.* Southern Illinois UP, 2010.

Your Offer; Your Benefit. Globethics.net, 2014.

Zein, Subhan. *Language Policy in Superdiverse Indonesia.* Springer, 2020.

INDEX

relationality in, 114
Tawhid in, 133–134, 142, 147, 149

labor
  intellectual, 23
  translingual, 42
language
  Bakhtin on, 46–48
  and borders, negotiating, 189
  control through, 68–70
  cosmopolitan orientation to, 189–193
  a discrete system, 189–190
  embodied, 104–105
  insurrection, link to, 70
  power of in national imaginings, 71
  sociological understanding of, 45–46
  spatiotemporal understanding, 44–45
  technicalization of, 67–70
  transformation in, 34
language of thought, 121, 148
learning, transformative, 37
limit-situations, 36, 43
listening
  across difference, 201, 205–206, 221
  with intent, 9
  intersectional, 7
  to learn, 5–6
  for mutual commitments, 6–8
  rhetorical / feminist rhetorical, xix–xx, 7, 9

meaning-making
  body's role in, 8
  discursive energy fields in, 27
  Engelson's locus of, xviii
  Faqih (Kodir, Faqihuddin Abdul), 112–115, 129
  languages/audience borderland, 28

power, negotiating with to produce, 44, 46
meaning-making practices, interpreting, 20
mind/body duality, 37, 111
modernity, 18–22, 27
mubadalah
  performing for gender justice, 138–142
  theorizing, 129–138
Mubadalah Movement, 114, 170
Muslim population, 72
Muslim women, agency, 26, 213

negotiation, translingual, 32, 39, 111
neoliberalism, 191
Nina (Noor, Nina Mariana). See Noor, Nina Mariana (Nina)
Ninik (Wafiroh, Nihayatul). See Wafiroh, Nihayatul (Ninik)
Noor, Nina Mariana (Nina)
  agency, 168, 173–174
  border thinking, 154, 168–172, 230
  code-switching, 170
  discursive energy field, 153
  English-medium knowledge, localizing, 174–179
  female agency, defined, 165
  "Gender and Feminism" course, 170–173
  identity, 154–155, 168–169, 173–175, 178
  Islam/female agency duality, challenging, 169
  on Islamic vs. Western feminism, 173
  language beliefs, 155–157
  literacy narrative, tactical networking in, 80
  motivation, 179
  overview of work of, 184–186
  pedagogy, multilingual, 170–173
  photograph of, 144p

AUTHOR

Amber Engelson is a professor of English and director of writing at Massachusetts College of Liberal Arts. She teaches first-year writing and undergraduate courses in global comparative rhetorics, feminist rhetorics, writing center theory and praxis, and creative nonfiction. In addition to teaching, she directs MCLA's Writing Studio and coordinates the college's first-year writing program as well as campuswide WAC initiatives. Her work has appeared in *College English, Literacy in Composition Studies*, and various edited collections.

BOOKS IN THE CCCC STUDIES IN WRITING & RHETORIC SERIES

The Hands of God at Work: Islamic Gender Justice through Translingual Praxis
Amber Engelson

Queer Techné: Bodies, Rhetorics, and Desire in the History of Computing
Patricia Fancher

Living English, Moving Literacies: Women's Stories of Learning between the US and Nepal
Katie Silvester

Recollections from an Uncommon Time: 4C20 Documentarian Tales
Edited by Julie Lindquist, Bree Straayer, and Bump Halbritter

Transfer in an Urban Writing Ecology: Reimagining Community College–University Relations in Composition Studies
Christie Toth with Joanne Castillo, Nic Contreras, Kelly Corbray, Nathan Lacy, Westin Porter, Sandra Salazar-Hernandez, and Colleagues

Teachers Talking Writing: Perspectives on Places, Pedagogies, and Programs
Shane A. Wood

Materiality and Writing Studies: Aligning Labor, Scholarship, and Teaching
Holly Hassel and Cassandra Phillips

Salt of the Earth: Rhetoric, Preservation, and White Supremacy
James Chase Sanchez

Rhetorics of Overcoming: Rewriting Narratives of Disability and Accessibility in Writing Studies
Allison Harper Hitt

Writing Accomplices with Student Immigrant Rights Organizers
Glenn Hutchinson

Counterstory: The Rhetoric and Writing of Critical Race Theory
Aja Y. Martinez

Writing Programs, Veterans Studies, and the Post-9/11 University: A Field Guide
Alexis Hart and Roger Thompson

Beyond Progress in the Prison Classroom: Options and Opportunities
Anna Plemons

Rhetorics Elsewhere and Otherwise: Contested Modernities, Decolonial Visions
Edited by Romeo García and Damián Baca

Black Perspectives in Writing Program Administration: From the Margins to the Center
Edited by Staci M. Perryman-Clark and Collin Lamont Craig

Translanguaging outside the Academy: Negotiating Rhetoric and Healthcare in the Spanish Caribbean
Rachel Bloom-Pojar

Collaborative Learning as Democratic Practice: A History
Mara Holt

Reframing the Relational: A Pedagogical Ethic for Cross-Curricular Literacy Work
Sandra L. Tarabochia

Inside the Subject: A Theory of Identity for the Study of Writing
Raúl Sánchez

Genre of Power: Police Report Writers and Readers in the Justice System
Leslie Seawright

Assembling Composition
Edited by Kathleen Blake Yancey and Stephen J. McElroy

Public Pedagogy in Composition Studies
Ashley J. Holmes

From Boys to Men: Rhetorics of Emergent American Masculinity
Leigh Ann Jones

This book was typeset in Adobe Garamond Pro and
Myriad Pro by Barbara Frazier.
Typefaces used on the cover include Garamond and News Gothic Std.
The book was printed on 50-lb., white offset paper.